Nutritional Aspects of Food Processing and Ingredients

Nutritional Aspects of Food Processing and Ingredients

Edited by

C.J.K. Henry and N.J. Heppell
School of Biological and Molecular Sciences
Oxford Brookes University
Oxford, UK

A Chapman & Hall Food Science Book

An Aspen Publication®
Aspen Publishers, Inc.
Gaithersburg, Maryland
1998

Orders: (800) 638–8437
Customer Service: (800) 234–1660

About Aspen Publishers • For more than 35 years, Aspen has been a leading professional publisher in a variety of disciplines. Aspen's vast information resources are available in both print and electronic format. We are committed to providing the highest quality information available in the most appropriate format for our customers. Visit Aspen's Internet site for more information resources, directories, articles, and a searchable version of Aspen's full catalog, including the most recent publications: **http://www.aspenpub.com**
Aspen Publishers, Inc. • The hallmark of quality in publishing
Member of the worldwide Wolters Kluwer group.

Editorial Services: Rose Gilliver
Library of Congress Catalog Card Number: 98–70876
ISBN: 0–7514–0401–2

Printed in Great Britain

1 2 3 4 5

Contents

6   Nutrition and genetically engineered foods   112
CLAIRE DOMONEY, PHIL MULLINEAUX and ROD CASEY

7   Use of food ingredients to reduce degenerative diseases   136
IAN JOHNSON

Contributors

Ursula Arens British Nutrition Foundation, High Holborn House, 52–54 High Holborn, London WC1V 6RQ

Eithne Cahill Kellogg's UK, The Kellogg Building, Talbot Road, Manchester M16 0PU

Rod Casey Department of Applied Genetics, John Innes Centre, Norwich NR4 7UH

Claire Domoney Department of Applied Genetics, John Innes Centre, Norwich NR4 7UH

Ian Johnson Institute of Food Research, Norwich Laboratory, Norwich Research Park, Colney NR4 7UA

Patrick A. Morrissey Department of Nutrition, University College Cork, Ireland

Phil Mullineaux Department of Applied Genetics, John Innes Centre, Norwich NR4 7UH

Kathryn O'Sullivan Kellogg's UK, The Kellogg Building, Talbot Road, Manchester M16 0PU

David Richardson Nestlé UK Ltd, St George's House, Croydon, Surrey CR9 1NR

Andrew J. Rosenthal School of Biological and Molecular Sciences, Food Science and Nutrition Section, Oxford Brookes University, Gipsy Lane, Oxford OX3 0BP

Tony Sheehy Department of Nutrition, University College Cork, Ireland

R. James Stubbs Rowett Research Institute, Bucksburn, Aberdeen AB21 9SB

Susan Sungsoo Cho Kellogg Company, W.K. Kellogg, Institute for Food and Nutrition Research, 2 Hamblin Avenue East, Battle Creek, Michegan 49016–3232, USA

Introduction: from foraging to farming to food technology

C.J.K. HENRY and N.J. HEPPELL

This book contains chapters related to modern advances in food technology and its relationship with nutrition. However, it is useful to begin this review by examining how man has exploited plants and animals for his food supply throughout the ages.

The acquisition of food by our ancestors was by hunting and gathering a broad range of wild plants and animals. This meant that the need for food preservation was minimal, especially in tropical climates where seasonality was less evident. With the evolution of farming and the domestication of animals, however, the need to store foods increased. Other factors, such as the migration of workers from farmland to cities during and after the Industrial Revolution enhanced this requirement. The need for food preservation to enable transportation of food, to overcome the seasonal availability of foods and to ensure a safe, continuous supply of nutritious food is still important today. However, nutritious food has also expanded into satisfying demand for a range of other attributes desired from food, e.g. convenience, reduction in preparation time, novelty, new flavors and textures and other factors relating to demographic changes. The food engineer has also contributed greatly in ensuring that large production rates of safe, high quality food are possible and thereby reducing the cost of food through the economy of scale. This industrialization of food has resulted in the food industry becoming one of the largest industry sectors in the industrially-developed world. The contrast between the delivery of food in the industrially-developed countries and in the "Third World" has hardly been greater.

To determine the food acquisition strategy used by our forbears for food gathering and preservation, we have to rely either on archaeological evidence or studying the ethnography of existing hunter–gatherer tribes. While the former may shed light on the types of plants and animals used by our ancestors, the latter will be more likely to provide better insights into the social aspects of food use. Table 1 shows the range of plant species used by two present-day hunter–gatherer tribes, the Tlokwa of Botswana and the Alyawara of central Australia (Grivetti, 1979). This shows the large and varied number of species which comprise their diet. They do not rely on any particular food staple, utilizing animals, insects, seeds, leaves, stalks, roots and even flowers.

Table 1. Number of plant species used by hunter–gatherers

Hunter-gatherer group	No. of plant species used	
	Total	Type
Alyawara (Central Australia)	92	36 Seeds 32 Flowers 26 Fruits 8 Roots
Tlokwa (Botswana)	126	22 Leaves and stalks 31 Roots 47 Fruits 23 Barks and resins 3 Mushrooms

This large number of species as a food source is in direct contrast to the situation throughout the world today, where the staples (defined as a food source which contributes significantly to the energy content of the diet) used globally number merely 17 (Table 2). This is a direct consequence of the introduction of agriculture. Its development has been to produce large quantities of a limited range of plants, rather than the more inefficient method of small quantities of a larger number of crops. Over the ages, variants of the plant staples have been modified to give greater yields, to grow in less favourable conditions or with

Table 2. Plants used as staple foods today

Common name	Latin name
Rice	*Oriyza sativa*
Wheat	*Triticum* spp.
Maize	*Zea mays*
Sorghum	*Sorghum vulgare*
Millet	*Eleusine coracana*
Rye	*Secale cereale*
Oat	*Avena* spp.
Potato	*Solanum tuberosum*
Sweet potato	*Ipomoea batatas*
Taro	*Colocasia esculenta*
Yam	*Dioscorea* spp.
Cassava	*Manihot esculenta*
Sago	*Metroxylon* spp.
Arrowroot	*Maranta arundinaceae*
Teff	*Eragrostis tef*
Bread fruit	*Artocarpus altilis*
Barley	*Hordeum vulgare*

increased disease resistance as a priority, further reinforcing the limited range of crops it would be efficient to produce.

The reduction in the number of species in the diet should, theoretically, lead to greater nutritional deficiencies and is, indeed, true in developing countries with a limited range of cultivated or naturally-occurring plant species, giving rise to macro- and micronutrient deficiencies (Latham 1979).

Although the number of staple crops is few in modern, Western society, the number of different food products made from these staples is vast. Wheat is one of the most common staples produced in the world, even considering the limited climatic conditions required for growth. Remarkably, wheat can be transformed into over 1500 food products, each with very different structural characteristics and sensory properties. A list of some of the more common products is given in Table 3. Similar, though smaller, tables can be made for the other food staples (e.g. rice, corn and potato).

These products are often made using ancient cooking recipes and techniques, but have been taken over by the modern food technologist and changed into products which can be produced in large quantities and with extended keeping qualities. Further development of the food industry, with its accent on new product development has resulted in an ever-increasing number of food products from the existing staples, into areas never considered previously (or never even considered desirable!). These include the development of snack foods, foods for use with microwave ovens, mycoprotein, 'fast food' or the conversion into non-food bulk chemicals for use in the chemical industry.

Table 3. Selected list of foods manufactured from wheat

White bread	Pitta bread
Cookies	Chapatti
Crackers	Poori
Pretzel	Parotha
Doughnut	Upma
Breakfast cereals	Naan bread
Pasta	Rava idli
Baguette	Ravadosa
Roll	Tempura batter
Croissant	Halwa
Brioches	Jalebi
Stollen	Roti
Scone	Tanoor bread
Cake	Baladi bread
Shortbread	Barbari bread
Noodles	Couscous
Waffle	Bulgar
Pancake	Bameah
Steamed bun	Kanofeah
Dumpling	

Present day technologies

The preservation of foodstuffs is achieved by stopping growth of microorganisms and enzyme action using one or more of the following techniques:

1. physical methods, such as drying, freezing, chilling, thermal processing,
2. chemical methods, by control of pH, redox potential, atmosphere, preservatives or antimicrobial compounds
3. a combination of (1.) and (2.) above,

The majority of the current food processes shown in Table 4 have been developed this century, but particularly in the period just after World War II when food supply was an urgent issue in many European countries. Although these technologies were effective in ensuring that a sufficient quantity of food was available, the nutritional and organoleptic quality was a secondary consideration and the poor quality of some products during the 1940s was responsible for consumer aversion to that technology for at least a decade or so.

These days, the drive for preserved or extended shelf-life foods is more likely to be increased convenience, required by changes in lifestyle to one which is more busy but involves less manual work, together with an increase in general availability of refrigerators, freezers and microwave ovens. At the same time, there is a demand for 'fresher-tasting' or less 'processed' foods and a general increase in the awareness of nutritional issues, all of which has stimulated the search for processing methods which will still extend shelf-life effectively but also have minimal impact on the organoleptic quality and biochemical nature of the foodstuff.

New food technologies

The requirements for any new food processing technology are that the product is at least as safe as the traditional or currently-used process, and has at least some, or preferably all, of the following:

Table 4. Traditional and modern food processing technologies

Traditional processes (prehistoric)	Current processes
Sundrying	In-container sterilization (retorting)
Oven drying	Aseptic (UHT) processing
Smoking	Pasteurization (HTST)
Salting	Irradiation
Pickling	Spray drying
Fermentation	Freeze drying
(Freezing)	Extrusion cooking
	Freezing and chilling
	Membrane processing
	Modified atmosphere packaging
	Microwave and radiofrequency heating
	Use of fluidized beds for freezing and drying

- has high convenience and greater ease of storage (preferably ambient conditions),
- is fresher, more natural and has less change over raw or freshly-cooked product,
- has better organoleptic quality, including texture, colour and flavour,
- has better nutritional value, but does not have a greater energy density,
- is cheaper on the supermarket shelf.

All the above facets are advantages that can be perceived by the consumer. Care must be taken to ensure that, if the new technology changes the characteristics of an established product in any way, the consumer actually considers this an advantage to themselves and will accept the changes. For example, if a canned product is replaced by an aseptically-processed and packaged one, the changes in the container material indicate some change has taken place and, unless the product has a superior taste or lower cost, the consumer may not accept, or indeed may mistrust, the product change.

There are some emerging technologies that are either available now or may be technologically possible in a few years time. These will now be considered and the implications for the nutritional status of the products considered.

Aseptic processing

Aseptic processing, or ultra high temperature (UHT) processing, is one where a continuous flow of the product is heated to a high temperature, held at that temperature for the time required for sterilization, then cooled and packed into a presterilized container under aseptic conditions. The use of heat exchangers appropriate to the product characteristics means that a faster rate of heating and much higher temperatures can be achieved than possible for in-container processes; temperatures in the region of 135–150°C are used compared to 118–125°C for the latter. To achieve sterilization, therefore, a very short holding time is required (about 3–6 s) and, due to the difference in sensitivities of microbial death and of chemical change to temperature changes, much less biochemical change in the food occurs.

The aseptic processing of low viscosity liquids, such as milk, fruit juice and cream is very common, and of medium to high viscosity 'pure' liquids is rapidly becoming established, with an increasing number of products on the market such as puréed soups, cook-in-sauces and gravies. The major difficulty arises when solid food particulates are present in the food, i.e. dishes containing meat, vegetable or fruit lumps. In all conventional heat exchangers, the liquid phase is heated first, and heat then has to transfer to the particle surface and through it to its thermal centre. The relatively slow rate at which the latter occurs means that the liquid phase will be overheated with subsequent quality deterioration. The rate of heat transfer into the particle when it is being transported by a flowing liquid is largely unknown (Lewis and Heppell, 1998), although current research work, reviewed by Maesmans *et al.* (1992), is under way to measure it under these difficult circumstances. With this information, the thermal process received by the centre of the particle may be predicted using mathematical models. Techniques to measure the received thermal process are also under development, using bacterial spores or other markers entrapped in particles, reviewed by Van Loey *et al.* (1996).

One major development has been the use of Ohmic heating to overcome these problems, where the foodstuff is heated by passing an electric current through the food which heats due to its electrical resistance. If particles are present in the liquid, and if their electrical conductivity is the same as the liquid that carries them, the particles and liquid heat at the same rate, approximately 1°C/s, which is much faster than is possible by conduction heat transfer. Special design of the electrodes stops surfaces heating up, which further improves product quality. Even though cooling is by conventional heat exchanger, the overall process gives a better quality product, with less overheating of the liquid phase than is possible using conventional aseptic processing equipment, and it is superior to the best in-container sterilization system for this type of food. No other sterilization effect is observed other than by the heat generated by the electrical current.

Other improvements in aseptic processing of particulate foodstuffs may be possible by use of the Stork Rota-Hold Selective Holding Section in which particles are held back in the holding section by using slowly-rotating fork blades that allow liquid to pass through quickly. It can therefore be arranged that the different phases, and also different particle ranges, can have their relevant optimum residence times, giving a higher quality product and minimizing overprocessing.

The extent to which aseptic processing may replace in-container sterilization, or canning is dependent on the physical nature of the product. Low and medium viscosity liquid products are common, such as flavoured milk, evaporated milk, custard, soya milks, tomato products, soups and cook-in sauces. Commercial products containing particulate products are less common, but include soups and cook-in sauces as well as a range of sauces and fruit products produced using the Ohmic process. Both the Ohmic and conventional heat exchanger systems have been approved by the FDA in the USA.

High-pressure processing

The use of high pressure to inactivate microorganisms was first investigated in 1899 by Hite (1899) but has only been recently reassessed as a preservation technique, especially in Japan, although with increasing interest in other countries. The technique uses pressures of 100–1000 MPa (1000–10 000 atmospheres) applied to the food at ambient, or relatively low, temperatures for periods of about 10 to 30 min.

The microbiological effect is mainly on vegetative cells where the changes induced by the pressure are still under investigation but include changes to morphology, biochemical reactions, genetic mechanisms and cell membrane and cell walls (Hoover *et al.*, 1989). Bacterial spores are much less affected by high pressure treatment directly, but their germination is promoted and subsequent cell death may occur. The use of temperatures higher than ambient, about 40°C, greatly enhances germination and so give greatly increased spore death. Hayakawa (1997) showed how the effect of a high pressures and elevated temperatures above 75°C for periods up to 240 min, followed by rapid decompression to ambient pressure will disrupt spores physically by bursting their coats. However, the effect of this on anything other than purely liquid foods would be extreme!

The effect of high pressure treatment on biochemical components of foods can be quite severe. Proteins are known to denature (egg protein will coagulate), polysaccharides may gelatinize, lipids may solidify and biomembranes denature (Knorr, 1997), but enzymes are often highly pressure resistant. The effect on micronutrients has been little studied, though Donsi *et al.* (1997) found little effect on Vitamin C, β-carotene and total carotenoids in orange juice. These authors also examined components related to flavour and colour of the juice and found the organoleptic quality to be little affected. The organoleptic quality of pressure-treated foods is generally found to be superior to other preservation methods.

It seems unlikely at present that high pressure treatment of foods will replace conventional preservation treatments to any great extent, although commercial products are available in Japan. Pressure treatment plants are large, expensive and require careful engineering to accommodate the pressure. The systems are generally batch, although a continuous system for liquids has been developed (Sionneau *et al.* 1997) capable of up to 380 MPa at 200 L/h, suitable for pure liquid foodstuffs only, obviously requiring an aseptic packaging system. All these factors mean that the product is relatively expensive and it is expected that high pressure technology will generally find a niche market for small production of high quality, high priced products or products where the protein and polysaccharide changes give unusual textural characteristics (Mertens, 1995).

Pulsed electric field

The use of pulsed electric field (PEF) as a non-thermal sterilization method has recently become the subject of much research effort. The method relies on applied voltage in the region of 12–50 kV/cm across the food product, applied in multiple short pulses, between 0.1 and 10 Hz, each with a duration of microseconds. The treatment can be applied either as a batch or in continuous flow at temperatures from chilled to ambient, although the application of electrical pulses causes some heating of the foodstuff. The effect of the treatment on microbial cells appears to be due to formation of pores in the cell membrane when the trans-membrane potential is higher than 1V and subsequent permeation of small molecules causes swelling and disruption of the cell membrane (Vega-Mercado *et al.*, 1997).

The majority of work has been on pasteurization of foods, or sterilization of high acid foods (pH<3.7), as inactivation of spores is much more difficult due to their size and lower electrical conductivity (Marquez *et al.*, 1997). However, these authors found that a reduction in *Bacillus cereus* spores of over five log cycles was obtained with a 50 kV/cm field strength at 25°C and the spores were completely destroyed, enlarged or had holes in it. The damage appeared not to be reversed after 30 days storage.

Several foods have been treated using PEF, especially fruit juices, milk, yoghurt, liquid egg and pea soup. Although product quality has been reported as good, and certainly better than equivalent thermal processing, the method does induce some chemical changes. Inactivation of enzymes has been found, especially lipase, plasmin in milk and proteinase from *Ps fluorescens* but only low levels of inactivation of alkaline phosphatase or denaturation of other proteins has been detected. Other components have been little studied, Grahl and Maerkl (1996) show little loss of vitamin C or A, the loss generally increasing with electrical potential. They also found no significant deterioration in taste.

Generally, the technique has potential, especially for pasteurization or sterilization of high acid foods where nutritional benefit over thermal processing may be found.

Other advances

There are other, less well developed, food processing techniques which may, in time, be valuable in improving the nutritional and organoleptic quality of foodstuffs, either as a preservation method in themselves or as methods of intensifying conventional processes. Methods presently under investigation include the use of ultrasound or sonic energy with heat, intense light pulses and the use of natural antimicrobial compounds. There is also considerable work in progress in improving hurdle technology, modified atmosphere packaging with the use of intelligent packaging and microwave or radio-frequency processing. It is to be hoped that some, if not all, of these techniques will eventually find there way into commercial use.

References

Donsi, G., Ferrari, G., Di Matteo, M. and Bruno, M.C. (1997) High pressure stabilization of orange juice. *Engineering & Food at ICEF 7 (1).* Sheffield Academic Press, UK.

Grahl, T. and Maerkl, H. (1996) Killing of microorganisms by pulsed electric fields. *Applied Microbiology and Biotechnology,* **45,** (1/2), 148–157.

Grivetti, L. (1979) Kalahari agro-pastoral hunter-gatherers. *Ecology of Food and Nutrition,* **7,** 235–256.

Hayakawa, I. (1997) High pressure technology in sterilization of biomass by adiabatic expansion of water. *Engineering & Food at ICEF 7 (1)*. Sheffield Academic Press, UK.

Hite, B. H. (1899) The effect of pressure in the preservation of milk. *West Virginia Agricultural Experiment Station Bulletin* , **58**, 15–35.

Hoover, D.G., Metrick, K., Papineau, A.M., Farkass, D.F. and Knorr, D. (1989) Biological effect of high hydrostatic pressure on food microorganisms. *Food Technology*, **43**, 99–107.

Knorr, D. (1997) Engineering aspects of novel non-thermal food processes. *Engineering & Food at ICEF 7(1)*. Sheffield Academic Press, UK.

Latham, M. C. (1979) *Human Nutrition in Tropical Africa. FAO Food and Nutrition Series* no.11. FAO, Rome.

Lewis M.J. and Heppell N.J. (1998) *Continuous-flow Processing of Liquid Foods*. Blackie, London.

Marquez, V.O., Mittal, G.S. and Griffiths, M.W. (1997) Destruction and inhibition of bacterial spores by high voltage pulsed electric field. *Journal of Food Science* , **62** (2), 399–401, 409.

Maesmans, G., Hendrickx, M., De Cordt, S., Fransis, A. and Tobback, P. (1992) Fluid to particle heat transfer coefficient determination of heterogeneous foods: a review. *Journal of Food Processing and Preservation*, **16** (1), 29–69.

Mertens, B. (1995) in *New Methods of Food Preservation* (ed. G.W. Gould), Chapter 7. Blackie, Glasgow.

Sionneau, M., Bouix, M., Vasseur, J. and Pontvianne, P.M. (1997) Continuous high pressure treatment of milk with different discharge devices. *Engineering & Food at ICEF 7(supp)*. Sheffield Academic Press, UK.

Van Loey, A., Hendrickx, M., de Cordt, S., Haentjens, T. and Tobback, P. (1996) Quantitative evaluation of thermal processes using time-temperature integrators. *Trends In Food Science & Technology*, **7**, (1), 16–26.

1 The addition of nutrients to foods

DAVID P. RICHARDSON

Introduction

Several nutrients have been added to food and drink products around the world as public health measures and as effective ways of ensuring the nutritional quality of the food supply. Additions of some nutrients have also formed the basis of marketing strategies in product development (Richardson, 1993). The main criteria for selecting nutrients to add to foods are that they are shown to be safe, effective and beneficial to the nutritional status of the target population groups (Brady, 1996a,b). Long-term solutions to micronutrient deficiencies rest on the provision of adequate quantities of all micronutrients from a well-balanced diet. Food-based approaches around the world include strategies to improve the availability of a variety of foods, food preservation methods to maximize nutrient retention, and addition of nutrients to suitable food carriers. Nutrition education is also an important and parallel long-term strategy.

The aim of this chapter is to review the rationale, benefits and risks associated with the responsible addition of nutrients to foods. The safety and quality of foods are fundamental to any initiatives, as is the need to avoid inappropriate additions, which could undermine consumer credibility and mislead consumers about the role of enriched foods in a healthy, balanced diet. The addition of nutrients requires an understanding of local or national dietary patterns and of the nutritional status of the population or target groups. Major technical challenges are also involved in adding nutrients to foods, including the identification of suitable dietary vehicles, the selection of appropriate compounds and the manufacturing technologies to be applied (Berry Ottaway, 1993). Nutrient additions to ordinary foods and the use of claims can also create difficulties because of the lack of common rules and approaches within the European Union (EU) and in other countries. Current practices and legislation, which differ considerably in approach and degrees of restrictiveness, can also sometimes interrupt free trade.

Whereas the addition of nutrients can undoubtedly improve the nutritional status and health of those segments of the population that are vulnerable and susceptible to deficiencies, there is also increasing awareness of the role of some foods, nutrients and non-nutrients, that can give positive nutritional and physiological benefits. Consumer interest in the link between diet and health is increas-

Reproduced with permission from *Proceedings of the Nutrition Society* (1997) vol. 56, pp 807–825

ing and there are many opportunities for developing foods that could have positive effects on health (Young, 1996).

Definitions and terminology

General agreement on terminology has been reached within Codex Alimentarius Commission (Codex Alimentarius Commission, 1994) and further clarification has been suggested by the Nordic Council of Ministers (Tema Nord, 1995). For the purposes of this book, the term *nutrient addition* refers to the addition of micronutrients, primarily vitamins and minerals. Amino acids and other substances with nutritional value, for example fatty acids, fibres and macronutrients such as proteins, carbohydrates and fats, may also be used as additions. *Restoration* refers to the addition of nutrient(s) to a food to replace naturally occurring nutrients that are unavoidably lost during the course of good manufacturing practice in the preparation and preservation of food or during normal storage and handling procedures. The levels of such nutrients are restored to those that were present in the edible portion of the food before processing, storage or handling, e.g. iron and B vitamins to flours. *Fortification* usually refers to the addition of one or more nutrients to a food, whether or not it is normally contained in the food, where the level of nutrients present makes the food a 'richer' source. These enrichment practices are used for public health reasons to prevent or correct a demonstrated deficiency or risk of suboptimal intakes in a population or specific population groups, e.g. the addition of iodide to salt, and to produce quality products with enhanced nutritional value, e.g. breakfast cereals. *Standardization* refers to the addition of nutrients in order to compensate for natural or seasonal variations in nutrient levels, e.g. vitamin C to juices. *Substitution* refers to additions of nutrients to a substitute product to obtain the level of nutrient in the food that the substitute is designed to resemble or replace, e.g. fat replacers in margarine. In practice a combination of these different types of nutrient additions, is often used.

General principles for the addition of nutrients to foods

The addition of nutrients to foods requires careful attention to food regulations, labelling, nutritional rationale, cost, the acceptability of the product to consumers and a careful assessment of technical and analytical limitations for compliance with label declarations (Richardson, 1990). The level of essential nutrients should not have any harmful effects on the consumers' nutritional status or health; excessive additions should be discouraged and information on food labels should not over-emphasise or distort the role of a single food or component in enhancing good health. Within the Food and Agriculture

Organization of the United Nations/World Health Organization (FAO/WHO) Food Standards Programme, the Codex Alimentarius Commission (1994) has adopted a number of basic principles (Table 1.1) to achieve any one or a combination of restoration, fortification, standardization and substitution, and to ensure the appropriate nutrient additions to special purpose foods, such as those for special dietary use.

These principles apply to the addition of nutrients to foods around the world as public health measures, when foodstuffs are enriched compulsorily, and also when proprietary foods and enriched voluntarily. If there are widespread deficiencies or a likelihood of deficiencies, then the solution is usually compulsory enrichment at local, regional or national levels, as appropriate. Increased attention is also being given to the addition of nutrients to food aid commodities, particularly foods used for emergency and refugee feeding. The levels of specific nutrients must be appropriate for the given situation, bearing in mind the cumulative amounts from other sources in the diet. More detailed discussion of the criteria for addition of nutrients can be found in Tema Nord (1995), FOA (1996) and Codex Alimentarius Commission (1994).

Regulatory aspects

Principles and practices of nutrient addition vary considerably and a survey by Tema Nord (1995) showed a number of approaches:

Table 1.1 Ten general principles for the addition of nutrients to foods (adapted from Codex Alimentarius CAC/GL 09-1987, amended 1989, 1991)

---

1. The essential nutrient should be present at a level which will not result in either an excessive or an insignificant intake of the added essential nutrient considering amounts from other sources in the diet.
2. The addition of an essential nutrient to a food should not result in an adverse effect on the metabolism of any other nutrient.
3. The essential nutrient should be sufficiently stable in the food under customary conditions of packaging, storage, distribution and use.
4. The essential nutrient should be biologically available from the food.
5. The essential nutrient should not impart undesirable characteristics to the food (e.g. colour, taste, flavour, texture, cooking properties) and should not unduly shorten shelf-life.
6. Technology and processing facilities should be available to permit the addition of the essential nutrient in a satisfactory manner.
7. Addition of essential nutrients to foods should not be used to mislead or deceive the consumer as to the nutritional merit of the food.
8. The additional cost should be reasonable for the intended consumer.
9. Methods of measuring, controlling and/or enforcing the levels of added essential nutrients in foods should be available.
10. When provision is made in food standards, regulations or guidelines for the addition of essential nutrients to foods, specific provisions should be included identifying the essential nutrients to be considered or required and the levels at which they should be present in the food to achieve their intended purpose.

- *general permission*: nutrient addition is regulated by legislation that specifies the foods and/or nutrients permitted; levels of permitted nutrients might also be specified
- *individual authorization*: nutrient addition is not permitted unless permission is specifically applied for from the authorities
- *notification*: nutrient addition is permitted but notification is required
- *free nutrient addition*: there are no authorization procedures or restrictions governing nutrient additions to foods, or no legislation.

Table 1.2 summarizes the approaches and underlying legislation on addition of nutrients to ordinary foods in the 17 countries surveyed. For example, in the UK a liberal approach has been successfully and safely adopted for almost 50 years, and additions of nutrients are not restricted in terms of types of food, nutrients or nutrient levels provided there is compliance with Section 7 of the Food Safety Act 1990 (Ministry of Agriculture, Fisheries and Food, 1996a) and they are not injurious to health. Typically, if a general claim is made for 'a useful source' or 'with added', then the daily intake (described as the quantity of food that can reasonably be expected to be consumed in a day) must contain at least one-sixth of the recommended daily amount (RDA) of two or more of the scheduled micronutrients. For a food to be claimed generally as a 'rich' or 'excellent' source of vitamins and minerals, then the typical daily amount consumed must contain at least half of the RDA of two or more of the scheduled micronutrients (Ministry of Agriculture, Fisheries and Food, 1996b). For specific claims for named vitamins and minerals, these conditions must be complied with in respect of every micronutrient named. The percentage of the RDA in a quantified serving and the number of servings must also be declared on the pack. According to the Nutrition Labelling Directive 90/469/EEC (European Commission, 1990), vitamins and minerals can only be declared when they are present in significant amounts, and must be declared when a claim has been made. As a rule, a significant amount means 15% of the RDA that is supplied by 100 g or 100 ml of a food, or per package of a food if the package contains only a single portion. In contrast to the UK, the addition of nutrients is strictly controlled in Denmark, Finland, Norway and Sweden, whereas Belgium adopts a middle approach whereby additions of vitamins and minerals are allowed for all foods, but notification is needed.

Examples of additions of nutrients to foods

Four categories of foodstuffs suitable for the addition of nutrients can be identified (du Bois, 1987):

(a) foods for special dietary uses
(b) foods having lost nutrients during manufacture
(c) foods resembling a common food (substitute products)
(d) staple foods representing ideal vehicles for nutrients.

Table 1.2 Principles underlying legislation on addition of vitamins and minerals to ordinary foods (Tema Nord, 1995)

Country	Legislation on nutrient addition	Legislation based on — General permission	Individual authorization	Notification	Free	Positive list with nutrients specified	Remarks
Austria	No (except salt)				X	No	Nutrient addition is free as long as no health hazards exist and labelling does not mislead or deceive
Belgium	Yes	X		X		Yes	Nutrient addition allowed for all foods but notification is needed Minimum and maximum final levels of nutrients in foods are defined
Denmark	Yes	X*	X			Yes	* For flours, oatflakes, cereals and juices only
Finland	Yes	X*	X			No	* For margarines only
Germany	Yes	X				Yes	Addition of named vitamins permitted without limitations For vitamins A and D maximum levels given
Greece	Yes	X*	X			No	* For margarines, fat emulsions and salt only
Iceland	Yes	X*		X		No	* For margarines only
Italy	No		X			No	Nutrient addition allowed to ordinary foods only if approved by Ministry of Health
Luxembourg	No				X	No	Nutrient levels should not be high enough to exceed RDI
Netherlands	Yes					No	Nutrient addition prohibited except compulsory additions to margarines and breadsalt, and optional addition to salt
Norway	Yes	X*	X			No	* For margarines, butter, oils, salt and goat whey, and cheese only
Sweden	Yes	X*	X			Yes	* For fat-reduced milk, oils, salt, flours and pasta only
Switzerland	Yes (for vitamins)	X				No	Addition of named vitamins allowed to all foods, maximum limits set
UK	Yes				X	No	Addition not restricted, provided not injurious to health
Australia	Yes	X				Yes	Foods, allowed nutrients and their levels specified
Canada	Yes	X				No	Foods, allowed nutrients and their levels specified
USA	Yes	X				No	Food standards specify what nutrients may be added Nutrients must be added to substitute food

RDI = recommended daily intake.

(a) Foods for special dietary uses

The EU Directive on Foods for Particular Nutritional Uses 89/398/EEC (PARNUTS; European Commission, 1989) sets out the general principles governing the composition and marketing of foods for *PAR*ticular *NUT*ritional use*S*, or dietetic foods as they are more commonly known. The Directive covers foodstuffs for which the composition and preparation are specifically designed to 'meet the particular nutritional requirements of the persons for whom they are mainly intended'. They must have a special composition or manufacturing process and be clearly distinguishable from everyday foodstuffs for normal consumption. Although the Directive requires the development of specific Directives for nine categories of dietetic foods, only three of these have been adopted. These are the Directive on Infant Formulae and Follow-on Formulae 91/321/EEC (European Commission, 1991), the Directive on Processed Cereal-based Foods and Baby Foods for Infants and Young Children 96/5/EC (European Commission, 1996a) and the Directive of Foods Intended for Use in Energy-restricted Diets for Weight Reduction 96/8/EC (European Commission, 1996b). This last Directive comes fully into force in 1 April 1999 and requires that single-meal replacers contain 30% of the daily requirements for the vitamins and minerals listed in the annex to the Directive. The remaining product categories are still being debated by Member States and, to date, the draft proposals have still to be developed. Although the issues go beyond the scope of this chapter, another requirement in Directive 89/398/EEC (European Commission, 1989) is the adoption of a positive list of nutrient sources permitted for use in PARNUTS products. Lists are now included as Annexe III to Directive 91/321/EEC (European Commission, 1991) and as Annexe IV to Directive 96/5/EC (European Commission, 1996a). The establishment of advisory lists of nutrients and nutrient compounds was also recommended by the Codex Alimentarius Commission in 1994 and the FAO in 1996, taking into account new scientific and technological developments and data on safety, bioavailability and stability as well as other relevant information.

(b) Foods having lost nutrients during normal manufacture, storage and
   handling

In the UK there are requirements for the compulsory addition of certain micronutrients to bread and flour (Ministry of Agriculture, Fisheries and Food, 1996c). It is compulsory to fortify extracted flours with iron (16.5 mg/kg), calcium (940 to 1560 mg/kg), thiamin (2.4 mg/kg) and niacin (16 mg/kg). The addition of vitamins A and D to skim-milk powder, of vitamin D to evaporated milk, of vitamin C to the preparation of instant potato and to some juices and nectars are examples of voluntary vitamin restoration in the UK. A comprehensive review of the mandatory and voluntary additions of nutrients to wheat flour and margarine worldwide is in a report of an FAO Technical Meeting (FAO, 1996). Although some losses of nutrients are inevitable, particularly losses of the more labile nutrients in any wet process, many manufacturers endeavour to conserve nutrients with attention to good quality assurance and manufacturing practices.

(c) Foods resembling a common food

The principle of substitution underlies the regulations in many countries for adding vitamins A and D to margarine (e.g. Germany, Austria, Greece, Iceland, The Netherlands, Norway, Sweden, Australia, Canada and the USA). In the UK, the compulsory addition began at the start of World War II as part of a major public health measure to prevent rickets. By law, margarine must be enriched to contain 800–1000 μg retinol (vitamin A) and 7.05–8.82 μg vitamin D per 100 g (Ministry of Agriculture, Fisheries and Food, 1996d) to make it comparable with butter, which contains typically 520–970 μg of retinol and 0.63–1.00 μg vitamin D per 100 g.

In 1991, the Committee on Medical Aspects (COMA) published a report by its Working Group, which advised on the need in the UK for continued mandatory fortification of margarine with vitamins A and D and whether this requirement should be extended to all fat spreads other than butter. Food manufacturers had begun to develop a range of low-fat and reduced-fat spreads in response to consumer demand. These types of products are not subject to specific legislation and they were taking a growing proportion of the total yellow fats market. Fortification of these products is not mandatory, but the Working Group recommended that the manufacturers should be encouraged to continue and extend the practice of voluntary fortification of these products with vitamins A and D to the levels currently required for margarine (Department of Health, 1991a).

The fat replacer Olestra™, which was granted approval for limited use in the USA in 1996, must be fortified with vitamins A, D, E and K. Olestra is a unique food component that can be used as a non-digestible substitute for fat. It is a sucrose polyester and because of its chemical compositions, it passes undigested through the body and adds no fat or calories to the diet. On 24 January 1996, after a long review of the safety data and concerns about Olestra's nutritional effects, the Food and Drug Administration (FDA) approved its use as a direct human food additive in a limited range of snack foods, such as flavoured and unflavoured crisps, snack products and crackers (Food and Drug Administration, 1996). These uses include frying, because it is the only fat replacer that can withstand high temperatures (Giese, 1996). One of the concerns about the use of Olestra is that fat-soluble vitamins dissolve readily in it as it moves through the digestive tract and the nutrients are carried out of the body before they can be absorbed from the intestine (Blackburn, 1996). Hence, the FDA decided that Olestra must be fortified with all four vitamins to compensate for the amounts that are not absorbed. The FDA also requires the label of any food containing Olestra to bear the following statement, which reflects the nutritional concerns: 'This product contains Olestra. Olestra may cause abdominal cramping and loose stools. Olestra inhibits the absorption of some vitamins and other nutrients. Vitamins A, D, E and K have been added'. Proctor and Gamble, the manufacturer which developed this novel fat-based substitute, and the FDA are continuing to monitor and evaluate the safe use of Olestra (G. Allgood, personal communication).

In the UK, COMA (Department of Health and Social Security, 1980) laid down the general principle that 'any substance promoted as a replacement or an alternative to a natural food should be nutritionally equivalent in all but unimportant aspects of the natural food which it would simulate'. Thus, in 1980, the Department of Health and Social Security gave their recommendations and specifications for the nutritional quality and use of textured vegetable protein (TVP) foods, which simulate meat. The Codex Alimentarius Commission has also stated that nutritional equivalence means being of a similar nutritive value in terms of quantity and quality of protein and in terms of kinds, quantity and bioavailability of essential nutrients. For this purpose, nutritional equivalence means that essential nutrients provided by the food being substituted, and that are present in a serving or portion or 100 kilocalories of a food at a level of 5% or more of the RDA of the nutrient(s), are present in the substituted or partially substituted food (extender) in comparable amounts.

(d) Staple foods

Foods that are to be used to supply nutrients must be likely to be widely consumed in quantities that will make a significant contribution to the diet of the target population. Hence, nutrients are often added to staple foods such as wheat, rice, maize, bread, pasta, sugar, vegetable oils, liquid and powdered milk products, and breakfast cereals as well as dietary components such as salt, tea, monosodium glutamate (MSG), etc.

A good example of such additions is the fortification of several foods with vitamin A. Vitamin A deficiency causes the deaths of approximately 500 000 children each year in developing countries and xerophthalmia is the most widespread nutritional disorder that results in blindness in man (Underwood, 1994). In most developing countries there is no legislation covering addition of vitamin A to foods and the practice is voluntary, requiring concerted action with partners such as grant and aid agency groups, technical agencies, the food industry and consumer groups. Vitamin A fortification of several foods including wheat, rice, salt, sugar and MSG, for developing countries has been worked on with various degrees of success (Bauernfeind and Arroyave, 1986; Murphy et al., 1992). However, there are a number of technical and logistical problems associated with the development of suitable forticants and carrier foods (Murphy, 1995).

Another good example of the fortification of a suitable dietary vehicle is the iodization of salt for the general population. Salt has been used successfully and, in general, safely for over 70 years in programmes around the world to prevent iodine deficiency disorders (IDD). Hetzel (Hetzel *et al.*, 1987; Hetzel, 1989) drew attention to the fact that visible goitre was only one of a series of consequences of inadequate iodine intake. He demonstrated that insufficient iodine during early foetal development resulted in inadequate development of the baby's brain because insufficient iodine-containing thyroid hormones were available. It is now realized that iodine deficiency may actually contribute to the process of under-development by limiting the development and learning capacity of children. 'Cretinism' is a term that embraces the most severe forms of damaged persons and it is related to the severity and duration of iodine deficiency, particularly in the children of mothers who themselves are iodine deficient and frequently goitrous (Stanbury, 1996).

Edible salt has been the favoured carrier for iodine owing to its widespread use, effectiveness, the simple technology involved and low cost. Iodized salt can be used in the home and in a wide variety of commercially prepared foods. Salt iodization began in Switzerland in 1922 and today most countries have either mandatory controls or voluntary programmes to eliminate the public health problem of IDD (FAO, 1996). The levels of fortification that have been used range from 30 to 200 ppm and the Codex Alimentarius Commission standards for food-grade salt permit the use of the sodium and potassium salts of iodides and iodates. The iodide compounds are cheaper, more soluble and have a higher iodine content (therefore less is needed to achieve the same level of iodization than the corresponding iodates). Major considerations need to be made in the choice between iodides and iodates. Iodates are generally more stable under high moisture, high ambient temperature, sunlight, aeration and the presence of impurities, compared with the iodide compounds. The use of iodized salt in commercially prepared foods, however, needs to be harmonized in Europe to remove barriers to trade.

Simple goitre is probably the easiest of all human diseases to prevent if there is action and good co-operation between governments, salt producers and refiners, and international agencies (Alnwick, 1995). It is United Nations (UN) policy that all salt programmed for food and distribution to beneficiaries has to be iodine fortified and of the 109 countries where IDD is a problem, most have already passed laws that require all salt to be iodized. Many more countries are following suit to meet the UNICEF challenge to eliminate this public health problem by the year 2000. Iodine fortification programmes should be continued and extended vigorously so that instances of newly susceptible persons, and especially of developmentally damaged children, become very rare (Stanbury, 1996).

Health and safety aspects

There is a substantial need for objective, scientific evaluations of the safety of micronutrients and for the determination of agreed safe intakes that provide acceptable margins of safety from any adverse effects. Several assessments have been undertaken: four government-commissioned reviews (Ministry of Agriculture, Fisheries and Food, 1991; The Netherlands Food and Nutrition Council, 1993; Australian National Food Authority, 1994; University of Toronto, 1996) and two comprehensive industry-sponsored reviews (Shrimpton, 1995, 1996). These sources of information, together with the COMA report on dietary reference values and the 'guidance on high intakes' (Department of Health, 1991b), provide the basic data for developing risk categories for individual micronutrients (Table 1.3). The data show the RDAs, where these have been set by the European Commission (Directive 90/496/EEC; European Commission, 1990), typical UK daily intakes (Office of Population Census and Surveys, 1990; Shrimpton, 1995), summaries of adverse effects and best estimates of upper, safe, daily intakes. In 1994, the Food and Nutrition Board in the USA defined the upper safe level as the level of intake of a nutrient or a food component that appears to be safe for most healthy people and beyond which there is concern that some people will experience symptoms of toxicity over time. Most substances will cause harmful effects at some level of intake and any assessment of the levels of micronutrient additions, or the food categories of which nutrients may be added, needs to be based on demonstrated risk using scientific risk assessment methods.

The traditional approach to estimating safe levels of vitamins and minerals for enrichment purposes and for nutritional supplements on free sale has tended to be based on an arbitrary multiple of the RDA. However, recent developments in nutrition science have drawn attention to the shortcomings of a single RDA and pointed to the need for the development of an 'upper safe level' reference point for both short-term and long-term consumption (see Table 1.3 for references). Since additions of nutrients to foods are usually based on delivering a predetermined proportion of the RDA, any review of current recommendations would impact on enrichment practices. Similarly, the principle in some countries of restricting nutrient addition to foods primarily on the basis of 'correcting demonstrated nutrient deficiency', as judged by classical nutrition methods, is no longer appropriate. It cannot be emphasized enough that the inadequacies of the scientific basis for RDAs for 'optimal health' and the difficulties in assessing safe levels of nutrient additions to the food supply underlie the current restrictions on the levels of micronutrient additions, the food categories to which nutrients may be added and the inconsistencies in practice and legislation between different countries and trading partners. For the UK food industry to be innovative and competitive there are increasing economic advantages that can be achieved through regulatory efficiencies and harmonization. Shrimpton (1995) proposed that 'any micronutrient may be consumed in an amount that is less than that for which an adverse effect has been confirmed either in peer-reviewed scientific literature or in responsibly monitored practice'. There is a need for caution, and in such dynamic areas of research and dietary experience and practice the subject area should be reviewed at regular intervals.

Table 1.3 Categories of risk for individual micronutrients

Nutrient	Unit daily usage	EU labelling RDA[a]	Typical daily intake from diet[b]	Maximum total safe daily intake[c]	Guidance on high (toxic) level[d]	Adverse effects in humans
Category 1: Low risk and no known adverse effects						
Thiamin	mg	1.4	1.8	50	500–3000 (n.e.)	No known effects
Riboflavin	mg	1.6	2.0	200	n.e.	No known effects
Vitamin B$_{12}$	μg	1	7.0	3000	n.e.	No known effects
Pantothenic acid	mg	6	6.0	1000	n.e.	No known effects
Biotin	μg	15.0	39	2500	n.e.	No known effects
Niacin (amide)	mg	18	40	500	n.e.	No known effects
β-carotene	mg	—	1.9	25	3000	Reversible yellowing of subcutaneous fat and skin discoloration
Vitamin E (α – TE)	mg	10	10	800	3200 (n.e.)	No known effects
Category 2: Low risk and acceptable safety margin						
Vitamin C	mg	60	75	1000	2000 (n.e.)	Gastrointestinal distress and diarrhoea at 10–15 g/day; reported pro-oxidant effects, excessive iron absorption
Vitamin B$_6$	mg	2	2.5	200[e]	500–7000	Sensory neuropathy of extremities
Folic acid	μg	200	300	1000	n.e.	Masking of B$_{12}$ deficiency and pernicious anaemia; interferes with effectiveness of anticonvulsant drugs; neurotoxic in epilepsy patients at high oral intakes
Calcium	mg	800	900	1500–2500	n.e.	Hypercalcaemia; urinary stone formation (in predisposed persons); inhibition of absorption of other essential nutrients, e.g. iron, zinc, manganese
Magnesium	mg	300	310	700	3000–5000	Diarrhoea; neurological disorders
Iodine	μg	150	225	1000	5000	Rare cases of hypersensitivity
Potassium	mg	—	3200	n.e.	17600 (n.e.)	Hyperkalaemia in sensitive individuals

Table 1.3 Continued

Nutrient	Unit daily usage	EU labelling RDA[a]	Typical daily intake from diet[b]	Maximum total safe daily intake[c]	Guidance on high (toxic) level[d]	Adverse effects in humans
Category 3: Known risk and narrow safety margin						
Vitamin A (RE)	µg	800	1200	3000–3300	6500 (9000)	Teratogenic; liver damage
Vitamin D	µg	5	3.5	20	50 (1500)	Hypercalcaemia; kidney damage
Selenium	µg	—	63	200	750 (900)	Neurological disorders; hair loss; paralysis; nail and skin disorders
Iron	mg	14	13	60–75	100	Relates to hereditary disorders of iron uptake and storage; high chronic iron and alcohol intakes leads to liver disease; formulation of free radicals
Zinc	mg	15	11	30	75–300	Copper deficiency induction
Copper	mg	—	1.5	9	n.e.	Toxicity from diet rare; acute, massive dose causes epigastric pain, nausea, vomiting and severe diarrhoea
Phosphorus	mg	800	1400	1500–3000	4500 (n.e.)	Hypercalcaemia
Category 4: Uncertain risk, little safety data						
Vitamin K	µg	—	80	n.e.	n.e.	Haemolytic anaemia
Chromium	µg	—	—	1000	n.e.	None from dietary sources
Manganese	mg	—	4.6	20	n.e.	May interfere with iron absorption
Molybdenum	µg	—	128	300	1000–1500	Elevated plasma uric acid level at intakes of 10–15 mg/day for prolonged periods

n.e. = not established. TE = tocopherol equivalent. RE = retinol equivalents.
[a] European Commission Nutrition Labelling Directive 90/496/EEC (European Commission, 1990).
[b] Office of Population Census and Surveys (1990).
[c] Data from Shrimpton (1995, 1996), University of Toronto (1996), Hathcock (1996) and The Netherlands Food and Nutrition Council (1993).
[d] Department of Health (1991a,b). Toxic levels are shown in parentheses.
[e] At the Food Advisory Committee (FAC) of 26 June 1997, members endorsed advice from the Committe on Toxicology that in view of nerve damage reported from prolonged high levels of B_6, intake from dietary supplements should not exceed 10 mg/d (FAC, 1997). The subject of an upper safe level of vitamin B_6 therefore requires further careful scientific consideration.

Table 1.3 attempts to categorize the risk for individual micronutrients. Category 1, low-risk nutrients, contains nutrients with few or no adverse effects, including thiamin (vitamin B_1), riboflavin (vitamin B_2), vitamin B_{12}, pantothenic acid, biotin, niacin (amide), beta-carotene and vitamin E (alpha-tocopherol). Category 2, low-risk nutrients with known adverse effects but a wide safety margin, consists by nutrients such as vitamin C, pyridoxine (vitamin B_6), folic acid, calcium, magnesium, iodine and potassium. Category 3 lists known risk nutrients, i.e. those that are known to have adverse effects at higher levels with a relatively narrow safety margin, such as vitamin A, vitamin D, selenium, iron, zinc, copper and phosphorus. Category 4 consists of nutrients with uncertain risks, i.e. no known dietary related adverse effects and little safety data.

The Netherlands Food and Nutrition Council (1993) evaluated the potential negative consequences of adding nutrients to foods and concluded that, with the exception of vitamins A, D and folic acid, there are no indications that the addition of vitamins to foods needs to be restricted on public health grounds. For trace elements, only selenium and possibly copper and zinc were identified as potential risks. In the case of minerals with relatively high RDA, such as calcium, phosphorus and magnesium, in practice there is little risk of excessive intake through the consumption of the individual foods to which these minerals have been added since the addition of large quantities of these minerals would have a marked effect on the organoleptic properties of the food. Again, a cautious approach is needed should a situation develop where a large number of foods to which small amounts of these minerals are added and consumed. Among all the trace elements, selenium must be regarded as carrying the highest risk because of the narrow margin of safety (Clydesdale, 1991).

There have been relatively few reports of hypervitaminosis or other harmful effects of excessive intakes of essential nutrients resulting from the consumption of foods to which they have been added (Tema Nord, 1995). In 1953–55 a clinical survey in the UK found 204 cases of hypercalcaemia in infants resultant from the excessive ingestion of vitamin D fortified foods. This observation led to the cessation of the vitamin D fortification of milk and highlights the need for thorough risk assessments. There is a possibility that the frequent consumption of foodstuffs with added category 3 nutrients could lead to a high cumulative intake of some nutrients, thereby increasing the risks of acute or chronic intoxication and an imbalance in nutrient supply. However, in practice the use of enriched foods has rarely led to excessive intakes of essential micronutrients.

Technological aspects of micronutrient additions to foods

Industrially processed and prepared foods make important contributions to our dietary intakes and the nutrient content of foods is increasingly regarded as being a mark of quality. The levels of micronutrients can vary considerably in raw materials as a result of genetic differences, cultivation conditions, stage of maturity, and pre- and post-harvest treatments. Developments in process technology and food preparation techniques in the kitchen can have positive or negative effects on the levels of micronutrients in foods. Heat treatments (such as frying, roasting, blanching, boiling, pasteurizing, sterilizing, high-temperature/short-time (HTST)) drying, chilling, freezing, fermentation, milling, irradiation, etc. can all impact on nutrient retention.

Although minerals and trace elements can be lost if they leach out with the water used in the manufacturing process or in milling procedures, by far the greatest potential is for loss of vitamins. The losses may be due to the length of the process, the temperature to which the product is exposed or the conditions, such as presence or absence of air, water or acidity, nutrient–nutrient interactions, nutrient–food matrix interactions, etc. The mechanical processes to which a product is subjected and any structural changes in the food influence nutrient retention. The treatment and preparation of foods in the home and in catering establishments can also dramatically influence nutritional value.

Because of the heterogeneity of the chemical structures of vitamins, their stabilities range from being relatively stable to very unstable. Berry Ottaway (1993) summarized the factors that can influence the rate of vitamin content, both endogenous vitamins and those added as forticants:

- temperature
- moisture
- oxygen
- light
- pH
- oxidizing and reducing agents
- the presence of metallic ions (e.g. iron, copper)
- the presence of other vitamins
- other components of food, such as sulphur dioxide
- a combination of the above.

In order to improve stability, vitamins are available in coated or encapsulated forms. Coating agents include gelatin, edible fats, starches, sugars and gums. In most cases where a number of vitamins are being added, a nutrient premix is prepared with the nutrients dispersed in a compatible base. This technique has a number of advantages in terms of good manufacturing practice: there is greater accuracy with the level of addition, the premix is dispersed throughout the product and, from the operational point of view, a premix can be used to manufacture a number of defined batches or days' production. In addition, analytical tests can be reduced by measuring 'tracer' nutrients to check each batch. When nutrients are required in microgram amounts per serving, great care has to be taken.

In the UK, the Food Labelling Regulations (Ministry of Agriculture, Fisheries and Food, 1996b) permit nutrition claims for six minerals (calcium, phosphorus, magnesium, iron, zinc and iodine) and twelve vitamins (A, C, E, D, thiamin, riboflavin, niacin, folic acid, biotin, pantothenic acid, B_{12} and B_6). These regulations require the indication of minimum durability (best before date) for most foods and the percentage of the RDA of every vitamin and mineral named in the claim present in a quantified serving to be stated on the label. Hence, the food technologist must have a good understanding of the extent to which the food processes and distribution system could affect nutrient retention to establish a realistic shelf-life and to adjust the overages of the less stable vitamins above the level of the declared values to ensure that all the declared values are met over the period of the life of the product (Institute of Food Science and Technology, 1997). The risk of excessive intakes must take into account cases of additions of nutrients where the actual level being added and present at the beginning of the shelf-life is greater than the declared level because of the need for overages (Tema Nord, 1995).

Additions of nutrients to foods are generally made in order to improve their nutritional value and there is no advantage at all for manufacturers to process products in such a way as to reduce nutritional value. Similarly, if nutrients are added, care is taken to ensure that as much as possible is used and retained. There are no indications that the increasing consumption of industrially prepared foods has led to reductions in the supply of essential micronutrients among different groups of the population, nor is there any evidence that the possibility of adding nutrients has led the food industry to adopt process conditions that are less favourable for the retention of these nutrients in manufactured foods.

When foods have added nutrients attention must also be paid to their bioavailability. Assessments of the degree of risk from nutrient excesses or deficiencies cannot be made without an evaluation of the bioavailability of the nutrients as well as the amounts of nutrients in foods and diets as a whole. In the case of iron, significant progress has been made in understanding the wide variations in bioavailability as a result of the form of chemical iron and the food and diet consumed. While meals with a large meat component are an excellent source of iron, many cereal and vegetable foods contain large quantities of phytate, polyphenols and other constituents that bind iron, rendering it unavailable for absorption (British Nutrition Foundation, 1995). Some iron salts added to foods are affected by the same inhibitory factors as the iron already present in the food. The use of readily bioavailable iron compounds in food enrichment, however, presents the food industry and legislators with a major dilemma. Forms of iron that are easily added to foods without causing adverse changes in colour, taste or stability are generally poorly absorbed, whereas the highly bioavailable forms of iron, such as ferrous sulphate, may affect the storage and organoleptic properties of the final product for the consumer (Richardson, 1983). Although considerable research has been devoted to identifying and modifying the factors governing the bioavailability of iron, the addition of iron to food can be technically difficult and expensive.

Attempting to add nutrients such as calcium and magnesium also presents potential problems with colour, flavour, texture and quality control. Table 1.4

illustrates the sensorial impact of some sources of calcium and magnesium. For any added nutrient, the technological problems increase as a higher proportion of the RDA is included per serving, or as the serving size decreases. Close attention therefore must be paid to nutrient additions in terms of shelf-life stability and sensory acceptability.

Nutrition and disease prevention

Folic acid and prevention of neural tube defects

There is now compelling evidence that the majority of neural tube defects (NTDs) can be prevented by an adequate intake of periconceptional folate (Selhub and Rosenberg, 1996). This relationship between a vitamin and a reduction in the risk of disease is the culmination of over 25 years of research and has highlighted a number of challenges for nutrition science policy. These challenges include the ways in which folate intake can be increased, the risks and benefits of food fortification, and the opportunity to make health claims on the labels of foods and dietary supplements.

NTDs develop very early in pregnancy (18–30 days after conception) and hence folate nutritional status is important in the periconceptual period before a woman knows she is pregnant. Practically, good nutrition must be maintained throughout the child-bearing period. Folate intake can be increased in three complementary ways: by taking a folic acid supplement, by eating folate-rich

Table 1.4 Sensorial evaluation of calcium and magnesium salts

Calcium Salts

Source	%Ca	Flavour/taste
Lactate	13.5	Neutral
Ascorbate	10.3	Medicinal
Phosphate	17–38	Sandy/bland
Citrate	24	Tart/clean
Gluconate	9.3	Bland
Chloride	36	Salty/bitter
Carbonate	40	Soapy/lemony

Magnesium Salts

Source	%Mg	Flavour/taste
Lactate	10	Neutral
Citrate	10	Taste/bland
Gluconate	5.5	Neutral
Carbonate	28	Soapy
Oxide	60	Sandy

foods or by eating foods fortified with folate. Humans obtain most of their folate from fruits and vegetables, and typical intakes are 0.15–0.2 mg/day. Folate intake therefore needs to be increased about threefold to reach the level of 0.4 mg/day, the amount of folate known to be effective against NTDs, and which does not mask the diagnosis of pernicious anaemia and/or vitamin B_{12} deficiency.

Many countries have issued public health advice recommending a combination of dietary and supplemental means to increase periconceptional folate intake and many have also recommended fortification of food with folic acid. In the USA the FDA and the Centres for Disease Control and Prevention (CDC) concluded that the development and implementation of a fortification programme for the addition of folic acid to the food supply could be effective in increasing the folate intake of women of child-bearing age. Because the FDA has a mandate to set fortification levels that are safe for all population groups, and because the effects of long-term high intakes of folic acid are not well known, the FDA ruling has been designed to keep folic acid intake under 1 mg per day. Fortification will be mandatory from 1 January 1998 (Anon., 1996) and folic acid must be added to flours, breads, corn meals, rice, noodles, macaroni and other grain products at a level of 140 µg/100 g. These foods were chosen for folate fortification because they are staple foods and have a long history of being successful vehicles for improving nutrition by reducing the risk of classic nutrient deficiency diseases. In the UK, efforts are being made to improve further the knowledge about folate and NTD prevention (Health Education Authority, 1996), and an increasing number of breads and cereals are being fortified with folic acid. For example, the level of folic acid added to breakfast cereals is between 50 and 100 µg per serving and a number of soft-grain breads contain 105 µg per serving. These additions, but not the levels, are governed by the Food Labelling Regulations 1996.

Currently there is discussion on whether to make fortification mandatory and the UK food industry has stated that if the medical view is that addition of folic acid to flour would be a safe and effective means of reducing the incidence of NTDs, a statutory approach should be followed (Food and Drink Federation, 1996). The scientific issues and the risks and benefits of folic acid fortification to prevent NTDs have been reviewed by Daly et al., (1995), Wald and Bower (1995), and Bower and Stanley (1996). Interestingly, the synthetic form of the vitamin folic acid used in fortification practices and supplements is more stable and more bioavailable than folate from natural foods (Cuskelly et al., 1996).

In the UK, food law prohibits claims that a food has the ability to prevent, treat or cure disease. However, it is possible to draw attention to the beneficial role of nutrients within a food either on the pack or in advertising and other promotional activities. These means of communication are effective ways of raising public awareness and supporting other programmes aimed at increasing population folate intake. In the USA, in the Federal Register of 14 October

1993, the FDA proposed to authorize a health claim about the relationship between folate and the risk of NTDs on food labels. In the final rules on folic acid fortification, effective from 1 January 1998, manufacturers will be allowed to make the claim on labels that fortified products contain folic acid and that an adequate intake of the nutrient may reduce the risk of NTDs. It should be noted that unenriched cereal-grain products without folic acid added will continue to be available to consumers who do not wish to use fortified products.

In conclusion, the addition of folic acid to foods will continue to attract interest from academia, government, consumer and industry sectors with respect to the application of scientific knowledge and the issues of voluntary versus mandatory fortification, bioavailability, level of addition, risks and benefits, health claims and freedom of choice.

Folic acid and prevention of cardiovascular disease

Research has also shown that an elevated plasma homocysteine concentration is an independent risk factor for cardiovascular disease (CVD) and stroke (Scott and Weir, 1996), that such elevations are widespread in the normal population and that dietary folic acid at levels found in existing fortified products, such as breakfast cereals, have a lowering effect on homocysteine (Ward et al., 1996). Hence, the benefits of folic acid used in fortified foods to achieve optimal folate status may well have implications for reducing the risk of CVD as well as NTDs.

Future developments

In 1911, when Casimir Funk enriched the language with the new word 'vitamine', a combination of the words 'vital' and 'amine', he could not have realized how far the research of this area would develop and the extent to which additions of nutrients to foods would benefit public health around the world. For a variety of reasons, however, many people still do not achieve the RDAs for specific essential micronutrients. It is important for socio-economic reasons, such as changing lifestyles, decreasing energy intakes and the existence of vulnerable population groups, such as women of child-bearing age, the elderly, slimmers, those who may not be able to afford the variety of foods necessary for a healthy balanced diet and those who do not have the knowledge to make adequate food choices, to continually re-evaluate the public health issues associated with the additions of nutrients to foods. Advances in nutrition science have provided increasing evidence that intakes of essential micronutrients not only prevent deficiency states but also have the potential to optimize physical and mental performance, and reduce the risk of chronic disease and disability.

The addition of nutrients to foods is one of the safest ways of ensuring the nutritional status of populations and individuals because the large quantity of a food one would have to eat to reach the potentially hazardous level of the few nutrients that are known to be toxic at high level limits the risk substantially. Generally, there are few significant safety concerns arising from foods with added nutrients. Intakes are generally well within safety limits and the risk of nutrient overdosing and imbalance is outweighed by the benefits of public health. The UK has a long tradition of adding essential nutrients to foods and enrichment practices have been carried out safely and effectively for over 50 years. Enriched foods that are familiar and enjoyable already contribute significantly to the UK diet (Brady, 1996a,b) and the food industry in many parts of the world has demonstrated that it has taken, and will continue to take, a responsible and sensible approach to both statutory and voluntary additions of nutrients to foods. Products with enhanced nutrient density have increased the chances that most people will meet RDAs and have virtually eradicated vitamin and mineral malnutrition. The industry is committed to giving active co-operation and support to achieve food security for all (FAO/WHO, 1992).

The scientific evidence for the roles of vitamins and minerals (e.g. antioxidant functions, hormone-like actions, optimization of the immune function and metabolic controls) indicates that the daily requirements go beyond the levels of intake required for prevention of clinical disorders (Walter, 1995). Increasingly data show that diets rich in antioxidant micronutrients are associated with a lower risk of premature death from coronary vascular disease and cancer (Gey, 1995), and governments are being quick to recognize the economic significance of illness and disease prevention. These advances, which demonstrate the potential disease-preventing role of certain nutrients at levels well above the RDAs raise a number of key issues, not least that the additions are safe. With responsible fortification procedures, and addition levels usually as fractions of the RDA per serving, it is actually quite difficult, both for technological and sensory reasons and because food intakes are limited, to exceed the upper safe levels. In those cases of nutrients where there are narrow safety margins, a careful risk–benefit analysis is required. Absence of significant risk is fundamental to the acceptance of any enrichment practice.

Although RDAs are often criticized, they have a very important and established role. They provide governments with a set of criteria for a minimal level of food provision and nutritional security. RDAs are also the standard for the addition of nutrients in food enrichment and the basis for nutrition labelling purposes. If RDAs are to be changed, it is essential to have substantial scientific agreement on broad and consistent evidence. At the present time such evidence is not available and it is extremely difficult to define higher amounts of single nutrients for any disease prevention action (Walter, 1995). Although there is general accord on RDAs, there needs to be a greater move towards harmonization on upper safe levels of daily dietary intakes over time. Progress in this area would help develop the new concept of optimal health and stimulate further research into the relationship between higher micronutrient intakes and the potential reduction of the risk of certain diseases.

The harmonization of current practices and legislation has advantages and disadvantages and several issues have been raised by the Commission of the European Community (1991) and more recently by Mathioudakis (personal communication). Although mutual recognition by Member States is one option, the harmonization option is gaining support, and hence there will need to be a thorough consideration of the purpose of nutrient additions, i.e. the determinant principles for policy, mainly safety and nutritional need, as well as the implications for consumer understanding and dietary habits. Nutrient additions certainly need to be part of a broader strategy, which should include nutrition education and information. Although concerns have been expressed that consumers may be led to choose products on the basis of their added nutrient content rather than an overall nutrient profile, there is no evidence to support this. There is, however, no doubt that more attention must be given to information and education about the importance of enriched foods and the role of individual nutrients in a healthy diet. Declarations on foodstuffs can help to provide that information, as long as they are consistent with the Food Labelling Regulations 1996. Restrictions on the use of health claims, e.g. statements such as 'folic acid reduces the risk of NTDs', also need to be reviewed. If health claims are true, do not mislead and are based on sound scientific evidence, they should be permitted on food packages (Richardson, 1996). Similarly, public health arguments for and objections to the restriction of additions of micronutrients to foods must be supported on the basis of objective scientific evaluations.

The addition of nutrients to foods requires a balanced, flexible and pragmatic approach, especially if the quantitative estimates of benefits outweigh any risk and hazard, taking into account all relevant scientific evidence, The inflexible application of absolute principles, such as upper limits of intake based on arbitrary multiples of RDA and concepts based solely on clinical deficiency states, needs to be continually re-evaluated in the light of new scientific research. The regulations that are moving towards the standardizing of food legislation throughout the EU, for free trade and comparable food standards, are going to have to keep up with the science, particularly when consumers and governments are seeking ways to achieve health benefits and reduce the risk and incidence of chronic disease. Responding to consumer demand is part of being in the food industry and here there are opportunities to take a leadership role by developing new products that meet the needs and expectations of consumers. It is, however, necessary to continually review policies, principles and practices, and encourage industry, governments, academic institutions, international agencies, scientific societies, trade associations and consumers to create the opportunities for dialogue and partnerships for sustainable improvements in the nutritional and health status of populations and individuals.

References

Alnwick, D. (1995) Solving iodine deficiency. *Chemistry and Industry*, 392.

Anon. (1996) Final rules on folic acid fortification. Federal Register, **61**, 8781–8797.

Australian National Food Authority (1994) Revised Draft Standard A9. Vitamins and Minerals Reconsideration Report.

Bauernfiend, J.C. and Arroyave, G. (1986) Control of vitamin A deficiency by the nutrification of food approach, in *Vitamin A Deficiency and its Control* (ed J.C. Bauernfiend), Academic Press, New York, pp. 359–388.

Berry Ottaway, P. (1993) *The Technology of Vitamins in Food*, Blackie Academic & Professional, Chapman & Hall, London.

Blackburn, H. (1996) Sounding board: Olestra and the FDA. *New England Journal of Medicine*, **329**, 984–986.

Bower, C. and Stanley, F.J. (1996) Issues in the prevention of spina bifida. *Journal of the Royal Society of Medicine*, **89**, 436–442.

Brady, M.C. (1996a) Addition of nutrients: the importance to public health. *British Food Journal*, **98**(9), 3–11.

Brady, M.C. (1996b) Addition of nutrients: current practice in the UK. *British Food Journal*, **98**(9), 12–19.

British Nutrition Foundation (1995) Iron: nutritional and physiological significance. *The Report of the British Nutrition Foundation's Task Force*, Chapman & Hall, London.

Clydesdale, F.M. (1991) Mineral additives, in *Nutritional Additions to Food: Nutritional, Technological and Regulatory Aspects* (eds J.C. Bauernfiend and P.A. Lachance) Food and Nutrition Press, Trumbull, Connecticut, pp. 87–108.

Codex Alimentarius Commission (1994) General principles for the addition of essential nutrients of foods, vol. 4, CAC/GL 09–1987 (amended 1989, 1991).

Commission of the European Community (1991) Diet integraters. A discussion paper prepared by DGIII III/3767/91. Commission of the European Community, Brussels.

Cuskelly, G.J., McNulty, H. and Scott, J.M. (1996) Effect of increasing dietary folate on red cell folate: implications for prevention of neural tube defects. *Lancet*, **347**, 657–659.

Daly, L.E., Kirke, P.N., Molloy, A., Weir, D.G. and Scott, J.M. (1995) Folate levels and neural tube defects: implications for prevention. *Journal of the American Medical Association*, **274**, 1698–1702.

Department of Health (1991a) The fortification of yellow fats with vitamins A and D. *Report on Health and Social Subjects No. 40*, HMSO, London.

Department of Health (1991b) Dietary reference values for food energy and nutrients for the United Kingdom. *Report on Health and Social Subjects No. 41*, HMSO, London.

du Bois, I. (1987) Food enrichment: legislation in Europe. *Bibliotheca Nutritio et Dieta*, **40**, 69–81.

European Commission (1989) Council Directive 89/398/EEC on the approximation of the laws of the Member States relating to foodstuffs intended for particular nutritional uses. *Official Journal of the European Communities*, **L186**, 27–32.

European Commission (1990) Council Directive 90/496/EEC on nutrition labelling. *Official Journal of the European Communities*, **L276**, 40–44.

European Communities (1991) Council Directive 91/321/EEC on infant formulae and follow-on formulae. *Official Journal of the European Communities*, **L175**, 35.

European Commission (1996a) Council Directive 96/5/EC on processed cereal-based foods and baby foods for infants and young children. *Official Journal of the European Communities*, **L49**, 17.

European Commission (1996b) Council Directive 96/8/EC on foods intended for use in energy-restricted diets for weight reduction. *Official Journal of the European Communities*, **L55**, 22.

FAC (1997) FAC 6/907 press release, 4 July 1997.

FAO (1996) Food fortification: technology and quality control. *Report of an FAO Technical Meeting, 20–23 November 1995*, FAO, Rome.

FAO/WHO (1992) Nutrition and development – a global assessment. International Conference on Nutrition, FAO/WHO, Rome.

Food and Drink Federation (1996) Addition of nutrients. Submission to the Committee on Medical Aspects Working Group reviewing the nutritional status of the population. Food and Drink Federation, London.

Food and Drug Administration (1996) Food additives permitted for direct addition to food for human consumption. Olestra: final rule. *Federal Register*, **61**, 3117–3173.

Gey, K.F. (1995) Cardiovascular disease and vitamins. *Bibliotheca Nutritio et Dieta*, **52**, 75–91.

Giese, J. (1996) Olestra: properties, regulatory concerns and applications. *Food Technology*, **50**, 130–131.

Hathcock, J.N. (1996) Vitamin and mineral safety (draft), Council for Responsible Nutrition, Washington, DC.

Health Education Authority (1996) *Folic acid campaign*, Health Education Authority, London.

Hetzel, B.S. (1989) *The Story of Iodine Deficiency: an International Challenge to Nutrition*, Oxford University Press, Oxford.

Hetzel, B.S., Dunn, J.T. and Stanbury, T.B. (eds) (1987) *The Prevention and Control of Iodine Deficiency Disorders*, Elsevier Press, Amsterdam.

Institute of Food Science and Technology (1997) Nutritional enhancement of food: benefits, hazards and technical problems. *IFST Technical Monograph 5*, Institute of Food Science and Technology, London.

Ministry of Agriculture, Fisheries and Food (1991) Dietary supplements and health foods. *Report of a Working Group*, HMSO, London.

Ministry of Agriculture, Fisheries and Food (1996a) The Food Safety Act 1990. SI Number 1383, in *Food Law*, London, HMSO.

Ministry of Agriculture, Fisheries and Food (1996b) The Food Labelling Regulations 1996. SI Number 1499, in *Food Law*, HMSO, London.

Ministry of Agriculture, Fisheries and Food (1996c) The Bread and Flour Regulations 1995. SI Number 3202, in *Food Law*, HMSO, London.

Ministry of Agriculture, Fisheries and Food (1996d) The Spreadable Fats (Marketing Standards) Regulations 1995. SI Number 3116, in *Food Law*, HMSO, London.

Murphy, P.A. (1995) History of technology development for vitamin A fortification of foods in developing countries. *FAO Technical Communication on Food Fortification*, FAO, Rome, pp. 65–76.

Murphy, P.A., Smith, B., Hauck, C.C. and O'Connor, K. (1992) Stabilisation of vitamin A in a synthetic rice premix. *Journal of Food Science*, **57**, 437–439.

Office of Population Census and Surveys (1990) *The Dietary and Nutritional Survey of British Adults*, HMSO, London.

Richardson, D.P. (1983) Iron fortification of foods and drinks. *Chemistry and Industry*, **13**, 498–501.

Richardson, D.P. (1990) Vitamin fortification and implications for health. *Journal of Micronutrient Analysis*, **7**, 223–227.

Richardson, D.P. (1993) Food fortification, in *The Technology of Vitamins in Food* (ed P. Berry Ottaway), Blackie Academic & Professional, Chapman & Hall, London, pp. 283–245.

Richardson, D.P. (1996) Functional foods – shades of grey: an industry perspective. *Nutrition Reviews*, **54**(11), S174–S185.

Scott, J.M. and Weir, D.G. (1996) Homocysteine and cardiovascular disease. *Quarterly Journal of Medicine*, **89**, 561–563.

Selhub, J. and Rosenberg, I.H. (1996) Folic acid, in *Present Knowledge in Nutrition*, 7th edn (eds E.E. Ziegler and L.J. Filer, Jr) ILSI Press, Washington, DC, pp. 206–219.

Shrimpton, D. (1995) *Essential Nutrients in Supplements*. European Federation of Health Product Manufacturers Associations, Surrey.

Shrimpton, D. (1996) Vitamins and minerals: a scientific evaluation of the range of safe intakes. Draft paper commissioned by the European Federation of Health Product Manufacturers Associations, Surrey.

Stanbury, J.C. (1996) Iodine deficiency and the iodine deficiency disorders, in *Present Knowledge in Nutrition*, 7th edn (eds E.E. Ziegler, and L.J. Filer, Jr), ILSI Press, Washington DC, pp. 378–383.

Tema Nord (1995) Additions of nutrients to food – principle and practices, Publication No. 643, Nordic Council of Ministers, Copenhagen, pp. 1–126.

The Netherlands Food and Nutrition Council (1993) *Report on the Addition of Essential Micronutrients of Foods*, The Netherlands, Food and Nutrition Council, The Hague.

Underwood, B.A. (1994) Vitamin A in human nutrition: public health considerations, in *The Retinoids: Biology, Chemistry and Medicine,* 2nd edn, (eds M.B. Sporn, A.B. Roberts and D.S. Goodman) Raven Press, New York, pp. 211–227.

University of Toronto (1996) *Nutrient Addition to Foods in Canada: an Evaluation of Micronutrient Safety*, submitted to Health Protection Branch, Department of Nutritional Sciences.

Wald, N.J. and Bower, C. (1995) Folic acid and the prevention of neural tube defects. *British Medical Journal*, **310**, 1019–1020.

Walter, P. (1995) The scientific basis for vitamin intake in human nutrition. *Bibliotheca Nutritio et Dieta*, **52**, 1–177.

Ward, M., McNulty, H., McPartlin, J.M., Strain, J.J., Weir, D. and Scott, J.M. (1996) The response of plasma homocysteine to low dose folic acid supplementation in healthy male subjects. *Proceedings of the Nutrition Society*, **56**, 150A.

Young, J. (1996) Functional foods: strategies for successful product development. *Financial Times Management Report*, Pearson, London.

2 Technological factors in the development of low-calorie foods

ANDREW J. ROSENTHAL

Introduction

In a weight-conscious society where obesity and related illnesses are major causes of death, and where icons of beauty are portrayed by a thin stature, there are social pressures for consumers to believe that they are empowered to control their weight through selecting foods with a low-calorie content. Stimulated by the idea that individuals feel under pressure to select low-calorie analogues of conventional foods, the food industry has invested in the development of a variety of processes and products which enable the production of traditional foods but with a fraction of the calories.

The idea of reduced-calorie foods has led to a variety of paradoxes in the public's perception, such as being abstemious with the selection of low-calorie staple foods allows the selection of high-calorie treats or choosing foods with half the calories allows one to eat twice as much. Clearly this kind of logic is flawed and has no physiological benefit to the individual. Furthermore there is good evidence that the calorie deficit resulting from the selection of low-calorie foods over traditional items is made up for by additional food consumption. However, the demand for low-calorie foods has allowed the successful proliferation of such products in the market place.

The high-calorie food constituents that have been most frequently targeted are sugar and fat, which contain 4 and 9 kcal/g respectively. Figure 2.1 charts some high-calorie foods in relation to their calorie contribution from fat and total sugar; those most likely to be targeted for calorie replacement can be identified clearly.

To achieve a successful reduction in the calorie content of foods that contain significant amounts of sugar and fat, one needs to understand the roles these components play in foods and their interactions with other components present in the food during processing and subsequent storage. The influence of these components on rheological and thermal properties during processing, their effect on microbiological, chemical and physical stability during storage and the subsequent influence they have on the sensory properties of the food need to be considered before they can be removed or replaced.

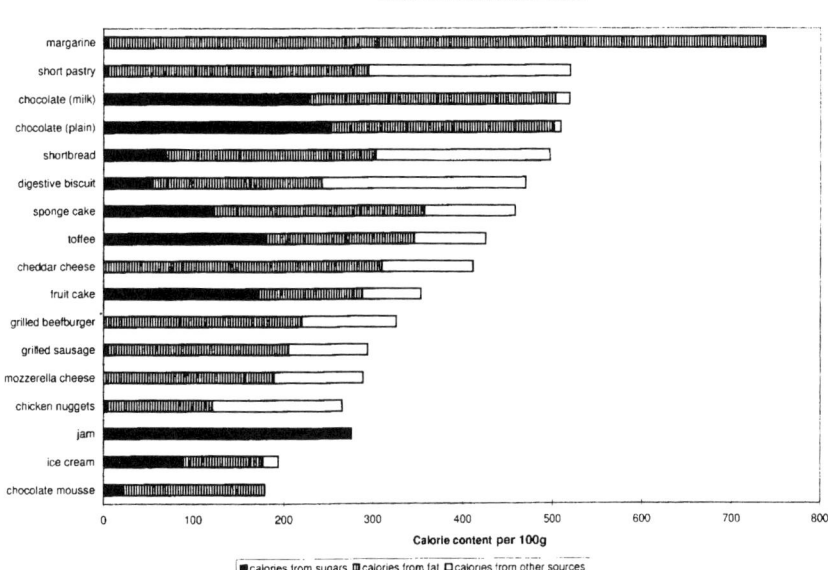

Figure 2.1   Energy content and contribution from fats and total sugars for selected foods

Functional properties of traditional food ingredients

The effect of individual food components on the sensory properties of finished products is often specific to the particular product being considered. However, some generalizations can be made for the sugars and fats present in foods.

Sugar

Many sugars are naturally present in foods; however, from a technological point of view the number of sugars that are used as ingredients in manufactured formulations is relatively small. While simple carbohydrate ingredients include glucose, fructose, lactose, maltose, mixtures of these (e.g. invert sugar), corn syrups and sugar alcohols (e.g. xylitol, sorbitol), all of which are used to limited extents, the use of the word 'sugar' is commonly considered to be synonymous with sucrose. This is not surprising when one considers that over 110 000 000 tons of sucrose have been produced annually, on a global scale, since 1990 (Lichts, 1996). Over a similar period, this figure translates as an average consumption of over 20 kg of sucrose per person per year (Lichts, 1996).

Sucrose is normally sold as a white crystalline solid, which dissolves readily in cold water with saturation at about 65% (w/w) at 25°C. Dilute solutions are

Newtonian, with viscosity in the region of 1.92 mPa.s for a 20% solution. As with other solutes, sucrose affects the colligative properties of water when in solution. It depresses the freezing point of water, giving a eutectic temperature of −9.5°C. Sucrose reduces the vapour pressure of water and when added to foods it reduces their water activity, thereby inhibiting the growth of micro-organisms. The increased osmotic pressure of a saturated sucrose solution creates a water activity of about 0.85, which is sufficient to prevent the growth of most bacteria and many yeasts.

Sucrose has a variety of functional and sensory properties in foods. One of the most characteristic properties it provides is the innate desirability of sweetness (Steiner, 1988). The availability and low price of sucrose has made it a standard for sweetness against which most other sweeners are compared. Such comparisons commonly include relative sweetness and cost for the same degree of sweetness. However, technological comparisons are possibly more important because there factors will decide whether the alternative sweetener is able to provide the appropriate nuances of flavour and texture with similar stabilities of temperature and pH as sucrose. In the past, it has been convenient to divide sweeteners, into bulk sweeteners which tend to be calorific, and intense sweeteners, which are used in such small quantities in foods that their calorie contribution can be virtually disregarded.

Our understanding of the theoretical basis of sweet taste is based on the work of Shallenberger and Acree (1967), who proposed that an electronegative group and a hydrogen atom on the sweet molecule (such as glycol groups in sugars) hydrogen bond onto complementary atoms on the receptors on the tongue. The distance between the atoms in the sweet substance is critical as it must match those of the receptors on the tongue (about 2.86 Å). The basic theory has been elaborated to account for the intensity of sweetness (Birch, 1987). When sucrose is placed in the mouth there is a rapid burst in the perceived intensity of sweetness, which then declines. With some of the intense sweeteners, however, there is a slower initial sensation that continues for many minutes. This slow initial response is related to the size of a large molecule that has been orientated correctly at the active site and the prolongation of the sensation is connected to the tenacity with which the molecule binds to the receptors on the tongue. Such effects need to be considered when selecting appropriate sweeteners for different applications because although such a lasting sweetness may be desirable on a low-sugar chewing gum, it may be a problem on a biscuit that is swallowed within moments of biting.

Sucrose is hygroscopic, binding to water through hydrogen bonding. A consequence of this water binding is that sucrose acts as a moistening agent, enabling relatively high quantities of water to be held within a solid or semi-solid food. Additionally, the water binding of sucrose provides the sense of bulk within foods that contributes to their texture. At high concentrations, sucrose binds water to the extent that it reduces water activity, thereby controlling microbiological growth and extending the shelf-life of fruit products. In addition to the sense of body and bulk produced by sucrose when present in solution, it also forms a glass when rapidly cooled from a molten state, allowing the production of a variety of confectionery products such as hard-boiled sweets, honeycomb and spun sugar, each of which has a characteristic texture.

Sucrose is instrumental in the development of many flavours and colours in processed foods. At high temperatures it undergoes caramelization, while in acid conditions it is hydrolysed, yielding the reducing sugars fructose and glucose which participate in the Maillard reaction.

As already mentioned, several strategies have been used to reduce sucrose in foods while maintaining the intensity of sweetness. Intense sweeteners such as saccharine, aspartame or acesulfame-k may be used at such low concentrations in food formulations that they act as low-calorie substitutes for sucrose. Diet versions of soft drinks may be produced by replacing the sucrose with iso-sweet concentrations of intense sweeteners; however, there is an obvious loss of body in the texture when the drink is in the mouth and when it is swallowed. Since the removal of sucrose in relatively simple foods results in such a marked difference in their sensory properties, then more complex high-sugar foods, such as cakes, will be at least as affected. If, as often happens, sucrose interacts with other food components during normal processing, then its removal results in an incomplete or altered product. This is the situation with cakes, in which sucrose plays a variety of roles. The propensity of sucrose to associate with water in the cake helps to maintain a soft moist crumb and also assists in preventing moisture loss, providing a long shelf-life and controlling staling. This water-binding capacity has been exploited in bakery products such as high-ratio cakes, which actually contain more sugar than flour. The removal of sucrose from high-ratio cakes results in a product akin to a brick. In practice it has been found necessary to modify a food formulation substantially when attempting to remove a major component such as sugar. One approach is to incorporate a low-calorie bulking agent as a partial or complete sugar substitute. However, the interactions that sucrose has with other components, such as water, starch or proteins, may not be identical to those of a different chemical compound.

By way of example, we can examine the role of sucrose in the baking of high-ratio cakes. In a conventional high-ratio cake air is incorporated in the fat phase of the batter during the mixing. During baking, the air cells expand and the starch begins to gelatinise, absorbing moisture from the batter. Simultaneously, the egg-white proteins denature, binding the starch and other components into a solid matrix. If we study the behaviour of starch while it is heated in the presence of excess water (>1.5 parts) we observe an endothermic transition, referred to as gelatinization (Donovan, 1979). Progressively reducing the water content results in the elevation of the temperature of the transition and a reduction in its enthalpy; however, a second endothermic transition occurs at a higher temperature and this has been attributed to the melting of the amylopectin crystallites. Similar behaviour is observed if the available water is reduced by the addition of sucrose (Spies and Hoseney, 1982). For a sugar replacer to be effective in cakes, it should behave in the same way as sucrose, that is it must raise the temperature of the endothermic transition temperature to the same extent. Several studies have looked at the phase transition of wheat starch systems containing the bulking agent polydextrose using relatively concentrated systems similar to those found in high-ratio cakes (Kim *et al.*, 1986; Pateras and Rosenthal, 1992). Pateras and Rosenthal found that polydextrose had virtually no effect on the protein denaturation temperature but substantially raised the starch gelatinization temperature such that the two events no longer coincided and the ungelatinized starch granules became embedded in the solid protein network. These granules then swelled at a higher temperature, breaking up the matrix and yielding a dense but friable cake crumb. In practice it was found that the cakes could only be substituted to about 25% by polydextrose before their sensory properties began to differ from the traditional all-sugar cake.

The inherent differences in chemical nature, and therefore in interactions with other components, of sugar replacers as opposed to sucrose requires modifications in recipe formulations, possibly by adopting other ingredients, to be considered. For example, it was observed that the main egg-white protein ovalbumin (which denatures at 84.5°C) transforms to s-ovalbumin (which denatures at 92.5°C) as the egg ages (Donovan and Mapes, 1976). It was postulated that controlled ageing of egg and its subsequent use in polydextrose-containing cakes could bring the protein denaturation temperature in line with starch gelatinization (Rosenthal, 1995). In practice this allows increased substitution of sucrose by polydextrose to about 50%.

The production of low-calorie products by replacing sugar with other components clearly must ensure that some properties of the normal food are satisfied for a successful product to be obtained.

Fats and oils

Food oils and fats are defined by their solubility in organic solvents, but since there are many such solvents representing a range of polarities and the degree of solubility of different lipid compounds varies in each, this working definition is actually rather vague. The variety of compounds that are soluble in organic solvents is broad, being heterogeneous in nature and often chemically dissimilar, but in practice food fats and oils are predominantly triglyceride materials.

Some workers have considered fat replacers in terms of *fat substitutes* and *fat mimetics*. Such a categorization works on the basis that a fat substitute is a compound which, like triglyceride, is soluble in an organic solvent, but by way of chemical structure is either not metabolised or not absorbed in the human digestive process. In contrast, a fat mimetic mimics the effects of fats and oils but is predominantly water soluble and would not be extracted with an organic solvent. As triglycerides are the predominant species in food oils and fats, chemists have assessed their structure and produced analogues that do not naturally occur and, as such, may not be used biologically. Triglycerides are made up of fatty acid esters of the glycerol and by using naturally occurring fatty acids to esterify a natural polyol, such as sucrose, sucrose esters and hence compounds such as Olestra™ can be produced. As such compounds are normally alien in our world, there has been some concern as to how they are to be disposed of. Fortunately they can be biodegraded and adsorbed on to waste-water solids during the activated sludge process of sewage disposal (McAvoy *et al.*, 1996). Another approach is to chemically modify natural triglycerides through hydrogenation, which allows the production of a mixture of *cis* and *trans* unsaturated fatty acid chains; as the *trans* isomers do not normally occur in nature they tend not to be used during digestion. In contrast, fat mimetics are a disparate group of chemicals which appear to have similar functional and/or sensory properties to oils and fats. Fat mimetics include water-soluble polysaccharides and protein hydrocolloids, as well as microparticulate proteins from foods such as egg and milk.

Bearing in mind that there are chemical differences in the solubility of these two categories of fat replacer and that neither fat mimetics nor fat replacers have any other common tie between their members, the rest of this chapter will treat all fat substitutes as a single group of unrelated compounds that possess sensory and/or functional properties similar to those of fats and oils. Furthermore, the terms fat substitute and fat replacer will be considered as synonymous and the former will not be used to describe a limited subset of materials.

Lucca and Tepper (1994) reviewed the functional properties that fats confer on the many food products in which they are major components. Foremost among these properties is the contribution that fats make to the sensory properties of foods. Fats and oils also interact with other components within food formulations during processing and give rise to characteristic textural properties. There appears to be some kind of biological propensity toward fatty foods, which is not understood, that results in a craving for such foods (Drenowski, 1990). In many cultures luxury foods or foods considered in high esteem tend to be those that have a high fat content. It has been suggested that one deciding factor in the enjoyment of fat is the smooth, creamy, homogeneous viscous mouthfeel. Fats tend to be plastic in behaviour and when they melt lubricating oils are produced. This is the desirable characteristic of cocoa butter: its unusually high melting point of 34°C, which happens to be just below the internal temperature of the mouth, elicits in chocolate the sensation of it melting away to a smooth creamy texture in the mouth.

Many fat substitutes create the same mouthfeel as fats and oils by offering a viscous yet homogeneous texture. For example, tapioca dextrin can be hydrated to form a gel that can be used to replace less than 50% of the oil in products like salad cream, providing a viscous smooth mouthfeel reminiscent of fat. In contrast to fats, which contain 9 kcal per gram, such carbohydrate materials contain only 4 kcal per gram on a dry basis. In addition, since they are hydrated with three parts water, they actually only contribute 1 kcal per gram (Haumann, 1986).

The resolving power of the tongue and palate to small particles is in the region of 3 μm. Particulate materials that have a diameter less than the resolving power of the tongue are perceived as smooth and homogeneous, and can therefore be used to mimic the smooth creamy mouthfeel of fats. Microparticulate materials that have been used in food formulations include microcrystalline cellulose, milk and egg proteins (e.g. Simplesse). Using whey proteins (by-products of cheese-making) in this way increases the value of milk as a raw material.

The characteristic properties of fats are frequently related to physical properties. The concept of melting point for fats is sometimes considered to be inappropriate, as fats are made up of mixtures of triglycerides. Each triglyceride has its own melting point, which is determined by the combination and order of the fatty acids present. Triglyceride mixtures therefore often exhibit varying properties with temperature, starting solid when cold, softening as some of the triglycerides melt and fully liquefying only when the temperature is above the highest triglyceride melting point. Where melting occurs over a broad temperature range technological indexes of behaviour, such as the slip point, have been adopted instead of distinct melting temperatures, which are more commonly associated with pure substances. One such index, used in margarines, relates the proportion of solid to liquid fat present at a particular temperature and is used to describe the texture and spreadability. Melting behaviour is further complicated by the ability of fats to crystallize into different polymorphic forms, each with its own characteristic melting point, crystal structure, molecular packing and distinctive properties. Polymorphism of fats is a deciding factor in their functional behaviour in foods. Apart from differences in melting point, the crystals have different shapes and properties. For example, in the case of chocolate, six polymorphic forms have been identified (types I–VI). The melting points of these polymorphs increase from type I to type VI. The most desired form, with its shiny surface, is type V and it is this polymorph that gives chocolate its characteristic appearance. If chocolate melts during storage and then cools slowly, the higher melting point type VI can form, giving a less desirable mottled appearance. The tempering step in chocolate manufacture is designed to preferentially form the favoured polymorph.

Fats and oils act as vehicles for flavour compounds. The β' polymorph is reputed to be necessary in bakery shortenings to ensure that air is incorporated in cake batters (Shepherd, 1969). Fat crystals have also been implicated in stabilizing the air cells formed within cake batters (Brooker, 1990). This stabilization has been attributed to the lower level of crystal–crystal interaction which allows the fact crystals to adsorb as a dense layer at the interface, thereby raising the interfacial viscosity to more than that of the ß polymorph (Ogden and Rosenthal, 1997).

Within emulsions, fats are of structural importance, providing one of the bulk phases. A high viscosity in the continuous phase helps to ensure emulsion stability. This can be achieved by the addition of hydrocolloids to the aqueous phase of an oil-in-water (o/w) emulsion. In the case of water-in-oil (w/o) emulsions, fat crystals present within the oil phase are found to adsorb onto the interface of the aqueous droplets and they can help to stabilize the emulsion. Moreover, as the crystals grow they form a matrix of solid crystals around the aqueous phase droplets (Berger, 1970).

People often ask why fried foods taste so good. The residual frying fats on the surface of a fried food have their own desirable textural characteristics but, in addition, chemical changes, such as the Maillard reaction, occur at the surface of the food during frying. The high temperature of the oil and the high heat transfer coefficient during frying ensures rapid heating of the food. The surface moisture is quickly lost and, with the temperature around 150°C, conditions are ideal for the development of the flavour, the slightly brittle crisp textures and the characteristic golden-brown colours associated with fried foods.

Other applications for which fats are used in the food industry include the enrobing and coating of confectionery products, and the formation of a moisture barrier in products like puff pastry. Obviously, with such a range of functions within food removal or replacement of fat must be examined on an individual product basis.

Mechanisms of calorie reduction

Simple removal of high-calorie components, with a proportionate rise in the concentration of all the other ingredients present, is a possible mechanism of calorie reduction. This has been very successful in certain foods, for example replacing whole milk by skimmed in some dairy foods. However, as discussed above, changes can occur in the functional properties of foods when sugar or fat is removed and generally one of three strategies is employed:

- calories may be diluted by the addition of air or water. In both cases the recipe and/or process will need modification to maintain the product's character.
- the high-calorie component may be substituted or partially replaced with one or more ingredients that have a lower calorie content but which contribute to the essential functional and sensory attributes that were previously offered by the fat or sugar. Reformulation is implicit in this approach and a variety of replacement ingredients is often required, for example sweeteners, bulking agents, colours, etc.
- a limited number of products may be produced in the conventional way and subsequently have the fat removed by solvent extraction to produce reduced-fat foods.

Calorie dilution

Food emulsions consist of two immiscible phases: a high energy oil phase and a lower energy aqueous phase. Food emulsions, such as margarines and salad creams, are therefore prime candidates for calorie reduction. The viscosity of emulsions is controlled partly by the presence of particles, which affect the flow, and partly by stabilizing agents, which increase the viscosity of the continuous phase. In the case of o/w emulsions, hydrocolloid stabilizing agents are often added to the aqueous continuous phase, thus maintaining a high viscosity. Increasing the hydrocolloid concentration further may result in the formation of a gel containing emulsified droplets of fat. Since the gelation of such materials depends more on the hydrocolloid concentration than on the droplet size and number, the fat content of an emulsion can effectively be reduced while maintaining its texture. Furthermore, the texture of many hydrocolloid materials is smooth and creamy, and such products may appear fat-like yet contain a fraction of the calories. The calorie content of such emulsions is further reduced by the fact that such hydrocolloids are used in relatively low concentrations. Various biopolymers have been used in this way, for example tapioca and potato dextrins (Chronakis, 1997).

In water-in-oil-in-water (w/o/w) emulsions oil droplets are suspended within an aqueous phase and the oil droplets themselves have a suspension of water droplets inside. Various approaches have been used to achieve such multiple emulsions, the preferred method being a two-stage homogenization. The first stage involves the formation of a fine droplet w/o emulsion using a lipophilic emulsifier and high shear rates in the homogenizer. The second step treats this primary emulsion as the oil phase in a second emulsification in which relatively low concentrations of a hydrophilic emulsifier and a relatively low pressure are used (Dickinson and McClements, 1996). Such an approach has been used by several workers to produce low-calorie food emulsions with similar rheological properties to their high-fat, high-calorie counterparts (Decindio and Cacace, 1995).

In the past, cynics have criticized the food industry for incorporating water in products. Techniques such as adding a glaze to prevent food from dehydrating during frozen storage have received scorn, with the suggestion that the industry is just adding water to boost the weight and make a higher profit, rather than adding value with a higher quality product. However, there seems to be a paradox in that for products such as ice cream, whipped desserts and mousses, which are often sold on a volume basis and may have additional air incorporated, the lightest and airiest texture is often seen as the best quality.

Ingredient substitution

Ingredient substitution involves the reformulation of products with partial or complete replacement of the high-calorie components (sugar and fat) by alternative ingredients that are of lower calorific content. As mentioned above, the alternative ingredients rarely behave in an identical way the originals and often more than one new functional ingredient needs to be incorporated to ensure that the sensory and functional properties of the high-calorie traditional food are maintained.

Low-calorie replacement ingredients originate from a variety of sources. Many are natural food ingredients that are either chemically or physically modified so that they are not broken down by the enzymes in the gut and are therefore not assimilated.

Frequently some product reformulation will need to be employed when calorie dilution is used so that the product retains its essential functional and sensory characteristics.

Calorie extraction

Solvent extraction has long been used to recover oil from seed cake in the manufacture of cooking oils. The essential properties of the solvents include purity and the ability to achieve complete separation after the extraction process. In the mid 1960s, organic solvents such as fluorochlorocarbons were used to reduce the fat content of deep-fried potato crisps or chips. The product was produced in the conventional way and the fat removed by solvent extraction (Nonaka *et al.*, 1974). One drawback of solvent extraction is the potential loss of desirable fat-soluble flavour compounds; this is relevant as many of the flavour volatiles in fried foods are produced during exposure to high temperatures.

In recent years, supercritical carbon dioxide has been used as a solvent for a variety of extraction processes in the food industry. Such extractions include the separation of oleoresins from spices or fatty fractions, such as phospholipids, or the separation of cholesterol from egg yolk. Supercritical carbon dioxide has also been used to produce low-fat foods by the extraction of fractions from conventional products. Solid foods, whose shape and structure are defined, such as flaked almonds can have almost half the fat removed without any appreciable loss in shape. The result is a lower calorie nut with lower bulk density and a relatively high protein content (Passey and Groslouis, 1993).

Food product groups

Several comprehensive reviews have been produced covering the range of calorie-replacing ingredients, for example Setser and Racette (1992). This section does not attempt to duplicate such overviews but seeks to consider the technological and sensory aspects of some calorie-reduced food products. While the calorie-replacing ingredients could be considered individually, they often interact with other components in a unique way and their behaviour can be better considered on a product basis.

Jams, soft drinks, sugar confectionery and chewing gum

Jams and conserves are traditionally produced by heating fruit and sugar to drive off water and so lower the water activity. The combination of heat treatment and low water activity preserves the product. In the UK, jam has a legal definition that requires a minimum sugar content of 65%. Low-sugar jams have been available for the diabetic market for many years. These products tend to use sorbitol or fructose as an alternative to sucrose, however, in practice, they tend not to reduce the total calories in the product (Thomas et al., 1992). A key consideration for sugar replacement in jams is the effect on the product shelf-life and, specifically, the reduction in water activity that any sugar replacer might bring about. Non-caloric materials with a high water-holding capacity, such as bacterial cellulose, have been suggested as bulking agents in low-sugar conserves (Okiyama et al., 1993).

Other diabetic products include sucrose-free pressed-tablet type mints which tend to use sorbitol, xylitol or erythritol in place of sucrose. Unlike sucrose, some of these sugars have negative enthalpy and give a cooling effect when they dissolve in the mouth; this can be a beneficial attribute in peppermint tablets. In addition to being suitable for diabetics, these products are usually claimed to be 'tooth-friendly' and do not cause dental caries. However, there is evidence to suggest that persistent use of these sugar alcohols encourages the microflora present in tooth plaque to adapt and break them down (Waller et al., 1993). Another important characteristic of pressed-tablet confectionery is the rate of dissolution; this controls flavour release. When using sugar alcohols in confectionery formulations it should be remembered that they produce a laxative effect when consumed in large quantities. This limits their use to products such as chewing gum.

It has been suggested that soft drinks are relatively simple systems that can have their calorie content reduced relatively easily by the addition of an intense sweetener. However, without the incorporation of some bulking agents the perceived viscosity is reduced. It is interesting to note that in the period since the launch of low-calorie carbonated soft drinks the sales of conventional sugared drinks has not declined. The development of a low-calorie product has essentially resulted in the creation of a new market. It is possible that the difference in mouthfeel between the conventional and the low-calorie drinks is in fact a desirable sensory attribute that appeals to the newly formed market.

Dairy products

Although its composition changes with season, breed and feed, the fat content of bovine milk is normally in the region of 4%. Removing this fat results in a change in the viscosity and colour of milk and this change in appearance markedly affects the perceived thickness and residual mouth coating of milk (Phillips et al., 1995). Attempts to enhance the colour of skimmed milk have included the addition of whiteners such as titanium dioxide.

Products with increased milk solids, such as cheese and yoghurt, often have a fat content substantially higher than 4%, making them prime targets for fat reduction. Tamime and co-workers (1994) have investigated the replacement of fat in yoghurt by particulate- and hydrocolloid-based replacers. Microparticulate fat replacers become incorporated into the casein and appear to form a bridge between adjacent casein chains giving a tighter structure than is present in yoghurts made with milk fat (Tamime *et al.*, 1995). Consequently, there is more separation of serum in reduced-fat yoghurts (Barrantes *et al.*, 1994a,b). Several fat replacers may be used to produce acceptable low-fat yoghurts and the sensory quality generally improves on storage (Barrantes *et al.*, 1994c).

Low-fat cheeses have a fat content that has been reduced by 50%, while reduced-fat cheeses have a fat content that is at least 25% less than the original fat content. Reduced-fat cheeses have been produced since the mid 1950s although, as with other low-calorie products, demand has mushroomed in recent years. Most of the work on fat replacement in cheese has tended to focus on a small number of cheeses, notably Cheddar and Mozzerella, although other products such as Gouda, feta, cottage cheese and goat's cheese have been investigated. Two basic approaches have been taken to achieve low-fat cheese, based either on modifications to the manufacturing procedure or on the incorporation of fat replacers.

As far as modifying the manufacturing procedure is concerned, increasing the moisture content of the cheese can provide some of the creamy mouthfeel previously offered by fat. The water content of the final cheese can be increased in a variety of ways, for example lowering the cook temperature, shortening the cook time or washing the curd (Drake and Swanson, 1995). The flavour of low-fat cheese can be a problem. Rapid growth of the starter culture can lead to accelerated acid production, which results in bitter flavours. It is considered better to have a small inoculum of starter culture to limit acid production and possibly to incorporate adjunct cultures, which produce specific flavour compounds through increased proteolysis. Some adjunct cultures are deliberately attenuated by heat treatment to achieve particular flavour nuances. Commonly used adjunct cultures include *Lactobacillus* spp. The growth conditions in Cheddar cheese require a salt concentration of 1.8%. Concern about salt concentrations and the likelihood that the market for low-fat cheese will be health conscious have prompted the development of low-fat, low-salt cheeses in which the sodium chloride has been replaced with potassium chloride (Zorrilla *et al.*, 1996).

A variety of fat replacers, including sucrose polyesters, microparticulate proteins and hydrocolloid products, such as pectin or gelatin, has been used to produce low-fat cheeses. While fat substitutes can successfully produce a similar mouthfeel to full fat cheese, they do not necessarily provide the flavour characteristics of the traditional product and some recipe compensation may be required. In practice, combining the approaches of modifying the manufacturing process and incorporating fat replacers may give optimum quality products.

The essential properties of a cheese have to reflect the use of which it is put, for example when it is an ingredient in pizza topping its meltability and rheological properties are fundamental. As described above for yoghurt, in Mozzerella cheese microparticulate fat replacers interact with the caseins from the milk, becoming embedded in the curd and forming links between adjacent bits of curd. Relatively large microparticulate fat replacers therefore create wide serum channels and a high degree of openness in the cheese. When melted (80°C), the fat-replaced cheese has a similar viscosity to conventional Mozzerella cheese (McMahon *et al.*, 1996).

Milk fat is often used as a food ingredient and consequently, when fat replacement is an issue, its melting characteristics and relative consistency at different temperatures are important. If sucrose polyesters are used to replace the milk fat in foods, then care must be exercised in the choice of the fatty acid esters because chain length will affect the hardness and melting characteristics of the fat-reduced food (Drake *et al.*, 1994).

Food emulsions

Numerous foods exist as emulsions, the small size of the dispersed-phase droplets giving rise to the desirable sensation of creaminess. The high-calorie oil phase of emulsion-based foods make them suitable for calorie replacement. Emulsion-based foods are typically luxury items and include ice cream, mousses, frozen desserts, salad cream, sandwich spreads, mayonnaise, butter and low-fat spreads. Emulsions must be stable to phase separation and attempts to replace fat within them must take this into account. Emulsions also occur as intermediate products in the manufacture of other items, such as cakes, and emulsion stability during processing is important in order that the final product succeeds.

Frozen desserts such as ice cream, as well as their non-dairy analogues and milk shakes, tend to be high-sugar, high-fat products, and prime candidates for calorie replacement. A variety of sugar and fat replacers have been tried in frozen milk systems and it has been found that temperature, in terms of both product melting and the solubility of ingredients, is a deciding factor on success. Using instrumental measurements of viscosity and over-run, it has been shown that carbohydrate-based fat mimickers are not able to achieve as high an over-run as conventional ice creams; moreover, they change the consistency and make the products less Newtonian (Schmidt *et al.*, 1993). In another study, Specter and Setser (1994) concluded that physical measurements of such systems did not correlate well with their sensory attributes and that dextrin-based fat replacers resulted in several adverse changes in sensory properties, including increased coarseness, increased wateriness and a decreased creaminess. These authors found that the most successful combination of fat replacers for calorie reduction in frozen dessert was polydextrose and aspartame, which adequately compensated for the textural characteristics conferred by sucrose as well as offering some compensation for those derived from the milk fat.

The sweet taste of ice cream can be maintained by using intense sweeteners in place of sugar, but bulking agents are still required to achieve comparable mouthfeel and to regulate the freezing point. The intensity of flavour volatiles is reduced at low temperatures and oil-soluble flavours are affected when fat is replaced by microparticulate- or hydrocolloid-based substitutes. Changes in flavour intensity become more apparent with storage and compensation for this in the product formulation is necessary (Graf and Roos, 1996).

Low-fat alternatives for butter are a burgeoning market. Several approaches have been taken in creating these products, for example the formation of multiple-phase emulsions that dilute the dispersed fat droplets by filling them with smaller droplets of water. Another approach is the incorporation of fat replacers into the formulation.

Although butter is normally stored refrigerated and spread at ambient temperatures, an allowance for temperature abuse needs to be considered when assessing the stability of low-fat spreads. Clegg and co-workers (1996) examined the effects of various hydrocolloids on the stability of low-fat margarines at temperatures around 34°C. They found that modified starches, maltodextrin and gelatin produced the most stable low-fat spread emulsions. Furthermore, changes in stability were accompanied by differences in sensory characteristics such as texture and flavour (Clegg et al., 1996). The melting characteristics of low-fat spreads are also important in producing the right mouthfeel; some starch-based, low-fat spreads have long melting profiles on heating, which contrast with the melt-in-the mouth behaviour of butter (Chronakis and Kasapis, 1995). Another important characteristic of butter is its rheological behaviour. Spreads should behave as plastic solids, that is to say they must resist small stresses and then start to flow when a minimum yield stress has been applied.

In addition to reducing the fat content of mayonnaise, the selective removal of specific fat components, such as cholesterol, has been attempted (Bringe et al., 1996). There are differences in the functional requirements of mayonnaise and salad cream compared to the emulsions discussed previously, for example their stability must be greater and subsequent shelf-life longer. Additionally, these products traditionally include raw egg and the need to pasteurize it for microbiological safety is of paramount importance. The protective influence of hydrocolloid materials on microbial stability during heat processing is well documented and rates of destruction of pathogens have been studied in these products. Examining a range of mayonnaise products, Erickson and Jenkins (1991) found that the inactivation kinetics of *Salmonella* spp. were unaffected by ingredient composition but the destruction of *Listeria monocytogenes* was directly correlated with aqueous phase volume fraction, thus the reduced-calorie mayonnaise dressings which they studied had a greater protective effect than the traditional mayonnaise and required a more severe time–temperature treatment.

Meat products

Reformed meat products, sausages and burgers have all been the target of fat replacement. The main approach to fat reduction within meat products is to increase the water-holding capacity of the meat. A certain amount of water is lost from meats as a result of post-mortem drip but further losses can occur if the meat is cured because the curing salts draw water and soluble proteins out of the flesh by osmosis. With the advent of mechanization in food processing, attempts were made to speed the curing process and to limit the amount of water lost during curing. One solution is to incorporate water-binding salts, such as phosphates, into the brining solution. A similar approach has been taken in enhancing the water-holding capacity of reformed meat products by the addition of phosphates. In the case of frankfurters, the addition of acid phosphate allows the incorporation of more connective tissue into the meat emulsion, thus adding to the value of the product and further diluting its fat content (Eilert *et al.*, 1996). The arguments for using phosphates in restructured meat products is not just one of economy; in addition to the ability to reduce the proportion of fat, added phosphates and water improve some textural characteristics such as juiciness, tenderness and overall palatability (Miller *et al.*, 1993).

Water binding of restructured meats has also been achieved by incorporating grain or bean flours, starches or purified hydrocolloid gums, such as carrageenan or cellulose esters. These materials bind water but tend to modify the texture of the product. By way of reiterating the need to reflect on the desired product characteristics when selecting a fat replacer, we will consider the use of λ-carrageenan, which several authors have investigated as a water-binding agent in low-fat meat products such as beef patties, restructured pork nuggets and bologna sausage. This gum appears to soften products, making beef patties, for example, juicier and more tender (Berry *et al.*, 1996). It also makes a firm product, such as bologna, softer than the normal high-fat version (Trius *et al.*, 1994).

The addition of low-fat protein extenders can also serve as a means of reducing the relative fat content of comminuted meat products. Lean meats, such as goat, can be incorporated into patties, allowing 60% of the beef to be replaced without trained sensory or consumer panels detecting any difference (James and Berry, 1977). Other extenders that have been used to extend protein and lower fat include connective tissue and soya flour.

Flour confectionery

Figure 2.2 shows various items of flour confectionery graphed according to their fat and sugar content. The products that would potentially benefit from calorie reduction can be clearly identified at the extremes of the axes. The incentive for producing healthy foods has been a significant impetus to the bakery industry, which has shown considerable interest in the possibility of reduced-calorie products. Butter has traditionally been used as the fat in most flour confectionery goods. Industrialization brought with it butter substitutes, such as shortenings, that, unlike both butter and margarine, are not emulsions and therefore contain little water. Butter, margarines and shortenings are used in many bakery products such as cakes, cookies, crackers, pastries, etc. It has been shown that the addition of certain surfactants to biscuit doughs and cake batters can help to

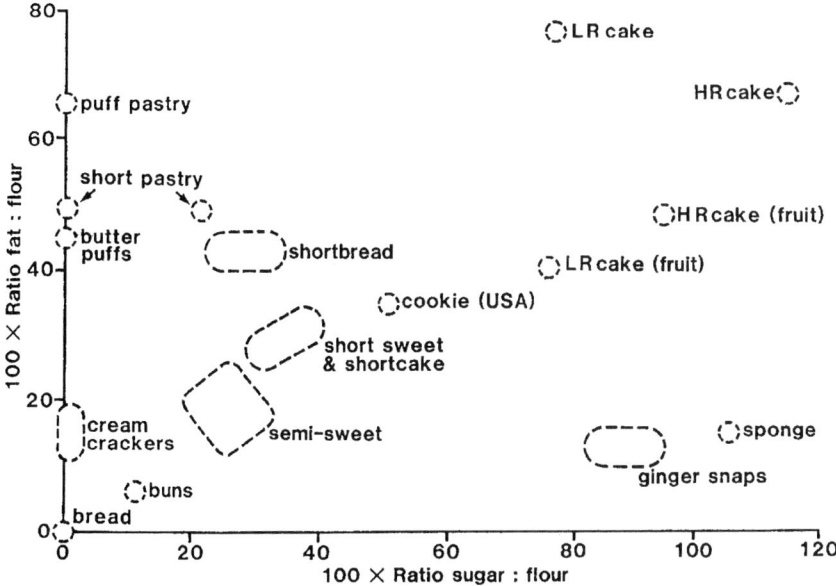

Figure 2.2 Sugar and fat contents (flour basis) of selected confectionery products (with permission from Mr S. Cauvain, Chorleywood and Campden Food Research Association).

maintain the texture of reduced-fat biscuits (Wootton *et al.*, 1967; Hutchinson *et al.*, 1977). Many commercial bakery shortenings include high levels of emulsifier.

In puff pastry, the fat is laminated into the dough and forms an impervious layer that traps steam during subsequent baking, resulting in the formation of a light, flaky, characteristic texture. Various approaches have been taken to reduce the calorie content of the laminating material. Kazier and Dyer (1995) rule out the use of carbohydrate-based fat replacers because their hydrophilic properties prevent them from being able to form an impervious layer, which means that steam is not trapped during baking. Instead it is necessary to use an oil-soluble, restructured lipid, such as a sucrose polyester, which will form a water-insoluble barrier.

Many types of sweet biscuits and cookies have been the subject of calorie replacement. As has been shown with some other foods, the simple removal of fat without the addition of any substitute leads to a hard biscuit, with a reduction in spread during baking and an undesirable white crust colour. The incorporation of emulsifiers helps to soften the dough, enabling some spread during baking and resulting in a softer biscuit (Srivastava and Rao, 1993). Since reducing the fat content of biscuits generally makes a harder product, it might be assumed that reducing the fat of soft dough-type cookies is more difficult to achieve. However, using oat fibre 30% of the fat can be replaced in soft-type chocolate chip or peanut butter cookies (Dougherty *et al.*, 1988). The increased water content required to handle the dough ensures a reduction in calories by one-third and also helps the cookies to rise during baking. Care has to be exercised to avoid large particles of oat fibre, which might result in a gritty mouthfeel. In another study, between 50 and 75% of the shortening in chocolate chip cookies was replaced by protein-based, lipid-based or carbohydrate-based fat replacers (Armbrister and Setser, 1994). However, some side effects resulted, including an increased mouth coating, a reduction in the fractureability and sensory firmness, and a reduction in the caramel flavours, compared to conventional cookies. Sanchez and co-workers (1995) used five different carbohydrate-based fat replacers, along with emulsifiers, to replace shortening fat in shortbread cookies. As the carbohydrate fat replacers are water-based hydrocolloids, higher levels of substitution lead to an increase in the moisture content, which in turn results in a denser and tougher biscuit. It was found that the lowest level of substitution that was investigated (35%) resulted in 'the least negative effects on the physical attributes' of the biscuits. Overall, it can be seen that studies on the replacement of fat in biscuits and cookies have not been altogether successful; only a limited reduction in the fat content has been achieved and replacement tends to result in characteristics not seen in the conventional product.

In cake batters the fat has several functions: it acts as a vehicle for some of the oil-soluble volatile flavour compounds, it traps air during mixing and during baking it becomes integrated into the protein matrix, adding to the tenderness of the final crumb. Complete substitution of fat in high-ratio cakes has been achieved using a variety of hydrocolloid-based fat replacers. However, this substitution led to a reduction in the batter over-run, which resulted in a reduction in the baked cake volume (Bath *et al.*, 1992).

The interaction of sugar and water in high-ratio cakes is discussed above. With more sugar than flour, the high-ratio cake normally has a moist crumb and good keeping properties. Several workers have investigated sugar and/or fat replacement in high-ratio cakes and found that bulking agents, such as polydextrose, can replace up to 30% of the sugar; higher levels of replacement result in adverse quality and a deterioration of the sensory qualities (Pateras and Rosenthal, 1992). Other substitutes, such as microcrystalline cellulose, have also been considered but no additional benefit has been found (Kamel and Rasper, 1988).

Staling and starch retrogradation affect the keeping quality of cakes. Differences between calorie-reduced cakes and conventional goods during storage have a bearing on shelf-life. With so many cakes and gateaux being sold as frozen products, there is a need to consider the freeze–thaw stability of hydrocolloid-based fat replacers. Smith (1984) undertook a study in which a fat replacer based on a mixture of starch and guar gum was substituted for all the shortening in a yellow cake recipe. The resulting cake was of good quality with a uniform cell structure, a tender crumb and a good colour. When subject to three freeze–thaw cycles the cake maintained its initial moisture content, a result which differed from the three commercially available yellow cakes that were used as controls.

Bakery fillings and coating mixtures are conventionally based on a fatty formulation. Usually such materials have a continuous phase of fat into which sugar, milk solids and cocoa are dispersed. When the coating is in the mouth the fat melts, releasing the flavours and the characteristic creamy mouthfeel. If the continuous phase is replaced with a water-soluble hydrocolloid, such as microcrystalline cellulose, then the sugar present forms a concentrated solution, which may be pumped to the enrobing machines in the factory. When the mixture is cooled, the sucrose solution becomes saturated, the solids present dominate and the mixture sets. The higher temperature in the mouth causes the coating to liquefy, releasing flavour and the same characteristic creamy mouthfeel of a fat (Izzo, 1995).

Frying oils and batters

The high fat content, yet desirable characteristic flavours and textures, of fried foods make them important targets for fat replacement. The high temperatures involved in frying make most of the hydrocolloid-based and microparticulate fat mimetics unsuitable for frying oil substitution. High-boiling, non-calorific fat replacers, such as sorbitol esters or polyorganosiloxanes, may be used as alternatives.

A different approach to reducing fat uptake during deep-fat frying is the incorporation of materials that provide barrier properties in the batter or breaded layers of the food. For example, an edible film of hydroxypropyl methylcellulose can reduce the fat uptake of chicken pieces by one-third (Balasubramaniam *et al.*, 1997).

Fried food analogues, such as oven-ready foods, often have coatings or batter mixtures that contain fats. The intention is that during cooking the coatings will yield some of the flavours and textures of their fried counterparts.

Conclusions

The promise of low-calorie foods has enticed our society and captivated food scientists. Because a simple reduction in high-calorie constituents often results in a change in the sensory and/or functional properties of the food, a number of alternative routes to calorie reduction are used. These approaches include the substitution of high-calorie components with one or more functional ingredients, calorie dilution and extraction of high-calorie constituents after production.

References

Armbrister, W. and Setser, C. (1994) Sensory and physical properties of chocolate chip cookies made with vegetable shortening or fat replacers at 50 and 75% levels. *Cereal Chemistry*, **71**(4), 344–351.

Balasubramaniam, V., Chinnan, M., Mallikarjunan, P. and Phillips, R. (1977) The effect of edible film on oil uptake and moisture retention of a deep-fat fried poultry product. *Journal of Food Process Engineering*, **20**(1), 17–29.

Barrantes, E., Tamime, A., Muir, D. and Sword, A. (1994a) The effect of substitution of fat by microparticulate whey protein on the quality of set type natural yoghurt. *Journal of the Society of Dairy Technology*, **47**(2), 61–68.

Barrantes, E., Tamime, A. and Sword, A. (1994b) Production of low-calorie yoghurt using skim milk powder and fat substitute. 4. Rheological properties. *Milchwissenschaft – Milk Science International*, **49**(5), 263–266.

Barrantes, E., Tamime, T. and Sword, A. (1994c) Production of low-calorie yoghurt using skim milk powder and fat substitute. 3. Microbiological and organoleptic qualities. *Milchwissenschaft – Milk Science International*, **49**(4), 205–208.

Bath, D., Shelke, K. and Hoseney, R. (1992) Fat replacers in high ratio layer cakes. *Cereal Foods World*, **37**(7), 495–500.

Berger, K.G. (1970) Fats as structural components of foods. *Food Manufacture*, **45**, 60.

Berry, B., Joseph, R. and Stanfield, M. (1996) Use of electrical stimulation, hot processing and carrageenan for processing low-fat ground-beef patties. *Meat Science*, **42**(1), 111–123.

Birch, G. (1987) Chemical aspects of sweetness, in *Sweetness* (ed. J. Dobbing), Springer, London.

Bringe, N., Howard, D. and Clark, D. (1996) Emulsifying properties of low fat, low cholesterol egg-yolk prepared by supercritical CO_2 extraction. *Journal of Food Science*, **61**(1), 19.

Brooker, B.E. (1990) The adsorption of crystalline fat to the air–water interface of whipped cream. *Food Structure*, **9**, 223.

Chronakis, I. (1997) Structural–functional and water-holding studies of biopolymers in low fat content spreads. *Food Science and Technology Lebensmittel-Vissenschaft und Technologic*, **30**(1), 36–44.

Chronakis, I. and Kasapis, S. (1995) A rheological study of the application of carbohydrate protein incompatibility to the development of low fat commercial spreads. *Carbohydrate Polymers*, **28**(4), 367–373.

Clegg, S., Moore, A. and Jones, S. (1996) Low fat margarine spreads as affected by aqueous phase hydrocolloids. *Journal of Food Science*, **61**(5), 1073–1079.

Decindio, B. and Cacace, D. (1995) Formulations and rheological characterisation of reduced-calorie food emulsions. *International Journal of Food Science and Technology*, **30**(4), 505–514.

Dickinson, E. and McClements, D. (1996) *Advances in Food Colloids*, Blackie Academic & Professional, Chapman & Hall, London.

Donovan, J. (1979) Phase transitions of the starch water system. *Biopolymers*, **18**, 263–257.

Donovan, J. and Mapes, C. (1976) A differential scanning calorimetric study of conversion of ovalbumin to S-ovalbumin in eggs. *Journal of the Science of Food and Agriculture*, **27**, 197–204.

Dougherty, M., Sombke, R., Irvine, J. and Rao, C. (1988) Oat fibres in low calorie breads, soft-type cookies, and pasta. *Cereal Foods World*, **33**(5), 424–427.

Drake, M. and Swanson, B. (1995) Reduced- and low-fat cheese technology: a review. *Trends in Food Science and Technology*, **6**(11), 366–369.

Drake, M., Boutte, T., Younce, F., Cleary, D. and Swanson, B. (1994) Melting characteristics and hardness of milkfat blend sucrose polyesters. *Journal of Food Science*, **59**(3), 652–654.

Drenowski, A. (1990) The new fat replacement. *Postgraduate Medicine*, **87**(6), 111.

Eilert, S., Mandigo, R. and Sumner, S. (1996) Phosphate and modified beef connective tissue effects on reduced fat, high water added frankfurters. *Journal of Food Science*, **61**(5), 1006.

Erickson, J. and Jenkins, P. (1991) Comparative *Salmonella* spp. and *Listeria monocytogenes* inactivation rates in four commercial mayonnaise products. *Journal of Food Protection*, **54**(12), 913–916.

Graf, E. and Roos, K.D. (1996) Performance of vanilla flavour in low fat ice cream. *ACS Symposium Series*, **633**, 24–35.

Haumann, B. (1986) Getting the fat out. *Journal of the American Oil Chemists Society*, **63**(3), 278–288.

Hutchinson, P., Baiochi, F. and Vecchio, A.D. (1977) Effect of emulsifiers on the texture of cookies. *Journal of Food Science*, **42**, 399.

Izzo, M. (1995) Trimming fat from compound coatings with microcrystalline cellulose. *Cereal Foods World*, **40**(5), 361–362.

James, N. and Berry, B. (1997) Use of chevon in the development of low fat meat products. *Journal of Animal Science*, **75**(2), 571–577.

Kamel, B. and Rasper, V. (1988) Effects of emulsifiers, sorbitol, polydextrose, and crystalline cellulose on the texture of reduced calorie cakes. *Journal of Texture Studies*, **19**, 307–320.

Kazier, H. and Dyer, B. (1995) Reduced fat pastry margarine for laminated dough in puff, Danish and croissant applications. *Cereal Foods World*, **40**(5), 363–365.

Kim, K.-O., Hansen, L. and Setser, C. (1986) Phase transitions of wheat starch water systems containing polydextrose. *Journal of Food Science*, **51**(4), 1095–1097.

Lichts, F. (1996) *World Sugar and Sweetener Yearbook*, Lichts Gmbh, Ratzeburg.

Lucca, P. and Tepper, B. (1994) Fat replacers and the functionality of fat in foods. *Trends in Food Science and Technology*, **5**, 12–19.

McAvoy, D., Shimp, R., Namkung, E. and Hand, V. (1996) The fate of Olestra, a fat substitute, during conventional waste water treatment. *Water Environment Research*, **68**(2), 169–177.

McMahon, D., Alleyne, M., Fife, R. and Oberg, C. (1996) Use of fat replacers in low fat mozzarella cheese. *Journal of Dairy Science*, **79**(11), 1911–1921.

Miller, M., Andersoen, M., Ramsey, C. and Reagan, J. (1993) Physical and sensory characteristics of low fat ground beef patties. *Journal of Food Science*, **58**(3), 461–463.

Nonaka, M., Hautala, E. and Weaver, M. (1974) Reducing oil content to fried potatoes by immersing in oil-free difluorodichloromethane. US Patent 3846572.

Ogden, L. and Rosenthal, A. (1997) The effect of fat crystal polymorphism at the sunflower oil–water interface. *Journal of Colloid and Interface Science*, **191**, 38–47.

Okiyama, A., Motoki, M. and Yamanaka, S. (1993) Bacterial cellulose. 4. Application to processed foods. *Food Hydrocolloids*, **6**(6), 503–511.

Passey, C. and Groslouis, M. (1993) Production of calorie-reduced almonds by supercritical extraction. *Journal of Supercritical Fluids*, **6**(4), 255–261.

Pateras, I. and Rosenthal, A. (1992) Effects of sucrose replacement by polydextrose on mechanism of structure formation in high ratio cakes. *International Journal of Food Science and Nutrition*, **43**(1), 25–30.

Phillips, N., McGiff, M., Barbano, D. and Lawless, H. (1995) The influence of fat on the sensory properties, viscosity and colour of low-fat milk. *Journal of Dairy Science*, **78**(6), 1258–1266.

Rosenthal, A. (1995) Application of aged egg in enabling increased substitution of sucrose by litesse (polydextrose) in high-ratio cakes. *Journal of the Science of Food and Agriculture*, **68**, 127–131.

Sanchez, C., Klopfenstein, C. and Walker, C. (1995) Use of carbohydrate based fat substitutes and emulsifying agents in reduced fat shortbread cookies. *Cereal Chemistry*, **72**(1), 25–29.

Schmidt, K., Lundy, A., Reynolds, J. and Yee, L. (1993) Carbohydrate or protein based fat mimicker effects on ice-milk properties. *Journal of Food Science*, **58**(4), 761.

Setser, C. and Racette, W. (1992) Macromolecule replacers in food products. *Critical Review in Food Science and Nutrition*, **32**(3), 275–297.

Shallenberger, R. and Acree, T. (1967) Molecular theory of sweet taste. *Nature*, **216**, 480–482.

Shepherd, L.S. (1969) Bakery fats. *Food Manufacture*, **44**, 45.

Smith, P. (1984) Producing low calorie desserts. *Cereal Foods World*, **29**(7), 407–408.

Specter, S. and Setser, C. (1994) Sensory and physical properties of reduced calorie frozen dessert system made with milk fat and sucrose substitutes. *Journal of Dairy Science*, **77**(3), 708–717.

Spies, R. and Hoseney, R. (1982) Effect of sugars on starch gelatinization. *Cereal Chemistry*, **59**(2), 128–131.

Srivastava, A. and Rao, P. (1993) Studies on low fat soft dough biscuits. *Journal of Food Science and Technology – Mysore*, **30**(1), 21–24.

Steiner, J. (1988) Sweet and bitter in the mirror of behaviour, in *Food Acceptability* (ed. D.M.H. Thomson), Elsevier Applied Science, London, pp. 157–171.

Tamime, A., Barclay, M., Davis, G. and Barrantes, E. (1994) Production of low-calorie yoghurt using skim milk powder and fat substitute. 1. A review. *Milchwissenschaft – Milk Science International*, **49**(2), 85–88.

Tamime, A., Kalab, M., Muir, D. and Barrantes, E. (1995) The microstructure of set style natural yoghurt made by substituting microparticulate whey protein for milk fat. *Journal of the Society of Dairy Technology*, **48**(4), 107–111.

Thomas, B., Elkeles, R., Brenchley, S., Connor, H., Govindji, A., Hartland, B., Lean, M., Lord, K. and Southgate, D. (1992) British Diabetic Association discussion paper on the role of diabetic foods. *Diabetic Medicine*, **9**(3), 300–306.

Trius, A., Sebranek, J., Rust, R. and Corr, J. (1994) Low fat bologna and beaker sausage: effects of carrageenans and chloride salt. *Journal of Food Science*, **59**(5), 941–945.

Waller, S., Rolla, G. and Assev, S. (1993) Adaption of dental plaque to sorbitol after three months' exposure to chewing gum. *Scandinavian Journal of Dental Research*, **101**(2), 84–86.

Wootton, J., Howard, N., Martin, J., McOsker, D. and Holme, J. (1967) The role of emulsifiers in the incorporation of air into layer cake batter systems. *Cereal Chemistry*, **44**, 333.

Zorrilla, S., Castelao, E., Depiante, D. and Rubiolo, A. (1996) Proteolysis during ripening of low-fat fynbo cheese salted with a mixture of NaCl and KCl. *Australian Journal of Dairy Technology*, **51**(1), 6–7

3 Functional foods: prospects and perspectives

TONY SHEEHY and PATRICK A. MORRISSEY

Introduction

For many centuries there has been a deep-rooted belief that foods and herbs have health-giving and curative properties. In this century we have increasingly turned to drugs to treat, alleviate or prevent diseases. However, since the discovery of nutrients and with our increasing analytical capabilities at the molecular level, we have become more knowledgeable of the biochemical structure–function relationships of the myriad of chemicals that occur naturally in foods and their effects on the human body (Labuza, 1994). This has led initially to the rise in popularity of health foods and holistic medicine, which began in the 1970s, and now this area is being consolidated as newer scientific evidence emerges. One of the spin-offs of this movement is a change in emphasis from the negative aspects of foods (e.g. high fat, high salt, high cholesterol and artificial additives) towards the concept that certain foods or food ingredients can have a very positive impact on human health and well-being. The realization by consumers and food manufacturers alike that attention to diet, as part of a healthy lifestyle, can help reduce disease risk and promote health has created a lucrative market for a whole range of new products called 'functional foods'. Current sales of such products have been put at US $3 billion in Japan, US $3 billion in the US and US $3 billion in Europe, and it is estimated that the market will eventually reach 5% of the total developed world food expenditure (US $100 billion) (Young, 1996; Heasman, 1997). The increasing willingness of consumers to buy products from which health benefits are anticipated is being recognized by many of the world's major food companies and they have responded by developing new products such as prebiotics, probiotics, tailored fats/oils and vitamin-, mineral- or phytochemical-enriched foods to go alongside the more familiar low-fat, low-salt, or high-fibre foods that became common in the 1980s.

The functional foods concept has been helped by a number of factors. These include the increasing life expectancy of people in developed countries (often entailing longer hospital care), rising health-care costs and advances in food and ingredients technology. Moreover, the need for publicly funded research institutions to publicize their findings and the greater media coverage given to these findings and to health issues in general (Goldberg, 1994) have helped in popularizing functional foods. Many consumers are unable or unwilling to change their diet in the way that dietary guidelines envisage and are looking to the food industry for healthier versions of their favourite products (Southgate, 1997). The newly developing economic powers (most notably in the Asia-Pacific region) are seeking ways to ensure a healthy population and a productive workforce. In addition, it is anticipated that ongoing advances in technology for diagnosing genetic predisposition to disease, detecting the early stages of disease, and monitoring the effectiveness of therapy will motivate people to adopt dietary strategies that could involve functional foods (Young, 1996).

Definitions

Functional foods, nutraceuticals, designer foods and pharmafoods are all synonyms for foods that can prevent or treat diseases (Goldberg, 1994), with the term 'functional foods' being most common. However, to many people, this term seems vague and meaningless; after all, every food is functional in that it provides protein, energy, fibre or micronutrients. The proponents of the functional foods concept emphasize that for a food to be regarded as functional it must provide benefits over and above the nutrients required for normal health. Thus, Goldberg (1994) defined functional foods as 'any food or food ingredient that has a positive impact on an individual's health, physical performance or state of mind, *in addition* to its nutritive value'. A further difficulty with the term arises because 'functional' has traditionally been taken in food science to relate to the physico-chemical properties of food ingredients (e.g. water binding, viscosity, foaming and clarification). Referring to 'functional foods' or 'functional ingredients' in the context of health has, therefore, caused confusion. An alternative term, 'vitafoods' (meaning 'foods for vitality'), has been put forward in an attempt to get round this problem. Vitafoods are defined as 'foods and drinks to meet the needs of modern, health-conscious consumers, which enhance the bodily or mental quality of life, enhance the capacity to endure or flourish or enhance the capacity to recover from strenuous exercise or illness. They may also increase the health status of the consumer or act as a potential deterrent to health hazards' (Blenford, 1997). It remains to be seen whether we will be eating 'vitafoods' or 'functional foods' in the years to come.

The Japanese Ministry of Health and Welfare has highlighted three conditions that functional foods must satisfy (Goldberg, 1994). First, they are foods, not capsules, tablets or powders, which are derived from naturally occurring ingredients. Second, they can and should be consumed as part of the daily diet. Finally, they should have a particular function when ingested, serving to regulate a particular body process, such as enhancement of the biological defence mechanisms, prevention of a specific disease (e.g. heart and artery disease, cancer, hypertension or obesity), control of physical and mental conditions, or slowing down the ageing process. Within these specifications, a broad spectrum of functional foods is evident, some of which are well established and others that have only recently begun to emerge, including medical foods, dietary therapeutics, dietetic foods, fortified foods, sports foods, special foods for those with allergies or intolerances, foods for the elderly, foods for pregnancy or lactation, and infant foods.

At one extreme is the category of medical foods. These are foods formulated to be consumed or administered enterally under the supervision of a physician. They are intended for the specific dietary management of a disease or condition for which distinctive nutritional requirements based on recognized scientific principles have been established by medical evaluation (Schmidl and Labuza, 1994). Medical foods include nutritionally complete enteral formulations supplying all the required proteins, fats, carbohydrates, vitamins and minerals, incomplete enteral formulations that supply a single nutrient or combinations of nutrients in quantities insufficient to maintain the nutritional status of a normal, healthy individual, formulations manufactured specifically for individuals with inborn errors of metabolism, and oral rehydration solutions.

At the other end of the spectrum are fortified foods, such as B vitamin and iron-fortified cereal and flour products, or iodized salt. These are consumed by essentially the whole population. In many countries, fortification has been responsible for the virtual eradication of major nutritional deficiency diseases (e.g. iron-deficiency anemia, goitre and pellagra) (Sloan and Stiedemann, 1996) and it plays an important role in public health, as evidenced by the recent US Food and Drug Administration ruling (FDA) requiring that enriched bread, flour, pasta and other grains be fortified with folate to reduce the risk of neural tube defects (Anon., 1996a).

It is between these two extremes that much research and development activity is currently focused. This chapter concentrates on attempts to produce functional foods that could reduce the incidence of chronic diseases, including cardiovascular disease, cancer, obesity and osteoporosis, which are the main causes of morbidity and mortality today. The role of functional foods in improving mental capacity or physical performance, boosting the immune system, retarding ageing and aiding the birth of healthy babies will also be discussed. Where possible, examples of available foods and interesting ingredients will be given.

History of functional foods

The original concept of functional foods (or more correctly, 'physiologically functional foods') was born in Japan in the 1980s, where the term was used by industry to describe foods fortified with specific ingredients imparting certain health benefits. The concept was nurtured by the government because it was concerned about the ageing of the country's population and the resultant cost of health care (Japanese people have the longest life expectancy in the world) (Heasman, 1997). Dietary fibre was the first of the functional ingredients to be a commercial success and the sudden rise in demand for drinks containing high levels of fibre in the late 1980s is considered the start of the functional foods market in Japan and the rest of the world (Heasman, 1997). The product credited with being the first Japanese functional food is a dietary fibre-containing soft drink called Fibre-Mini (Otsuka Pharmaceutical), launched in 1988, which uses water-soluble polydextrose as its functional ingredient and is marketed for 'gut regulation'.

The subsequent boom in functional foods and beverages led to a demand for regulation from consumer groups and from leading companies in the sector (who sought to protect their reputations and prevent manufacturers making unreasonable or unjustified claims) (Heasman, 1997). In response, the state initiated a voluntary approval system in which the term 'functional foods' was actually dropped and replaced by the term 'foods for specific health use (FOSHU)'. FOSHU foods were defined by the Japanese Ministry of Health and Welfare as 'processed foods containing ingredients that aid specific bodily functions as well as being nutritious'. On provision of sufficient research data, FOSHU approval includes permission to make certain specified claims in food labelling relating to the benefits to health that consuming the product can be expected to produce (Ichikawa, 1994). Twelve categories of health-enhancing ingredients were recognized: dietary fibre, oligosaccharides, sugar alcohols, peptides and proteins, glucosides, alcohols, isoprenoids and vitamins, cholines, lactic acid bacteria, minerals, polyunsaturated fatty acids and others. The legislative guidelines and the approval process have been reviewed by Ichikawa (1994). Although initially regarded by many food manufacturers as being too strict and too costly, it appears that a growing number of companies are seeking FOSHU approval for their products because carrying a FOSHU logo has commercial value (Heasman, 1997). At the same time, many more new foods and beverages containing functional ingredients are being introduced without approval as FOSHU products. These rely on the presence of specific ingredients to sell the product.

Japanese products have mainly been aimed at promoting general gut health and the maintenance of healthy bones. However, interest in the west has focused more on the prevention of heart disease and cancer, although recent developments indicate that Europe is also becoming interested in the role of gut health in disease prevention (Young, 1997a). In the USA, the emphasis in the 1980s on low-fat, and low-cholesterol foods paved the way for foods containing fat substitutes (e.g. Simplesse™ and Olestra™) and enhanced levels of dietary fibre. There has also been substantial interest in foods containing n-3 fatty acids, the antioxidant (or, more correctly, 'redox') vitamins E, C and A/β-carotene, and phytochemicals. However, recent unfavourable clinical trials have had a negative impact on β-carotene. In Europe, the main focus has been on dietary fibres, oligosaccharides, n-3 fatty acids, garlic and β-carotene (Gardner, 1994), but interest in other types of functional and designed ingredients, such as those seen in the USA, has not developed. For example, fat replacements or substitutes are far less popular in Europe than in the USA.

Uses of functional foods

There is widespread recognition that diet plays an important role in the incidence of many diseases. In recent years accumulating evidence has pointed to a role for certain dietary components in the prevention of cardiovascular disease, some cancers, osteoporosis, inflammatory conditions and obesity. A considerable amount of attention has also been focused on the role of the diet in modulating the immune system, slowing the ageing process and in influencing mood and athletic or intellectual performance. The scientific evidence is much stronger for some of these roles than for others.

Cardiovascular disease

Cardiovascular disease (CVD) remains the single biggest cause of death in the world, despite many health promotion campaigns, accounting for some 50% of total deaths, even though death rates due to CVD have been falling in many countries over the last two decades. The classical risk factors of smoking, elevated blood cholesterol and hypertension, even if they are causal rather than adventitious, explain only about 50% of the variance in the incidence of the disease (Gey, 1986). The many anomolies in the lipid hypothesis, including the low incidence of CVD in France despite a fairly high intake of saturated fat in the population and the lower incidence of CVD in upper social classes in the UK despite higher fat intake and cholesterol levels, are discussed by Rosenman (1992) and Duthie and Brown (1994). The remaining variation is considered to be due to both genetic and environmental factors, and evidence from biochemical, epidemiological and cell culture studies points to dietary antioxidants as possibly explaining some of this variation (Duthie and Brown, 1994). These antioxidants include vitamin E and C, certain carotenoids, trace elements needed for the functioning of antioxidant enzyme systems, such as Cu, Zn, Fe, Mn and Se, and perhaps other compounds such as ubiquinone and flavonoids. The antioxidant hypothesis of CVD proposes that free-radical mediated oxidation of low-density lipoprotein (LDL), polyunsaturated fatty acids (PUFAs) and cholesterol is the key step in atherogenesis (Steinberg et al., 1989), setting in train a cascade of events including LDL uptake by scavenger receptors of macrophages, foam cell formation, platelet aggregation, thrombus formation and smooth muscle cell proliferation. The role of dietary antioxidants and endogenous antioxidant enzyme systems would be to prevent the oxidation of LDL PUFAs and cholesterol and thus inhibit the process in its earliest stages. However, before health authorities will be willing to recommend increases in antioxidant intakes, it will be necessary to establish whether the habitually low dietary antioxidant intakes observed in high CVD risk populations are causal or merely adventitious (Duthie and Brown, 1994).

Elevated plasma homocysteine is strongly associated with an increased risk of CVD and a preventative role for folate has been postulated on the basis that moderate elevations in plasma homocysteine can be reduced by increasing folate intake (Sanders, 1997). However, as yet there have been no intervention trials to test the hypothesis that lowering plasma homocysteine concentrations will decrease the risk of CVD.

To date, market activity has focused on exploiting the consumer's perception of the link between cholesterol reduction and maintenance of a healthy heart (Young, 1997a). The ingredients that have found the widest application with the promise of lowering blood cholesterol include soluble and insoluble fibres, and n-3 fatty acids. Others that are being promoted include palm oil and plant sterols.

Some companies have traditional products with high natural levels of these components, such as Quaker Oats (soluble fibre) and John West Mackerel Fillets (n-3 fatty acids) (Young, 1997a). Others have created products with enhanced levels of these ingredients. Kellogg's Common Sense Oat Bran Flakes use a photograph of a heart-shaped bowl of breakfast cereal on their packaging under the slogan 'The heart of a healthy breakfast'. The packaging states that this cereal is 'a rich source of oat-bran, which could help reduce your cholesterol level, as part of a low fat diet'. Jordan's Bran Crisp takes the oat bran–CVD connection even further by formulating their product in the shape of a heart. This product is enriched with both wheat bran and oat bran, and extensive information on both is given on the pack. In the UK, soluble fibre has also found application in fruit juices (Ribena Juice & Fibre) and yoghurt (J. Sainsbury). No doubt attempting to capitalize on interest in antioxidants, some high-fibre cereals (e.g. Kellogg's All-Bran Plus) are also being fortified with vitamins C and E.

Fish oils have important cardio-protective effects by being able to lower LDL cholesterol, promote vasodilation and inhibit platelet aggregration. BASF (Germany) have introduced a range of microencapsulated marine oils rich in n-3 fatty acids that can be incorporated in breads, pasta, cereals, soups and other foods. In Ireland, fish oils have already been added to bread and table spreads under the 'Live' brand name. The first branded spread product with n-3 oil in the UK was MD Foods' Pact, which was launched in 1995 in a heart-shaped box to emphasize its healthy properties (Hilliam, 1996). NutraSweet Kelco have developed technology to manufacture n-3 fatty acids via a controlled fermentation process. This will enable the food industry to obtain these active components of fish oils without relying on fish. An interesting application of this type of technology has been in the enrichment of laying-hen diets with certain powdered sea algae to produce eggs containing high levels of docosahexaenoic acid (DHA). DHA is an n-3 fatty acid that is found predominantly in fatty cold-water fish (e.g. salmon, herring and mackerel) and is therefore difficult to obtain for people who do not consume fish. Omega DHA Food GmbH (Germany) is marketing these Omega 3 eggs, each of which contains about 150 mg of DHA, roughly the average adult daily requirement. Sales of 100 million Omega 3 eggs were anticipated in 1996 (Anon., 1996b).

The Malaysian Palm Oil Promotion Council is currently very active in promoting palm oil as an ideal ingredient for margarines, biscuits, cake mixes, ice creams, chocolate and other foods, claiming that it has LDL cholesterol-lowering properties, a high tocopherol, tocotrienol and β-carotene content, and a fatty acid composition that requires little chemical modification. In contrast, other types of edible oils require hydrogenation, resulting in the formation of *trans* fatty acids, which have been implicated in CVD because they raise serum tryglycerides and LDL cholesterol and lowering HDL cholesterol (Willett *et al.*, 1993; Simopoulos, 1994).

There has also been significant market activity centering around the cholesterol-lowering properties of sitostanol, a saturated plant sterol (Miettinen *et al.*, 1995). The Raiso Group (Finland) has developed a technique for making sitostanol fat-soluble by esterifying it with fatty acids from vegetable oils, and the first commercial application was in Benecol margarine. This product has sold very well in Finland even though it is about six times more expensive than ordinary margarine (Young, 1997b). The company is now investigating the use of plant stanol esters in chocolate and ice cream, and believes that these esters could be used in any oil or fat product, as well as in products such as breakfast cereals.

Cancer

After heart disease, cancer is the second biggest cause of deaths in the world, accounting for 20% of all deaths. Although genetic predisposition continues to be viewed as a significant risk factor, evidence from cross-cultural and epidemiological studies suggests that approximately 30% of all cancer deaths may relate to diet (Eddy, 1986).

Manipulating dietary intake appears to be one of the relatively few realistic approaches to bring about a significant reduction in cancer risk (reviewed by Milner, 1994). Many foods, including carrots, cucumber, apples, strawberries, soyabeans, brussels sprouts, broccoli, peppers, leeks, fish and citrus fruits, are believed to contain anticarcinogenic components. Factors receiving attention include macronutrients, specific amino acids (methionine, cysteine, tryptophan, arginine), fatty acids (butyric acid, stearic acid, conjugated linoleic acid, *n*-3 fatty acids), vitamins (including vitamin A/carotenoids, vitamins C, D, E, choline, folate, B_{12}), minerals (Ca, Zn, Cu, Fe, Se, I) and non-essential dietary components (flavanoids, terpenes, thiocyanates/isothiocyanates, indoles, ellagic acid, sulphides) (Milner, 1994). Possible mechanisms of action include changing the activation/detoxification of foreign compounds, altering growth regulators such as intracellular cAMP concentrations and/or serving as anti-hormones (Milner, 1994). Micro-organisms (e.g. *Bifidobacteria* and lactic acid bacteria) could also be exploited for activating the immune system, which could be of benefit in cancer prevention (Young, 1997a).

Although not many consumers select foods specifically to reduce the risk of cancers, many have made some dietary changes, such as increasing fruit and vegetable intake, in line with dietary guidelines on healthy eating (Young, 1997a). In the late 1980s and early 1990s, emerging epidemiological evidence was interpreted as indicating that the protective factor in fruits and vegetables against cancer was vitamin C or β-carotene, rather than the mixture of over 150 phytochemicals in each fruit and vegetable (Herbert, 1996). Recent clinical intervention studies (Alpha-Tocopherol, Beta-Carotene Cancer Prevention Study Group, 1994; Albanes et al., 1995; Hennekens et al., 1996; Omenn et al., 1996) have cast considerable doubt on the efficacy of β-carotene for the prevention of cancers (indeed, there were indications of potential adverse effects in two large trials in populations at high risk due to long-term heavy chronic smoking) and raised questions about the appropriateness of adding high levels of any putative functional ingredient to processed foods with our current state of knowledge. They have also served to emphasize that the association of fruit and vegetable consumption with the prevention of cancer and other conditions might not reflect a causal relationship, but instead fruits and vegetables might appear protective only because people who eat more of them may smoke fewer cigarettes, drink less alcohol, eat less fat or consume fewer calories, or exercise more (Nestle, 1996). Dietary guidelines are designed to promote a healthful pattern of diet, activity and alcohol use. One or other aspect of that pattern may confer marginal health benefits that could become apparent in epidemiological studies, but it is the overall pattern that is most strongly associated with reduction of chronic disease risk (Nestle, 1996).

Obesity

Obesity is one of the most serious diet-related problems in the Western world, predisposing the subject to a number of disease conditions such as heart disease, hypertension and diabetes. A variety of approaches to weight control are practiced currently, including low-calorie versions of standard food and drink products, meal replacements, hypnosis, drug therapy and, in some cases, surgical intervention (Young, 1997a). However, these do not seem to have resulted in any decline in obesity levels and in fact the reverse appears to be happening.

One of the ways in which the high prevalence of obesity might be tackled could be by developing a broader range of products that induce satiety and therefore reduce energy intake. Food factors under investigation for this purpose include anorectic agents (such as caffeine, theobromine, thiamin and zinc) and dietary fibres or complex carbohydrates that delay stomach emptying, digestion and assimilation (Walqvist, 1994). There is also interest in food components that can increase energy expenditure by increasing the thermic effect of a given meal (e.g. capsaicin from chilli peppers) and in components that can alter the synthesis or distribution of body fat. Phytoestrogens (e.g. from soya products or clover) and milk peptides may be capable of altering fat distribution (Walqvist, 1994) and this could be beneficial since abdominal adiposity seems to be more predictive of chronic disease risk than peripheral adiposity.

DMV International Nutritionals (The Netherlands) produces Peptide FM, a mixture of enzymatic digests of blood globin, wheat protein and casein. The active peptides are said to interfere with fat metabolism by suppressing lipid absorption and activating the liver enzymes involved in tryglyceride clearance. The product is positioned as a fat metabolism enhancer and is aimed at foods for obesity control. Synthite Industrial Chemicals Ltd (India) produces hydroxycitric acid (HCA) from the dried fruit rinds of *Garcinia cambogia*. The company claims that HCA has anti-obesity properties because it inhibits lipid synthesis. It is marketed as an ingredient that could be incorporated into cookies, soft drinks, fruit juices and yoghurts. Kancor Flavours and Extracts Ltd (India), also supply extracts from *Garcinia cambogia* that are aimed at foods for the control of obesity. Further research and clinical work is necessary to support widespread use of such products.

Osteoporosis

Osteoporosis is defined as a disorder resulting from a combination of low bone mass (osteopenia) and low trauma fractures. The loss of bone mass usually occurs over many years. The disease cannot be cured; it can only be prevented or minimized (Dawson-Hughes, 1994). Hormone replacement therapy after menopause is considered the most effective measure against the disease. In addition, adequate consumption of calcium-rich foods is also important at all ages, but especially during periods of rapid growth, such as adolesence, with dairy products generally being the best vehicle.

Concern in Japan in the early 1990s over the lack of calcium in the national diet resulted in the launch of a wide range of calcium-fortified foods and drinks, with the latest also containing calcium absorption promoters (Young, 1997a). Of these, casein phosphopeptide, calcium citrate malate and vitamin D are most often used. Activity in the West has focused on the calcium enrichment of dairy products such as milk and children's desserts. For example, in Ireland, Golden Vale's SuperPlus low-fat milk is fortified with calcium, vitamins A and D, and folic acid. Extensive information is given on the packaging about diet and osteoporosis (as well as anemia and neural tube defects). In the USA, there have also been some cases of fortification of fruit juices, notably Tropicana's Pure Premium Plus orange juice containing calcium and antioxidants and Procter & Gamble's Hawaiian Punch with calcium and vitamin C (Sloan and Stiedemann, 1996). As yet, there has been very little use of calcium absorption promotors in calcium-enriched products in the West (Young, 1997a).

Neural tube defects

Neural tube defects (NTDs), including spina bifida, hydrocephalus, anencephaly and encephalocele, make a major contribution to infant mortality and mental and physical disability. Every year, approximately 4000 infants with neural tube defects are born in the USA, while worldwide nearly 400 000 are born with these conditions (Centres for Disease Control and Prevention, 1991). In 1991 it was estimated that the annual medical and surgical costs in the USA for all people with spina bifida exceed US $200 million (Centres for Disease Control and Prevention, 1991). It is now well accepted that folic acid can prevent most, though not all, neural tube defects (Anon., 1991; Medical Research Council Vitamin Study Research Group, 1991; Centres for Disease Control and Prevention, 1992; Expert Advisory Group, 1992; Oakley, 1993; Bower, 1996). In 1993, a recommendation was made that all women capable of becoming pregnant should consume 0.4 mg folate daily. In addition, those who have had a previous NTD-affected pregnancy should consult their physicians about the desirability of using 4.0 mg folate per day from at least 1 month before conception through the first 3 months of pregnancy (Centres for Disease Control and Prevention, 1993).

Humans obtain folate primarily from vegetables and fruits, and an average Western diet supplies 0.15–0.2 mg/day (Metz, 1995). Women of childbearing age would need to increase their intake two- to threefold to reach a level of 0.4 mg/day. This could be brought about by eating folate-rich foods, taking supplements or by fortifying staple foods. However, consumption of extra folate in natural foods is relatively ineffective in increasing folate status, presumably because of low bioavailability (Cuskelly et al., 1996). Furthermore, the critical need for folate occurs in the peri-conceptional period as the neural tube closes by the end of the sixth week after the last menstrual period. By this time a woman may not have even had confirmation that she is pregnant and might not have started taking steps to increase her folate intake or take supplements. In any event, about 40% of pregnancies are unplanned so advice on improving diet or taking supplements would be given too late in those cases (Bower, 1996). Recognizing these problems, the US FDA has mandated that folic acid be added to most enriched flour, breads, rice and other grain products (at a level of 0.14 mg/100 g). The final rules on fortification were published in the *Federal Register* of 5 March , 1996 (**61**: 8781–8797) and become effective on 1 January 1998. Unenriched cereal-grain products without folic acid will continue to be available to consumers who wish to avoid folic acid for whatever reason. The FDA decided not to extend fortification to fruit juices and dairy products because intakes of folate by very large segments of the US population could then reach several milligrams per day (Anon., 1996a). The effects of sustained higher intakes are not well known but may include neurotoxicity (Scott et al., 1991) and may complicate the diagnosis of vitamin B_{12} deficiency (Reynolds, 1991). Consequently, total folate consumption should be kept at less than 1 mg/day, except under the supervision of a physician (Centres for Disease Control and Prevention, 1993).

In Europe, an increasing number of breads, milks, breakfast cereals and breakfast bars are being fortified with folic acid. Important issues that need to be addressed include whether to make fortification of a staple food mandatory, as in the USA, and whether to place some limits on the range of foods currently being fortified, in the light of the possible harmful effects of high intakes.

Immunity

Blumberg (1994) reviewed the role of diet in maintaining normal immune defences in immunocompromised patients and promoting optimal immune function in healthy individuals to reduce their risk of infectious and chronic diseases. He concluded that a wide range of macro- and micronutrients have important effects on immune function. These include amino acids (e.g. arginine, glutamine), *n*-6 and *n*-3 fatty acids, some minerals (e.g. Se, Cu, Fe, Mn, Zn), fat-soluble vitamins (A, D, E), carotenoids and water-soluble vitamins (e.g. B_6, B_{12}, folate, C). In addition, there may be a dietary requirement of pre-formed purine and/or pyrimidine bases under situations of immune challenge. Phytochemicals (e.g. catechin, flavonoids from green teas and berries, γ-glutamyl allylic cysteines from aged garlic extract, triterpenoids from licorice and polyacetylenes from parsley, carrot and celery) also appear to influence immunologic activity and could be useful components of functional foods.

Mood, behaviour and intellectual performance

The possibility that certain food components could influence mood, behaviour and intellectual performance has stimulated interest in producing so-called 'mood foods' and 'smart foods'. The evidence to support a role for caffeine, amino acids and carbohydrates in the modification of mood and performance was reviewed by Meiselman and Lieberman (1994) who found that, on the whole, it is still rather unconvincing. Caffeine in moderate amounts generally increases vigilance and awareness and reduces fatigue. However, its effects on more complex tasks such as memory or learning are inconclusive, and it is unlikely to have robust effects on complex cognitive performance. Tryptophan at sufficient concentrations increases brain serotonin and induces a sedative-like effect but it is unlikely that this occurs when it is consumed at the levels found in foods. Although the supply of tryptophan for serotonin synthesis can be modified by high-protein or high-carbohydrate diets, the definitive effects of protein and carbohydrate-containing meals on human mood and performance have not been established.

Despite the lack of clear evidence for robust effects of the above foods or food components on mood and behaviour, products (and especially food ingredients) are beginning to appear aimed at capitalizing on consumers' desires to feel better, smarter or less stressed. These range from traditional plant extracts and herb teas, through 'new-age' soft drinks, to *n*-3 fatty acids and phospholipids.

Herbal teas have for many years been promoted for their relaxing and reviving properties. In the USA, sales of ready-to-drink herbal teas increased by 61% from 1994 to 1995 (Sloan, 1996). Recent additions to the drinks market have been carbonated waters flavoured with fruit juice and natural extracts, and fortified with vitamins and minerals. An example is AMÉ, containing grape and apricot juices, schizandra, limeflower, jasmine, gentian, Siberian and Korean ginseng, vitamins B_6, B_{12} and C, and iron. The herbs are said to have 'soothing, enhancing, energy-giving and restorative' properties, and to be capable of 'invigorating and enlivening the spirit' and 'comforting and relieving the mind'. Nuova Linnea SA (Switzerland) manufactures active ingredients from botanical sources, including *Ginkgo biloba* extract, which, it is claimed, maintains circulation to the brain, leading to improvement of memory.

In Japan, the *n*-3 fatty acid DHA became popular as a food ingredient in 1994, finding application in infant milk formulas and a range of processed foods, most of which are aimed at children (Young, 1997a). The rationale behind its use is the belief that DHA is important in brain development but is in short supply in standard infant formulas and in the diets of children. BASF (Germany) have introduced a microencapsulated fish oil powder called Dry *n*-3 5:25, which contains fish oil tryglycerides with a ratio of 5% eicosapentaenoic acid (EPA) to 25% DHA and is intended specifically for infant formulas.

Phospholipids are important building blocks of cell membranes and are essential for the normal funtioning of all body cells. Since the phospholipid composition of cell membranes can be influenced by diet, phospholipids are now being promoted as 'membrane foods'. Belovo (Belgium), which produces fine chemicals from eggs, has introduced DHA- and arachidonic acid (ARA)-enriched phospholipids, which it claims have beneficial effects on cognitive performance as well as protective effects against cardiovascular disease and various cancers. Eurochem (Germany) offers phosphatidylserine as a nutritional supplement, claiming that it has beneficial effects on certain types of memory disorders (e.g. Alzheimer's disease). Lucas Meyer GmbH (Germany), is also marketing phosphatidylserine (as LECI-PS) as a brain nutrient, claiming in its promotional literature that it can improve memory and learning, increase concentration under the stresses of work, establish a basic positive mood in the face of depression and regenerate mental capacity in cases of excessive alcohol consumption or due to ageing. LECI-PS is proposed as being suitable for addition to energy drinks, mineral waters, fruit vitamin drinks, iced coffee and other types of instant drinks. Similarly, Euticals SpA (Italy) produces glycerophosphorylcholine (GPC), which is being marketed in combination with L-glutamine, B vitamins, bilberry extract and manganese as a means of reducing memory decay and improving intellectual performance.

While the benefits of *n*-3 fatty acids (at least for normal brain development) in infants and young children appear to be well founded, those ascribed to the other ingredients appear more tenuous. It may well be that they can benefit certain very specific population sub-groups, but great care will be needed to avoid exploitation of consumers by misappropriation of beneficial effects from these subgroups to the normal population. Failure to deliver on these claims would greatly undermine the credibility of the functional food market as a whole.

Gut health

There is growing scientific evidence to support the concept that the maintenance of a healthy gut microflora may provide some protection against conditions such as diarrhoea, food poisoning and even some cancers (Schaafsma, 1997). This concept is, however, still in its infancy as there has been only a limited demonstration of efficacy in humans (Young, 1997a).

Europe and Japan have already experienced much activity in probiotic food products, particularly those that are milk-based. Yakult is a fermented milk drink that has been on the market in Japan for many years and is now arguably the world's leading mass marketed functional food product. It contains *Lactobacillus caseii Shirota* and is packaged in small bottles characteristic of the Japanese health drinks market (Hilliam, 1996). The use of probiotic cultures, particularly *L. acidophilus* and *Bifidobacterium*, underwent a boom in Europe in the late 1980s and early 1990s, especially in France. More recently, newer and more complex strains have been introduced. LC1 is a range of fermented dairy products from Chambourcy (Nestlé) containing a new strain of *L. acidophilus*, which is claimed to reinforce the body's natural defence mechanisms and is supported by a strong medical dossier (Hilliam, 1996). Gaio yoghurt from MD Foods (Denmark) contains Causido, a Caucasian lactic acid culture that is claimed to have cholesterol-lowering properties. Mona (The Netherlands) produces the Vifit range of dairy products containing *L. caseii GG*, for which beneficial effects have been reported, such as increased resistance of gut flora against invading micro-organisms and prevention and/or effective treatment of diarrhoea. Danone's Actimel is a yoghurt drink containing *L. caseii Actimel* that is claimed to 'balance the intestinal flora and support the body's natural powers of resistance'.

Another approach to the maintenance of gut health is the provision of substrates (prebiotics) that encourage the growth of preferred micro-organisms. Oligosaccharides that are not digested or absorbed by the small intestine reach the large intestine, where they are fermented by intestinal bacteria. Orafti (Belgium) manufactures RAFTILINE products which consist of six different types of inulin extracted from chicory roots. From inulin, Orafti produces RAFTILOSE, which consists of oligofructose liquids and powders. Both inulin and oligofructose stimulate the development of *Bifidobacteria* in the human colon (Coussement, 1997). Inulin is aimed as a fat/gelatin replacer (e.g. in chocolates, mousses, cheeses, breads, spreads and frankfurters) and oligofructose can replace carbohydrates (e.g. in muesli bars, milkshakes, chocolate milk drinks, ice cream, cakes and yoghurts). Borculo Whey Products (The Netherlands) has developed a prebiotic based on lactose called Elix'or. This contains galacto-oligosaccharides, which act as growth promoters for several beneficial intestinal bacteria such as *Bifidobacteria* and *Lactobacilli*. In contrast, hardly any putrefactive micro-organisms are able to use galacto-oligosaccharides.

Products that contain both pre- and probiotics are still rare in Europe (Hilliam, 1996). One of the first was Fyos, a fermented milk drink launched by Nutricia in 1994 in Belgium. It contained *L. caseii* and inulin. In 1995, the leading UK multiple retailer J. Sainsbury launched a fruit and fibre yoghurt containing inulin but no mention was made of its potential benefit to the digestive system.

Bowel functions and disorders

Diverticular disease, irritable bowel syndrome, haemorroids and constipation are all associated with the affluent Western diet, which is low in dietary fibre. Despite a rise in consumer awareness of the benefits of fibre, intakes are still well below those recommended. Breakfast cereals have long been a source of fibre and other products that have been enriched with fibre include wholewheat biscuits, crackers and breads. In the past, the addition of fibres to foods often resulted in the presence of undesirable flavours, appearance and texture. However, IDIRC (France) and Lyckeby Stärkelsen (Sweden) are among a number of companies now offering fibres that impart natural or neutral flavours, as well as having good textural and appearance characteristics. This should lead to a greater degree of fibre addition to biscuits, snack bars, meat products, confectionary and, ultimately, drinks, though the association of fibre with solid foods is still so strong that its addition to a liquid is not yet readily accepted by the average consumer (Young, 1997a).

Exercise and athletic performance

An enormous range of products is offered to athletes for the purpose of improving performance. However, in most cases, the advertised benefits are not supported by a sufficiently strong body of scientific evidence. One of the few nutritional products aimed at athletes that has been subjected to thorough scientific evaluation and shown to be effective is the sports drink (Brouns, 1997). Sports drinks are formulated to serve a variety of purposes, including supplying carbohydrate to the working muscles, preventing dehydration, allowing replacement of electrolytes lost during sweating, promoting hydration before the event and encouraging faster rehydration and glycogen repletion afterwards. At present, most of the commercial products (such as Gatorade, Lucozade Sport, Isostar and Powerade) are generally rather similar in composition, yet no single formulation is likely to meet all these requirements equally well. It is likely that there will be further intensive development in this area in the foreseeable future, with drinks becoming more tailored to individual sports. Greater attention to palatability will also be important as it has become apparent that the perception of the basic tastes (sweet, sour, salt, bitter) changes with increasing activity (Brouns, 1997).

Substances such as L-carnitine and certain peptides have received attention because of their possible influence on performance, fatigue and recovery. Biosint SpA (Italy) and Lonza Ltd. (Switzerland) supply L-carnitine, a compound formed in the body and consumed in the diet that is essential for energy production and fat metabolism. Some of the claims for supplementing the daily diet with L-carnitine include improved performance during physical exercise, raised energy, endurance and stamina, compensation for losses incurred after exhaustive exercise, and increased resistance to fatigue. However, Brouns (1997) considered that well-controlled human studies have failed to show any changes in muscle carnitine content, fat oxidation or performance after L-carnitine supplementation. DMV International Nutritionals (The Netherlands) has introduced Glutamine Peptide to the sports food and clinical nutrition markets. Glutamine is considered to become an essential amino acid during stress (e.g. strenuous exercise, surgery, burns) and it is suggested that glutamine-containing products may help to maintain plasma glutamine so that provision of this amino acid to the gut, muscles and immune cells is sufficient. The company believes that Glutamine Peptide may play a role in counteracting a number of phenomena associated with 'overtraining syndrome', such as decreased performance, depressed mood and increased susceptibility to infection. However, they recognize that further research is needed in order to substantiate these claims.

Ageing

As birth rates fall and life expectancy rises, age profiles in developed countries show a growing proportion of older people. For example, in the USA, about 12.8% of the population were over 65 years of age in 1995, but this figure is expected to double by the year 2050, at which time about 50% of the population will be over 45 (Hasler, 1996). These demographic changes have important implications with regard to the burden on national health care systems. In 1990, nearly 60% of new cancer cases in the USA occurred in those over the age of 65 and this trend can only be expected to continue into the next century. The possibility that foods could be designed to combat the physical and mental deterioration associated with ageing appeals to everyone wishing to maintain a high quality of life for as long as possible. However, it has a special appeal to governments eager to limit their burgeoning health care obligations.

In a wide range of animal species, life span can be increased significantly by restricting caloric intake while maintaining an appropriate intake of essential nutrients (Warner and Kim, 1994). The suggested mechanism is a reduction in the amount of oxidative damage to DNA, proteins or lipids arising from normal metabolic processes. This has given rise to the hypothesis that vitamins E and C, carotenoids, certain trace elements and non-nutrient compounds with antioxidant properties (e.g. ubiquinone, flavanoids) could help to retard the physical and mental degeneration that accompanies ageing, and perhaps even prolong the life span itself (Walton and Packer, 1980; Warner and Kim, 1994). Many of these nutrients and non-nutrients are clearly very effective in preventing or minimizing oxidative damage in selected experimental models. However, apart from a limited amount of work in elderly subjects indicating benefits for vitamin E in reducing cataracts (Robertson *et al.*, 1989), blood lipid peroxides (Wartanowicz *et al.*, 1984; Tolonen et al., 1988) and oral cancer (Gridley *et al.*, 1992) and maintaining immune function (Meydani *et al.*, 1990), studies in humans are lacking on whether or not higher intakes of antioxidants can result in a decrease in age-related pathology, let alone an increase in life span.

Future prospects

Functional foods potentially offer consumers many benefits (Hilliam, 1996). Most consumers believe that what they eat influences their health. Provided they can be assured that the claims made for functional foods are true, consumers are willing to believe that such foods will help them live longer and avoid certain medical conditions. Functional foods should also provide consumers with the psychological benefit of taking greater responsibility for their health. In a recent survey in the UK (Cathro and Morris, 1995), more than two-thirds of respondents were positive about the concept of functional foods, believing that the concept was a good or very good idea, while only 9% felt that it was a bad idea.

There are, however, some potential barriers to the widespread acceptance of functional foods that need to be borne in mind. The development of functional foods and the basic research to document marketing claims are expensive, and premium pricing will therefore be necessary for profitability (McNutt, 1994). Some consumers are suspicious that the promise of health benefits will be used as a marketing ploy simply to justify higher pricing (Hilliam, 1996) or to gain a competitive edge. This makes it absolutely imperative that claimed benefits associated with particular foods should be real, not imaginary. At present, in the UK at least, the purchasing of functional foods is biased towards the higher socio-economic groups, reflecting both awareness and price (Hilliam, 1996). It will be very important to achieve a pricing structure that ensures that consumers across the socio-economic spectrum can purchase functional food and drink products. This is particularly true now that growing attention is being given to the comparatively poor diet of the lower socio-economic groups (Young, 1997b). Clearly, any company that adopts a pricing structure that puts functional foods out of the reach of such groups could be criticized for creating a class of elitist foods. Other consumer concerns include whether functional foods are necessary if one is already eating a healthy diet, and whether they may lull consumers into a false sense of security and be used to complement for otherwise poor dietary habits (Hilliam, 1996).

The task of raising awareness and educating consumers is vitally important if functional foods are to fulfill their potential (Hilliam, 1996), but the question of who provides that education needs to be addressed. For many people, the media, especially television, are a major source of information about health and functional foods. The other important source is the product label itself. Health professionals are less important sources of information for most people, but the credibility of that information is high. In contrast, most consumers do not believe marketing claims from food companies and many doubt that scientists themselves understand what good nutrition really is (McNutt, 1994). Government credibility in relation to food issues tends to be low and in the UK is probably especially so after the BSE scare. Certainly, scientists need to communicate much more effectively (and without the use of jargon) with the general public (McNutt, 1994). They should explain to consumers that understanding the effects of foods on health is an evolving body of knowledge, and they should try, wherever possible, to be more quantitative in their messages about the beneficial effects of foods (e.g. how much is beneficial and how much is likely to be harmful) (McNutt, 1994).

A fundamental issue for the overall credibility of functional foods is that those involved in the industry should not mislead the public, whether explicitly or by inference, about the expected benefits of a product, ingredient or technology. A market as potentially lucrative as that foreseen for functional foods brings with it the possibility that excessive or inappropriate claims will be made, leading to exploitation of consumers. Lobstein (1996) referred to this as 'food quackery'. Claims such as 'may help maintain a healthy heart . . .' or 'for healthy hearts and minds . . .', though very appealing, are vague and may well be misleading. Some of the early entrants into the UK functional foods market were sharply criticized by the Advertising Standards Authority because it felt that the strong health claims being made on products and in advertising in relation to their ability to reduce blood cholesterol levels and, by inference, heart disease were likely to be exaggerated (Lobstein, 1996; Young, 1997b).

Lobstein (1996) discussed several practices that he considered should give rise to caution. First, the claimed benefits attributed to a product may be justified by reference to inappropriate studies. Consuming white bread to which fish oils are added is not the same as eating oily fish, and health benefits associated with oily fish consumption should not be appropriated to other products. Second, giving the impression that n-3-fatty-acid-fortified white bread can adequately substitute for oily fish consumption or that fibre-enriched soft drinks can substitute for a diet rich in naturally occurring dietary fibre is confusing and undermines attempts by governments to encourage consumption of oily fish, fruits, vegetables and wholegrain foods. Indeed, if the product is of poor nutritional quality, then supplementing it with a functional ingredient (e.g. fibre in soft drinks) only serves to reinforce poor dietary habits. Finally, the addition or promotion of high contents of vitamin A in foods (e.g. as one of the so-called 'ACE' vitamins) without mentioning the danger of foetal abnormalities in pregnant females who consume high amounts of this nutrient is dangerous. Care will also be needed to avoid excessive intakes of other components (e.g. iron, vitamin D and folic acid) as more and more products become enriched.

Regulations on claims are still evolving at European Union level and a formula for allowing certain types of health claims is being sought through ongoing discussions with regulatory, industry, academic and consumer bodies (Richardson, 1996). However, it seems prudent that health claims for functional foods should only be allowed if they follow government recommendations for healthy eating, if the claim relates to the food itself, when eaten in normal quantities, and not to some general property of any of its ingredients, and if manufacturers can produce the required degree of substantiation for the claim. Strict regulation of claims may initially give the appearance of stifling innovation and opportunity but in the long run will serve to protect the responsible manufacturer and inspire greater consumer confidence in the industry.

Conclusions

The thinking of nutritionists, in developed countries at least, has gradually moved away from the idea of 'deficient' versus 'adequate' diets towards the concept of 'optimal' nutrition. The evolving concept of functional foods is closely linked to that of optimal nutrition. Foods are being formulated and promoted on the basis that they can provide 'measurable' health benefits over and above the nutrients needed for normal function. As indicated in this chapter, the health benefits could include reduced susceptibility to heart disease, cancer, obesity, osteoporosis, infection or an NTD-affected pregnancy. However, it is clear that much more research is needed, including development of valid disease biomarkers, clinical trials and intervention studies, before a great many of these benefits can be properly measured and substantiated.

The success of functional foods will depend on many factors, including their safety, efficacy, taste, convenience and value. Of paramount importance is that products must be safe and claimed benefits must be real, not a commerical hype. In this regard, the comments of Herbert (1996), made in connection with antioxidant vitamin supplements, are worth repeating as they could just as easily be aimed at foods bearing health claims. They are:

1. No therapy is effective until it has been objectively, reproducibly and reliably demonstrated to be more effective than a suggestion, a placebo or doing nothing.
2. No therapy is safe until it has been objectively, reproducibly and reliably demonstrated to be as safe as doing nothing.
3. If there is any question with respect to safety, before using a product it must be objectively, reproducibly and reliably demonstrated that the potential for benefit exceeds the potential for harm.

Assuming that products are safe and effective, their taste and convenience must not be compromised or they will not sell. Consumers must be educated to see the value of such products and they must be able to afford them. The regulations governing the scientific evidence required to support claims must protect the consumer while not stifling innovation. It will be difficult to achieve a regulatory formula that pleases everyone, but the consumer's rights must come first.

In marketing functional foods it is important that they are promoted in the light of dietary guidelines for healthy eating and are seen as components of a healthy diet, rather than as a way of compensating for a poor diet. The core of sound eating and drinking is, and will continue to be, balance, variety and moderation within the framework of physical activity and a well-balanced perspective on life.

If the hurdles stated above can be overcome, the potential market for functional foods in the future would seem to be vast. Ultimately, as advances in science lead to more and more products with proven efficacy, the hope is that functional foods will be able to help improve and maintain the health and vitality of the greater part of the world's population; not merely the affluent few in developed countries, in the same way that fortification contributed to improving public health and eliminating deficiency diseases earlier this century. Time will tell whether or not this hope will become a reality.

References

Albanes, D., Helnonen, O.P., Huttunen, J.K., Taylor, P.R., Virtamo, J., Edwards, B.K., Haapakoski, J., Rautalahti, M., Hartman, A.M. and Palmgren, J. (1995) Effects of alpha-tocopherol and beta-carotene supplements on cancer incidence in the Alpha-Tocopherol, Beta-Carotene Study. *American Journal of Clinical Nutrition*, **62**, 1427S–1430S.

Alpha-Tocopherol, Beta-Carotene Cancer Prevention Study Group (1994) The effect of vitamin E and beta carotene on the incidence of lung cancer and other cancers in male smokers. *New England Journal of Medicine*, **330**, 1029–1035.

Anon. (1991) Folic acid and neural tube defects (editorial). *Lancet*, **338**: 153–154.

Anon. (1996a) Folic acid fortification. *Nutrition Reviews*, **54**, 94–95.

Anon. (1996b) Omega eggs sell well. *World Poultry*, **12**, 9.

Blenford, D.E. (1997) The significance of vitafoods, what they are and their potential, in *Proceedings of the 1st Vitafoods International Conference* (ed. D.E. Blenford), FoodTech Europe, Copenhagen.

Blumberg, J. (1994) Nutrient control of immune function, in *Functional Foods: Designer Foods, Pharmafoods, Nutraceuticals* (ed. I. Goldberg), Chapman & Hall, London, pp. 87–108.

Bower, C. (1996) Folate and the prevention of birth defects. *Australian Journal of Nutrition and Dietetics (Supplement)*, **53**, S5–S8.

Brouns, F. (1997) Functional foods for athletes, in *Proceedings of the 1st Vitafoods International Conference* (ed. D.E. Blenford), FoodTech Europe, Copenhagen.

Cathro, J.S. and Morris, L. (1995) *Functional and Healthy Foods: An In-Depth Review of UK Consumer Attitudes*. Leatherhead Food Research Association Special Report, Leatherhead.

Centres for Disease Control and Prevention (1991) Use of folic acid for prevention of spina bifida and other neural tube defects – 1983–1991. *Journal of the American Medical Association*, **266**, 1190–1191.

Centres for Disease Control and Prevention (1992) Recommendations for the use of folic acid to reduce the number of cases of spina bifida and other neural tube defects. *Morbidity and Mortality Weekly Report*, **41**, 1233–1238.

Centres for Disease Control and Prevention (1993) Recommendations for use of folic acid to reduce number of spina bifida cases and other neural tube defects. *Journal of the American Medical Association*, **269**, 1233–1238.

Coussement, P. (1997) Non-digestible oligosaccharides for functional foods, in *Proceedings of the 1st Vitafoods International Conference* (ed. D.E. Blenford), FoodTech Europe, Copenhagen.

Cuskelly, G.J., McNulty, H. and Scott, J.M. (1996) Effect of increasing dietary folate on red-cell folate: implications for prevention of neural tube defects. *Lancet*, **347**, 657–659.

Dawson-Hughes, B. (1994) Nutrition, exercise, and lifestyle factors that affect bone health, in *Nutrition in the '90s: Current Controversies and Analysis* (eds F.N. Kotsonis and M.A. Mackey), Marcel Dekker, New York, pp. 99–116.

Duthie, G.G. and Brown, K.M. (1994) Reducing the risk of cardiovascular disease, in *Functional Foods: Designer Foods, Pharmafoods, Nutraceuticals* (ed. I. Goldberg), Chapman & Hall, London, pp. 19–38.

Eddy, D.M. (1986) Setting priorities for cancer prevention. *Journal of the National Cancer Institute*, **76**, 187–199.

Expert Advisory Group (1992) *Folic acid and the prevention of neural tube defects*, Department of Health, London.

Gardner, J.C. (1994) The development of the functional food business in the United States and Europe, in *Functional Foods: Designer Foods, Pharmafoods, Nutraceuticals* (ed. I. Goldberg), Chapman & Hall, London, pp. 468–479.

Gey, K.F. (1986) On the antioxidant hypothesis with regard to arteriosclerosis. *Bibliotheca Nutritia Dietetica*, **37**, 53–91.

Goldberg, I. (1994) Introduction, in *Functional Foods; Designer Foods, Pharmafoods, Nutraceuticals* (ed. I. Goldberg), Chapman & Hall, London, pp. 3–16.

Gridley, G., McLaughlin, J.K., Block, G., Blot, W.J., Gluch, M. and Fraumeni, J.F., Jr (1992) Vitamin supplement risk and reduced risk of oral and pharyngeal cancer. *American Journal of Epidemiology*, **135**, 1083–1092.

Hasler, C.M. (1996) Functional foods: the Western perspective. *Nutrition Reviews*, **54**, S6–S10.

Heasman, M. (1997) The regulation of functional foods and beverages in Japan, in *Proceedings of the 1st Vitafoods International Conference* (ed. D.E. Blenford), FoodTech Europe, Copenhagen.

Hennekens, C.H., Buring, J.E., Manson, J.E., Stampfer, M., Rosner, B., Cook, N.R., Belanger, C., La Motte, F., Gaziano, J.M., Ridker, P.M., Willet, W. and Peto, R. (1996) Lack of effect of long-term supplementation with beta-carotene on the incidence of malignant neoplasms and cardio-vascular disease. *New England Journal of Medicine*, **334**, 1145–1149.

Herbert, V. (1996) Introduction: Symposium on prooxidant effects of antioxidant vitamins. *Journal of Nutrition*, **126**, 1197S–1200S.

Hilliam, M. (1996) Functional foods: The Western consumer viewpoint. *Nutrition Reviews*, **54**, S189–S194.

Ichikawa, T. (1994) Functional foods in Japan, in *Functional Foods: Designer Foods, Pharmafoods, Nutraceuticals* (ed. I. Goldberg), Chapman & Hall, London, pp. 453–467.

Labuza T. (1994) Foreword, in *Functional Foods: Designer Foods, Pharmafoods, Nutraceuticals* (ed. I. Goldberg), Chapman & Hall, London, pp. xi–xiii.

Lobstein, T. (1996) Feeding neurosis: functional foods serve commercial, not consumer, needs, in *Proceedings of Functional Food, Nutraceutical of Pharmaceutical?* (ed. S. Shaw), IBC UK Conferences, London, pp. 125–133.

McNutt, K.W. (1994) Consumers' views on functional foods, in *Functional Foods: Designer Foods, Pharmafoods, Nutraceuticals* (ed. I. Goldberg), Chapman & Hall, London, pp. 523–534.

Medical Research Council Vitamin Study Research Group (1991) Prevention of neural tube defects: results of the Medical Research Council Vitamin Study Research Group. *Lancet*, **338**, 131–137.

Meiselman, H.L. and Lieberman, H.R. (1994) Mood and performance foods, in *Functional Foods: Designer Foods, Pharmafoods, Nutraceuticals* (ed. I. Goldberg), Chapman & Hall, London, pp. 126–150.

Metz, J. (1995) Folate, B_{12}, and neural tube defects. *Medical Journal of Australia*, **163**, 231–232.

Meydani, S.N., Barklund, M.P., Liu, S., Meydani, M., Miller, R.A., Cannon, J.G., Morrow, F.D., Rocklin, R. and Blumberg, J.B. (1990) Vitamin E supplementation enhances cell-mediated immunity in healthy elderly subjects. *American Journal of Clinical Nutrition*, **52**, 557–563.

Miettinen, T.A., Puska, P., Gylling, H., Vanhanen, H. and Vartiainen, E. (1995) Reduction of serum cholesterol with sitostanol-ester margarine in a mildly hypercholesterolemic population. *New England Journal of Medicine*, **333**, 1308–1312.

Milner, J.A. (1994) Reducing the risk of cancer, in *Functional Foods: Designer Foods, Pharmafoods, Nutraceuticals* (ed. I. Goldberg), Chapman & Hall, London, pp. 39–70.

Nestle, M. (1996) Fruits and vegetables: protective or just fellow travellers? *Nutrition Reviews*, **54**, 255–257.

Oakley, G.P. (1993) Folic acid-preventable spina bifida and anencephaly. *Journal of the American Medical Association*, **269**, 1292–1293.

Omenn, G.S., Goodman, G.E., Thomquist, M.D., Balmes, J., Cullen, M.R., Glass, A., Keogh, J.P., Meyskens, F.L., Jr, Valanis, B., Williams, P.H.J.H., Jr, Barnhart, S. and Hammer, S. (1996) Effects of a combination of beta-carotene and vitamin A on lung cancer and cardiovascular disease. *New England Journal of Medicine*, **334**, 1150–1155.

Reynolds, E.H. (1991) Folic acid to prevent neural tube defects (letter). *Lancet*, **338**, 505–506.

Richardson, D.P. (1996) Functional foods – shades of gray: an industry perspective. *Nutrition Reviews*, 54, S174–S185.

Robertson, J., Donner, A.P. and Trevithick, J.R. (1989) Vitamin E intake and risk of cataracts in humans. *Annals of the New York Academy of Sciences*, **570**, 372–382.

Rosenman, R.H. (1992) Diet in haste; repent at leisure. *The Biochemist*, Aug.–Sept., 6–10.

Sanders, T. (1997) Products with specific health benefits against cardiovascular disease, in *Proceedings of the 1st Vitafoods International Conference* (ed. D.E. Blenford), FoodTech Europe, Copenhagen.

Schaafsma, G.J. (1997) Products with specific health benefits against digestive disorders, in *Proceedings of the 1st Vitafoods International Conference* (ed. D.E. Blenford), FoodTech Europe, Copenhagen.

Schmidl, M.K. and Labuza, T. (1994) Medical foods, in *Functional Foods: Designer Foods, Pharmafoods, Nutraceuticals* (ed. I. Goldberg), Chapman & Hall, London, pp. 151–179.

Scott, J.M., Kirke, P., O' Broin, S. and Weir, D.G. (1991) Folic acid to prevent neural tube defects (letter). *Lancet*, **338**, 505.

Simopoulos, A.S. (1994) Fatty acids, in *Functional Foods; Designer Foods, Pharmafoods, Nutraceuticals* (ed I. Goldberg), Chapman and Hall, London, pp. 355–392.

Sloan, A.E. (1996) America's appetite '96: the top 10 trends to watch and work on. *Food Technology*, July, 55–71.

Sloan, A.E. and Stiedemann, M.K. (1996) Food fortification: From public-health solution to contemporary demand. *Food Technology*, June, 100–108.

Southgate, D.A.T. (1997) Dietary fibres and resistant starch, in *Proceedings of the 1st Vitafoods International Conference* (ed. D.E. Blenford), FoodTech Europe, Copenhagen.

Steinberg, D., Parthasarathy, S., Carew, T.E., Khoo, J.C. and Witztum, J. (1989) Beyond cholesterol: modifications of low-density lipoprotein that increase its atherogenicity. *New England Journal of Medicine*, **320**, 915–924.

Tolonen, M., Sarna, S., Halme, M., Tuominen, S.E.J., Westermarck, T., Nordberg, U.-R., Keinonen, M. and Schrijver, J. (1988) Antioxidant supplementation decreases TBA reactants in serum of elderly. *Biological and Trace Element Research*, **17**, 221–228.

Walqvist, M.L. (1994) Functional foods in the control of obesity, in *Functional Foods: Designer Foods, Pharmafoods, Nutraceuticals* (ed. I. Goldberg), Chapman & Hall, London, pp. 71–86.

Walton, J.R. and Packer, L. (1980) Free radical damage and protection: relationship to cellular ageing and cancer, in *Vitamin E: a Comprehensive Treatise* (ed. L.J. Machlin), Marcel Dekker, New York, pp. 495–517.

Warner, H.R. and Kim, S.K. (1994) Dietary factors modulating the rate of ageing, in *Functional Foods: Designer Foods, Pharmafoods, Nutraceuticals* (ed. I. Goldberg), Chapman & Hall, London, pp. 109–125.

Wartanowicz, M., Panczenko-Kresowka, B., Ziemlanski, S., Kowalska, M. and Okolska, G. (1984) The effect of α-tocopherol and ascorbic acid on the serum lipid peroxide level in elderly people. *Annals of Nutrition and Metabolism*, **28**, 186–191.

Willett, W.C., Stampfer, M.J., Manson, J.E., Colditz, G.A., Speizer, F.E., Rosner, B.A., Sampson, L.A. and Hennekens, C.H. (1993) Intake of *trans* fatty acids and risk of coronary heart disease among women. *Lancet*, **341**, 581–585.

Young, J. (1996) A perspective on functional foods. *Food Science and Technology Today*, **10**, 18–21.

Young, J. (1997a) Functional foods market still to grow. *Food Ingredients and Analysis International*, **19**, 43–57.

Young, J. (1997b) Vitafoods – factors critical to success, in *Proceedings of the 1st Vitafoods International Conference* (ed. D.E. Blenford), FoodTech Europe, Copenhagen.

4 Nutritional enhancement of cereals by fortification

KATHRYN O'SULLIVAN, EITHNE CAHILL and
SUSAN SUNGSOO CHO

Introduction

The fortification of foods is an issue currently being discussed both nationally and internationally (Johnson *et al.*, 1988; American Dietetic Association, 1994; British Nutrition Foundation, 1994; McNamara, 1995). From a historical perspective, adding nutrients to foods dates back to 1833, when the French chemist Boussingault recommended adding iodine to table salt to prevent goitre in South America (American Dietetic Association, 1994). In 1918 Denmark fortified margarine (used as a butter substitute) with vitamin A concentrate, and in 1931 the USA fortified whole milk with vitamin D.

The addition of nutrients to breakfast cereals began in 1941. As grain is milled and processed into ready-to-eat breakfast cereals, some of the nutrient levels originally found in the grain are lost. Prior to World War II, cereal processing did not take account of these losses. During World War II, when food was in short supply, nutritionally dense foods (i.e. foods that provide significant quantities of nutrients per kilojoule) became more important to the diet. Cereal companies took a lead role in developing the technology to add vitamins and minerals to the product during the manufacturing process (fortification) (Johnson *et al.*, 1988).

Over the years cereal companies have spent considerable time identifying the nutrient requirements of populations around the world and developing fortified products to meet those needs. By 1943, 95% of breakfast cereals in the USA contained levels of thiamin, niacin and iron equivalent to those in whole grains. Other micronutrients were added later. Today, most breakfast cereals are fortified with a number of nutrients, measurably contributing to the nutritional quality of the Western diet (Morgan *et al.*, 1981; Morgan *et al.*, 1986; Walter *et al.*, 1993; McNulty *et al.*, 1994, 1996; Gibson and O'Sullivan, 1995). The morning meal is often regarded as the most important meal of the day. Nutritionists generally recommended that breakfast should provide one-fourth to one-third of the daily recommended intake of essential nutrients. After a 12- to 14-h overnight fast, the body needs energy to perform physical and mental work. Studies have shown that without breakfast some people have more difficulty performing physical work in the late morning hours, and students may not perform as well in the classroom.

The fortification of foods is governed by both mandatory and voluntary policies. In the UK and many other European countries food legislation requires that margarines be fortified with vitamins A and D to levels similar to those found in butter. Also in the UK there is mandatory fortification of flour with thiamin, niacin, calcium and iron. Many other foods, including breakfast cereals, are fortified on a voluntary basis.

The role of fortified breakfast cereals in human health

Many studies have investigated the impact of the consumption of fortified breakfast cereals on nutrient intake (Hoppner and Verdier, 1984; Kamel and Martinez, 1984; Wang et al., 1992; Saldanha, 1993; Sommerville and O'Reagan, 1993; Hammond, 1994; McNulty et al., 1996). Breakfast cereals are an ideal vehicle for food fortification. They are grain based and as a consequence are low in fat, high in carbohydrate and often high in fibre. Inadequate and poor intakes of vitamins and minerals are well documented in many parts of the world (Mostafa and

Table 4.1 Average nutrient composition of breakfasts* containing pre-sweetened ready-to-eat (RTE) cereal, non-sweetened RTE cereal or no RTE cereal (Morgan et al., 1981)

Nutrient	Pre-sweetened RTE ($n = 941$)	Non-sweetened RTE ($n = 949$)	No RTE ($n = 2527$)
Calories	370 ± 205†[b]	389 ± 211[b]	465 ± 293[a]
Total protein (g)	11 ± 7[c]	13 ± 7[b]	14 ± 9[a]
Total fat (g)	10 ± 10[b]	10 ± 10[b]	20 ± 16[a]
Total carbohydrate (g)	59 ± 32[b]	63 ± 33[a]	59 ± 42[b]
Total sugar (g)	35 ± 22[a]	32 ± 22[b]	32 ± 31[b]
Cholesterol (mg)	34 ± 44[b]	41 ± 68[b]	135 ± 173[a]
Crude fibre (mg)	0.3 ± 0.4[b]	0.6 ± 0.9[a]	0.3 ± 0.4[b]
Ascorbic acid (mg)	40 ± 50[ab]	43 ± 47[a]	37 ± 49[b]
Thiamin (mg)	0.62 ± 0.31[a]	0.58 ± 0.32[b]	0.32 ± 0.22[c]
Niacin (mg)	7.2 ± 3.7[a]	6.5 ± 3.9[b]	2.3 ± 2.1[c]
Riboflavin (mg)	0.94 ± 0.44[a]	0.85 ± 0.47[b]	0.47 ± 0.32[c]
Pyridoxine (µg)	741 ± 394[a]	722 ± 436[a]	226 ± 229[b]
Vitamin B_{12} (µg)	1.89 ± 1.28[a]	1.70 ± 1.47[b]	0.90 ± 1.72[c]
Folacin (µg)	108 ± 97[b]	131 ± 101[a]	70 ± 180[c]
Total vitamin A (IU)	1869 ± 1250[a]	1938 ± 1257[a]	907 ± 1365[b]
Vitamin D (IU)	122 ± 98[a]	109 ± 80[b]	50 ± 67[c]
Iron (mg)	4.7 ± 3.4[a]	4.4 ± 3.8[a]	2.7 ± 2.5[b]
Calcium (mg)	310 ± 192[a]	306 ± 184[a]	280 ± 221[b]
Phosphorus (mg)	294 ± 179[b]	350 ± 200[a]	318 ± 223[c]
Sodium (mg)	422 ± 258[c]	476 ± 258[b]	550 ± 484[a]
Potassium (mg)	541 ± 337[b]	624 ± 369[a]	536 ± 341[b]
Magnesium (mg)	54 ± 39[b]	66 ± 50[a]	53 ± 39[b]
Copper (µg)	383 ± 335[a]	381 ± 274[a]	296 ± 272[b]
Zinc (mg)	2.0 ± 2.8[a]	1.9 ± 3.6[ab]	1.7 ± 2.7[b]

* Classification is based on type of breakfast without regard to individual child's consumption patterns.
† Row means with the same letter are not significantly different ($P \leq 0.05$).

Nuwayhed, 1979; Amin, 1980; Sawaya, 1985; Sedrani, 1986; Stanek, 1990; Al-Shawi, 1992). There are numerous reports that breakfast cereals can serve as excellent vehicles, providing necessary iron and other micronutrients to children and adults (Albertson and Tobelmann, 1993; Morgan and Zabik, 1984).

Morgan et al. (1981) investigated the contribution of breakfast cereal to the breakfast meals of American children. Breakfasts including pre-sweetened breakfast cereals ($n = 941$), those including non-sweetened breakfast cereals ($n = 949$) and those with no breakfast cereal ($n = 2527$) were compared (Table 4.1). Breakfasts containing non-sweetened and sweetened cereals provided significantly greater amounts of thiamin, niacin, riboflavin, vitamins B_{12}, pyridoxine, vitamin A, vitamin D, iron, calcium and copper compared to breakfasts containing no cereals. Breakfasts containing either type of cereal on average had a higher content of all vitamins and minerals (except phosphorus and sodium) than did breakfasts that included no cereal. Pre-sweetened breakfast cereals have received some criticism as having a negative impact on dental health but this concern is not supported by controlled trials (Glass and Fleisch, 1974) or by longitudinal studies in which unlimited supplies of sweetened cereals were provided (Rowe et al., 1974).

Gibson and O'Sullivan (1995) examined the relationship between breakfast cereal consumption and total daily nutrient intakes on 2705 UK schoolchildren (Tables 4.2 to 4.4). The children were grouped according to the amount of cereal consumed per day: none; less than 20 g; 20–40 g; over 40 g (Table 4.3). For the nutrients examined, there was a highly significant and graded increase in vitamin and mineral intake with increasing cereal consumption and a simultaneous reduction in energy from fat from 39–40% among non-cereal consumers to 36–37% among children consuming a portion of cereal or more per day. The study demonstrated that children who eat breakfast cereal tend to have more desirable daily nutrient intakes than those who do not (Tables 4.3 and 4.4).

McNulty et al. (1996) reported micronutrient intakes in 1015 schoolchildren aged 12 and 15 in Northern Ireland between 1990 and 1991, and established the

Table 4.2 Number and percentages* of children in each cereal group (Gibson and O'Sullivan, 1995)

Breakfast cereal intake (g/day)	Boys				Girls				Total	
	10–11 years		14–15 years		10–11 years		14–15 years		10–15 years	
	n	%	n	%	n	%	n	%	n	%
0	100	(11)	93	(18)	166	(20)	144	(30)	503	(19)
1–20	211	(24)	80	(16)	301	(36)	103	(22)	695	(26)
21–40	315	(35)	141	(28)	242	(30)	160	(34)	858	(32)
>40	272	(30)	191	(38)	120	(14)	66	(14)	649	(24)
	898		505		829		473		2705	

* Percentages read downwards.

Table 4.3 Mean daily intake of energy and nutrients according to consumption of breakfast cereals (boys) (Gibson and O'Sullivan, 1995)

| | Boys 10–11 years | | | | | Boys 14–15 years | | | | |
| | Breakfast cereal intake group* | | | | | Breakfast cereal intake group* | | | | |
	0	1	2	3	MR test†	0	1	2	3	MR test†
Energy (kcal)	1960	1997	2033	2152	0,1,2,<3	2307	2372	2396	2654	0,1,2,<3
Fat energy (%)	39.2	38.5	37.3	35.9	3 <2<1,0	40.1	37.8	37.6	36.3	3< 2,1<0
Fat (g)	87	87	86	88	ns	105	102	102	109	ns
Carbohydrate (g)	250	258	268	291	0,1<2<3	286	308	311	357	0,1<2<3
Calcium (mg)	705	783	855	920	0<1<2<3	748	812	907	1025	0<1<2<3
Iron (mg)	9.1	9.5	9.7	10.6	0,1,2<3	11.0	11.5	11.8	13.2	0,1,2<3
Thiamin (mg)	0.8	1.0	1.2	1.5	0<1< 2<3	1.0	1.2	1.4	1.8	0,1<2<3
Riboflavin (mg)	1.1	1.4	1.7	2.1	0<1<2<3	1.2	1.5	1.8	2.4	0<1<2<3
Niacin (mg)	22	24	27	30	0,1<2<3	27	29	32	37	0,1<2<3
Vitamin B_6 (mg)	1.0	1.1	1.1	1.3	0,1<2<3	1.2	1.2	1.2	1.3	0,1,2<3

* Breakfast cereal intake group: 0 = non-consumers; 1 = 1–20 g/day, 2 = 21–40 g/day, 3 = >40 g/day.
† Multiple range test: < groups that are significantly different at the 95% confidence level.
ns = not significant.

Table 4.4 Mean daily intake of energy and nutrients according to consumption of breakfast cereals (girls) (Gibson and O'Sullivan, 1995)

	Girls 10–11 years					Girls 14–15 years				
	Breakfast cereal intake group*					Breakfast cereal intake group*				
	0	1	2	3	MR test†	0	1	2	3	MR test†
Energy (kcal)	1765	1781	1857	1996	0,1,2,<3	1762	1881	1906	2048	0<2,3
Fat energy (%)	39.6	38.8	37.4	35.9	3 <2<1,0	39.4	39.4	37.4	36.8	3,2<1,0
Fat (g)	79	78	79	81	ns	79	85	80	85	ns
Carbohydrate (g)	224	229	246	271	0,1<2<3	223	241	243	271	0,1,2<3
Calcium (mg)	628	675	753	826	0,1<2<3	579	680	736	830	0<1<2<3
Iron (mg)	8.1	8.1	8.9	9.6	0,1<2<3	8.4	9.3	9.6	10.3	0<1<3
Thiamin (mg)	0.7	0.9	1.1	1.3	0<1<2<3	0.8	1.0	1.2	1.4	0<1<2<3
Riboflavin (mg)	1.0	1.2	1.6	1.8	0<1<2<3	1.0	1.3	1.6	1.8	0<1<2<3
Niacin (mg)	20	21	24	27	0<1<2<3	21	24	26	28	0<1<2<3
Vitamin B_6 (mg)	0.9	1.0	1.1	1.1	0,1<2,3	1.0	1.1	1.1	1.2	0<1<3

* Breakfast cereal intake group: 0 = non-consumers; 1 = 1–20 g/day, 2 = 21–40 g/day, 3 = >40 g/day.
† Multiple range test: < groups that are significantly different at the 95% confidence level.
ns = not significant.

contribution of fortified breakfast cereal to overall nutrient intake (Table 4.5). Fortified breakfast cereal consumption categories were 0, 1–20, 1–40 and >40 g/day, which correspond to non-consumer, consumption of breakfast cereal two to three times weekly, consumption once daily and consumption more than once daily, respectively. Estimates of daily intake of micronutrients traditionally added to breakfast cereals, along with calcium and zinc at four levels of consumption of fortified breakfast cereal, are given in Table 4.5. Intakes of thiamin, riboflavin and niacin increased with increasing consumption of breakfast cereal in all sex–age groups. Vitamin B_6 intake was significantly different between the breakfast cereal consumption groups only in 12-year-old girls, who consumed more than 40 g/day of fortified breakfast cereal. In general, greater breakfast cereal consumption was associated with high vitamin B_{12} intake, except for boys aged 12 years. Folate intake significantly increased with increasing consumption of fortified breakfast cereal in the younger adolescents and was greater in girls aged 15, who consumed more than 20 g/day of breakfast cereal, and in 15-year-old boys, who consumed more than 40 g/day of breakfast cereal, compared with non-consumers of cereal or those consuming lower levels. In general, higher breakfast cereal consumption was associated with higher iron intake in all age–sex groups except 15-year-old boys. Calcium intake increased with increasing breakfast cereal consumption in all age–sex groups. Zinc intake was higher at breakfast cereal consumption levels greater than 20 g/day in 15-year-old boys and girls, and greater than 40 g/day in 12-year-old boys, while zinc intake increased with increasing breakfast cereal consumption in 12-year-old girls.

The Bogalusa Heart Study is an ongoing, 20-year epidemiological investigation of cardiovascular risk fact variables and environmental determinants in a pediatric population in Bogalusa, Louisiana, USA. The nutrient impact of breakfast cereals eaten at any time during the day on the total dietary intake of children and young adult participants has been examined in this study (Nicklas et al., 1995). Two cross-sectional surveys (1984–1985 and 1987–1988) of 10-year-old children who completed a 24-h dietary recall interview were included in this study (Table 4.6). Also included were data collected from 1988 to 1991 on young adults aged 19 to 28 years. The subjects were divided into two groups on the basis of their cereal consumption: (1) those who ate cereals (both pre-sweetened and unsweetened) at any time during the day and (2) those who ate none. For 10-year-old children, 21% consumed cereal sometime during the day. Sixty-three percent consumed cereal at breakfast, 36% ate it as a snack and 6% consumed it at two meals in a 24-h period. For young adults, 16% consumed cereal sometime during the day. Sixty-five percent ate it at breakfast, 24% ate it as a snack, and 5% consumed cereal at two meals in a 24-h period. Nutrient adequacy was assessed for the two cereal consumption groups. Mean nutrient intake of selected vitamins and minerals was compared to the RDA (recommended dietary allowance). For each recommended level given for vitamins and minerals, total daily intake was divided into the percentage of children and young adults less

Table 4.5 Daily intakes of micronutrients traditionally added to breakfast cereals, and calcium and zinc by fortified breakfast cereal consumption (values are means; 95% confidence intervals) (McNulty *et al.*, 1996)

Breakfast cereal consumption (g/day)	Sample size	Vitamin D (µg)	Thiamin (mg)	Riboflavin (mg)	Niacin (mg)	Vitamin B_6 (mg)	Vitamin B_{12} (µg)	Folate (µg)	Iron (mg)	Calcium (mg)	Zinc (mg)
Boys aged 12 years											
0	11	1.25	0.96	1.04	27.8	1.48	2.3	115	10.4	680	7.7
1–20	42	1.87	1.23	1.66	31.5	1.54	3.5	140	11.7	963	8.5
21–40	95	1.49	1.54	2.03	34.9	1.54	3.4	139	11.7	1073	8.9
>40	89	1.44	2.00	2.66	41.4	1.59	3.4	154	13.4	1223	9.9
P value		0.1593	<0.001	<0.001	<0.001	0.9001	0.0714	0.0027	0.0081	<0.001	<0.001
Boys aged 15 years											
0	20	2.58	1.33	1.62	35.7	1.83	3.3	148	14.2	1079	10.4
1–20	29	1.24	1.43	1.69	37.0	1.85	3.2	150	13.2	1032	9.9
21–40	95	2.14	1.75	2.32	41.8	1.80	3.9	162	14.0	1264	10.9
>40	94	1.94	2.26	3.22	49.0	1.90	4.6	189	15.4	1484	11.7
P value		0.0616	<0.001	<0.001	<0.001	0.6409	<0.001	<0.001	0.0587	<0.001	0.0103
Girls aged 12 years											
0	31	1.39	0.92	1.03	24.2	1.33	2.1	118	9.6	683	7.1
1–20	67	1.38	1.12	1.47	27.7	1.34	3.2	124	9.9	848	7.5
21–40	106	1.65	1.38	1.72	30.4	1.35	2.5	126	10.9	896	7.7
>40	34	1.84	1.79	2.35	37.3	1.58	3.4	155	12.7	1164	9.6
P value		0.018	<0.001	<0.001	<0.001	0.0043	<0.001	<0.001	<0.001	<0.001	<0.001
Girls aged 15 years											
0	49	1.69	0.95	1.09	25.5	1.40	2.2	127	10.1	742	7.2
1–20	85	1.85	1.11	1.35	29.1	1.45	2.7	127	11.0	805	7.8
21–40	60	1.86	1.41	1.96	33.3	1.51	3.2	155	12.5	1024	8.9
>40	27	1.74	1.63	2.04	33.8	1.48	2.7	169	13.0	1144	9.1
P value		0.7682	<0.001	<0.001	<0.001	0.4829	0.0124	<0.001	0.0012	<0.001	<0.001

than or equal to one-third of the RDA, from one-third to two-thirds of the RDA, greater than two-thirds of the RDA and exceeding the RDA. The predominant differences between the two consumption groups appeared in vitamin and mineral intake (Table 4.6). In both the 10-year-olds and the young adults the cereal groups consumed greater ($P < 0.05$) amounts of vitamin A, thiamin, riboflavin, niacin, vitamin B_6, vitamin B_{12} and folic acid, and greater amounts of iron. Cereal consumers among the young adults also had greater ($P < 0.05$) intakes of vitamin C, phosphorus, magnesium and calcium. Consistent with the findings on mean nutrient intake is the finding that a greater percentage of 10-year-olds and young adults who consumed cereals met at least two-thirds of the RDA for vitamin A, vitamin D, vitamin C, folate, iron and zinc, in contrast to those children and young adults who did not consume cereals (Table 4.7).

Similar findings have been reported by other workers (Crawley, 1993; Saldahna, 1993; Sommerville and O'Reagan, 1993; Albertson and Tobelmann, 1993; Morgan and Zabik, 1984), suggesting that fortified breakfast cereals have a strong benefical effect on intakes of important nutrients. Regular breakfast cereal eaters appear to be more likely to meet daily recommendations for nutrients compared to breakfast skippers and those who eat other types of breakfast foods (Crawley, 1993; Nicklas et al., 1995). The potential of fortification in contributing to micronutrient status appears to be particularly important for those on marginal diets of poor nutritional quality, namely children, pregnant and lactating women, the obese and the elderly.

Table 4.6 Average daily vitamin and mineral intake of 10-year-old children and young adults in the Bogalusa Heart Study by ready-to-eat cereal consumption pattern (Nicklas et al., 1995)

	10-year-old			Young adult		
Nutrient	Cereal	No cereal	P value	Cereal	No cereal	P value
Vitamin A (μg RE)	1671	1174	0.0001	2418	1273	0.0003
Vitamin B_6 (mg)	1.8	1.2	0.0001	4.2	1.8	0.0034
Thiamin (mg)	1.5	1.0	0.0001	3.0	1.4	0.0088
Niacin (mg)	20.0	1.0	0.0001	30.7	19.3	0.0016
Riboflavin (mg)	2.4	1.9	0.0001	3.8	1.8	0.0011
Vitamin B_{12} (μg)	5.1	4.5	0.0493	9.1	5.3	0.0001
Vitamin C (mg)	84.4	77.2		128.8	77.3	0.0011
Vitamin D (μg)	9.0	7.5	0.0067	8.5	4.9	0.0065
Vitamin E (mg)	6.2	6.7		12.5	10.8	
Folate (μg)	259.1	138.6	0.0001	431.3	192.0	0.0001
Calcium (mg)	1095	1110		970	644	0.0002
Sodium (mg)	3474	3714		3679	3441	
Potassium (mg)	2524	2384		2532	2187	
Phosphorus (mg)	1363	1321		1420	1146	0.0074
Magnesium (mg)	240.5	229.1		269.9	221.3	0.0368
Iron (mg)	12.6	9.0	0.0001	36.2	16.2	0.0060
Zinc (mg)	11.0	10.0		17.4	14.2	

RE = retinol equivalent.

Table 4.7 Cereal consumption and percentage of children and young adults in the Bogalusa Heart Study receiving more than two-thirds of the RDA (Nicklas *et al.*, 1995)

Nutrient	10-year-old		Young adult	
	Cereal (*n* = 119)	No cereal (*n* = 449)	Cereal (*n* = 82)	No cereal (*n* = 422)
Vitamin A (μg RE)	97.5	82.0	84.1	52.4
Vitamin B$_6$ (mg)	89.9	59.0	81.7	43.6
Vitamin B$_{12}$ (μg)	96.6	97.8	91.5	80.1
Niacin (mg)	92.4	71.9	89.0	65.6
Thiamin (mg)	95.0	68.8	86.6	48.6
Riboflavin (mg)	98.3	89.1	91.5	59.2
Vitamin C (mg)	82.4	65.9	65.9	47.6
Vitamin D (μg)	57.1	49.7	58.5	31.3
Vitamin E (mg)	49.6	54.1	54.9	54.5
Folacin (μg)	99.2	81.1	84.1	47.4
Calcium (mg)	84.0	75.7	87.8	34.1
Phosphorus (mg)	96.6	95.3	84.1	70.4
Magnesium (mg)	92.4	90.0	65.9	45.3
Iron (mg)	84.9	64.8	72.0	51.2
Zinc (mg)	79.8	72.6	72.0	48.8

RE = retinol equivalent.

In studies that have included an investigation of micronutrient status, significantly higher blood levels of nutrients, including riboflavin, thiamin, folate, retinol and beta-carotene, have been found in association with the consumption of fortified breakfast cereals (Herceberg *et al.*, 1996; Ortega *et al.*, 1996).

Children and pregnant and lactating women

Iron is a nutrient that deserves particular attention. Health professionals have had longstanding concerns regarding childhood iron deficiency and iron-deficiency anemia (Soemantri, 1985). It has been recognized for some time that iron deficiency affects all age groups and all socio-economic levels of society. In addition to the deleterious hematologic effects that iron deficiency is known to have more recently similar effects of a non-hematologic nature have been stressed, including the impact that iron deficiency and iron-deficiency anemia have on the capacity for performing several physical and mental functions (Cook and Lynch, 1986; Lozoff and Brittenham, 1986).

Iron deficiency or iron-deficiency anemia is particularly common among youngsters during infancy and early childhood, times when important aspects of brain development occur. Unfortunately, determination of iron depletion or iron deficiency in the absence of anemia in clinical practice is limited by the fact that most physicians still rely on measurement of hemoglobin concentration or hematocrit percentage to detect the child who is hematologically at risk.

To study the effectiveness of iron-fortified infant cereal in the prevention of iron-deficiency anemia, Walter *et al.,* (1993) compared iron-fortified rice cereal to unfortified rice cereal in infants who were exclusively breast-fed for more than four months and to iron-fortified formula in infants who were weaned to formula before four months of age (Table 4.8). The design was double blind in respect to the presence or absence of iron fortification in the cereal or formula and included 515 infants who were followed on the protocol from 4 to 15 months of age. Rice cereal was fortified with 55 mg of electrolytic iron per 100 g of dry cereal and infant formula fortified with 12 mg of ferrous sulfate per 100 g of dry powder, levels approximating those used in the USA. Measures of iron status were obtained at 8, 12 and 15 months. Infants with hemoglobin levels of <105 g/l were excluded from the study and treated. Among infants weaned to formula before 4 months, the cumulative percentages of infants excluded for anemia by 15 months were 8, 24 and 4%, respectively, in the fortified cereal, unfortified cereal and formula, and fortified formula groups ($P < 0.01$ unfortified versus either fortified group; the difference between the two fortified groups was not significant). In infants breast-fed for more than four months, the corresponding values were 13 and 27%, respectively, in the fortified and unfortified cereal groups ($P < 0.05$). Mean hemoglobin level and other iron status measures were in accord with these findings. It was concluded that iron-fortified infant rice cereal can contribute substantially to preventing iron-deficiency anemia. In a study of 2–5-year-olds in the UK, Payne and Belton (1993) have reported that breakfast cereals provide 10% of the total dietary iron intake.

Iron is also especially important for women. A woman's iron needs are increased substantially during pregnancy primarily to supply the growing foetus and placenta and to increase the maternal blood volume and red cell mass (Hallberg, 1988). Because this increased need for iron cannot always be met by the diet, daily supplements ranging from 30 to 60 mg are often recommended. It is thought that the lack of iron reserves can lead to an increased risk of anemia during pregnancy. Anemia is associated with a risk of premature birth and an increase in the incidence of morbidity and mortality of the foetus and/or mother (Bothwell *et al.,* 1979). Several other symptoms are associated with a lack of iron, such as decreased energy, apathy, sleepiness, irritability and lack of concentration and attention. Iron deficiency, with or without anemia, can lead to metabolic disturbances associated with detrimental changes to numerous enzy-

Table 4.8 Percent of infants showing haemoglobin < 105 (Walter *et al.,* 1993)

	8 months	12 months	15 months
Fortified cereal, unfortified formula	6.0	2.8	0
Unfortified cereal, unfortified formula	12.9	8.1	9.1
Unfortified cereal, fortified formula	3.2	0	1.4
Fortified cereal, breast fed	10.6	1.4	1.4
Unfortified cereal, breast fed	14.8	10.8	5.2

matic systems; this may affect the well-being of the pregnant women and have an effect on the development of her pregnancy.

In addition to iron, vitamins and also important for tissue growth and brain development during pregnancy (Bailey et al., 1983; Schuster et al., 1983; Romano et al., 1995; Yetley and Raider, 1995). An adequate intake of vitamins is important for both the mother and the foetus. Deficiency states may occur, even though they do not appear clinically in the mother. For example, vitamin B_6 is especially important in the development of the central nervous system. Folate is vital for cell division; however, its metabolism is altered during pregnancy. McPartlin et al. (1993) have calculated that folate requirements are increased particularly during the second and third trimesters of pregnancy owing to enhanced folate metabolism. Pregnant women, therefore, represent a group that requires larger intakes of these vitamins. Vitamins associated with regular consumption of breakfast cereals have been shown to be important for healthy babies. An analysis carried out at a London mother and baby clinic found that breakfast cereal consumption was associated with fewer low birth weight (LBW) babies in a group at high risk of LBW (Doyle et al., 1990).

There is now considerable evidence that an adequate intake of folic acid before conception can reduce the risk of a woman having a pregnancy affected by neural tube defects (NTDs) (Department of Health Expert Advisory Group, 1992; Romano et al., 1995; Yetley and Raider, 1995). NTDs result from the failure of the covering of the brain or spinal cord to close during early embryonic development (Yetley and Raider, 1995). Because the neural tube forms and closes between 18 and 27 days after conception, the defect may occur before a woman realizes she is pregnant. Studies during the periconceptional period have concluded that folic acid supplementation in this period is associated with a decrease in the risk of occurrence of NTDs (Smithells et al., 1983; Medical Research Council Vitamin Research Group, 1991). Another study, which was a prospective placebo control trial of over 4500 pregnancies in Hungary, showed a reduction in the risk of NTDs among patients who received folic acid supplementation (Czeizel and Dudas, 1992). These studies have resulted in the publication of recommendations with respect to the use of folic acid by women planning pregnancies by relevant bodies in the UK (Department of Health Expert Advisory Group, 1992) and the USA (Centers for Disease Control and Prevention, 1991; Schaller and Olson, 1996). In summary, the recommendation to women of childbearing age is to consume an additional 0.4 mg folic acid per day for the purpose of reducing the risk of having an NTD-affected pregnancy. For women who have had a previous child with an NTD, the daily dose range for prevention of recurrence appears to be between 0.8 and 4.0 mg folic acid, although the optimal dosage has yet to be found. The estimated dietary folate intake in the UK (Gregory et al., 1990) and in the US (Bailey, 1995) is approximately 200–210 µg/day or 50% of the public health service recommendation. It is clear that an increase in dietary folate may have positive health benefits. Research has shown that folic acid in the form of pteroyl (mono) glutamic acid, added to breakfast cereals or in supplement form, is effective in raising folate intake and red cell folate levels (Yetley and Raider, 1995; Bailey, 1995).

There is strong evidence relating the impact of folic acid fortified foods, including breakfast cereals, on both folic acid intake and folate status. In a study in Ireland, where NTD incidence is particularly high, Cuskelly et al., (1995) demonstrated the importance of fortified foods. This study assessed the effectiveness of providing extra folic acid in the diet by examining groups given folic acid supplementation as a pill, folic acid fortified foods (breakfast cereals and bread), foods rich in naturally occurring folate and dietary advice alone, and a control group with no folic acid intervention. Red blood cell folate status (an indicator of folate status) was measured before and after three months on the various diets. Both the supplementation and fortified food groups showed significant increases in red blood cell folate status. By contrast, although aggressive intervention with dietary folate (fruits and vegetables) or diet advice significantly increased intake of food folate, there was no significant change in red blood cell folate status. It was concluded that increased intakes of folic acid, either as a supplement or as fortified foods, seem to be very effective in increasing folate status and hence in reducing the prevalence of NTDs. Of interest it has been reported in the USA that among women of childbearing age fortified breakfast cereals contributed to 17.7% of their current folate intake (Keast et al., 1997).

It has been estimated that over 50% of pregnancies may be unplanned, therefore it is important to ensure that all women of childbearing age get adequate amounts of folic acid in their diets. According to the UK report by the Department of Health (1992), breakfast cereals fortified with folic acid are an excellent source of this vitamin. In the USA and Food and Drug Administration (FDA) have implemented a mandatory fortification of cereals to provide an additional 100 µg of folic acid per day, which took effect from January 1998. The decision to fortify with folic acid in the UK currently lies with individual food manufacturers on the basis of the voluntary recommendations to do so given by the Department of Health in 1992 to bread and breakfast cereal manufacturers.

Ageing adults

As individuals age there is a decline in lean body mass, physical activity and basal metabolic rates (Popkin et al., 1992). Although energy requirements decrease with age, the recommended dietary intakes for vitamins and minerals remain relatively constant. To meet these recommendations, the elderly must consume fewer calories without decreasing their vitamin or mineral intake. The UK Department of Health (1992) recommends that 'elderly people should derive their dietary intakes from a variety of nutrient-dense foods'. Among the elderly, a change in digestive secretions and in the mucous membranes along the alimentary tract could lead to a reduction in the rate of absorption of vital nutrients. It is also thought that the retention and storage abilities of some nutrients also deteriorate with age (Stare and McWilliams, 1981). Senior citizens tend to prefer foods that are shelf-stable, require little or no difficulty in preparation and are easy to chew and digest. Furthermore, they need foods that are nutrient dense. Foods that contribute carbohydrates, essential nutrients and little fat are ideal for meeting the needs of the elderly. A fortified breakfast cereal with milk is a food combination that meets the needs and interests of the elderly (Morgan, 1986, Morgan and Zabik, 1984).

Raised blood homocysteine is a recognized and independent risk factor for cardiovascular disease (CVD) (i.e. heart disease and stroke) (Selhub et al., 1993; Scott and Weir, 1996). Blood levels may be high due to genetic defects (e.g. homocysteinaemia), renal disease or inadequate levels of vitamin B_6, vitamin B_{12} and folic acid in the diet (Morbidity and Mortality Weekly Report, 1992). It has been estimated that 10% of the total population is at risk of CVD because of elevated homocysteine levels in the blood (50% of which is because of inadequate folic acid intakes).

Folate is essential for homocysteine metabolism and sub-optimal status of the vitamin is the most frequently cited reason for the elevation of plasma homocysteine. Research has shown that folic acid at levels reasonably added to food (i.e. 100–200 µg) can reduce homocysteine and hence, probably the risk of heart disease and stroke in adults (Ward et al., 1997). This evidence not only supports the importance of fortification, but also demonstrates that a simple intervention health strategy to encourage the consumption of fortified foods could effectively reduce the risk of CVD. There is also some evidence suggesting the benefit of folic acid in relation to colon (Giovannucci et al., 1993) and cervical cancer (Butterworth, 1992).

Tucker et al. (1996) examined the relationship between the intake of food group (and supplement) sources of folate and plasma folate and homocysteine concentrations among 885 elderly subjects in the Framingham Heart Study. Dietary data were collected by food-frequency questionnaire and blood samples analysed for folate and homocysteine concentrations. Top contributors to total folate intake were ranked. Major contributors to folate intake were breakfast cereals (13.3%), multivitamins (12.8%) and orange juice (12.4%). These rankings included consideration of the frequency of consumption and the prevalence of consumption in the population as well as the concentration of folate in each food source (Table 4.9). Plasma folate and homocysteine concentrations were also determined by quintile of intake frequency for breakfast cereals. Tucker et al. (1996) identified clear dose–response relationships for both plasma folate and homocysteine with increased quintile of breakfast cereal and of fruit and vegetable use. Frequent consumption of these foods was associated with higher folate and lower homocysteine concentrations. Folate and homocysteine concentrations followed a clear and significant dose response with frequency of intake of breakfast cereals, and fruits and vegetables, respectively, aft er adjustment for age, gender, total energy intake and use of folate supplements (Tables 4.9 and 4.10).

Table 4.9 Major contributors to folate intake in the Framingham Heart Study cohort for men and women aged 67 to 95 years (Tucker *et al.*, 1996)

Rank	Source	% Contribution	Men	Women
1	Cold cereal	13.3	1	2
2	Multivitamins	12.8	3	1
3	Orange juice	12.4	2	3
4	Pizza	3.3	4	5
5	Iceberg lettuce	3.2	7	4
6	Spinach, cooked	2.8	6	6
7	White bread	2.6	5	10
8	Bananas	2.6	8	7
9	Romaine/leaf lettuce	2.4	9	9
10	Oranges	2.3	13	8
11	Potatoes	2.2	11	11

Table 4.10 Folate and homocysteine status by quintile of average weekly frequency of breakfast cereal intake in the Framingham Heart Study (Tucker *et al.*, 1996)

Frequency mean	Folate intake (μg/day (CI))	Plasma folate (nmol/L (CI))	Homocysteine (μmol/L (CI))
0.1	257	7.9	12.4
2.1	309	9.2	12.0
4.6	350	11.3	11.3
6.6	384	12.8	10.8
10.2	414	13.5	11.0
P for trend	0.0001	0.0001	0.0001

More frequent use of cereals was associated with higher plasma folate concentrations ($P < 0.001$), ranging from 7.9 nmol/l at intakes of 0 to 0.5 servings per week to 13.5 nmol/l when cereal was consumed daily. The association between cereal intake and homocysteine level also showed a strong dose response at lower levels of intake, but appeared to plateau at about 5 to 6 servings per week.

Obese and overweight people

Obesity has become one of the most important public health problems in the Western world (Martin *et al.*, 1995). People have access to an abundance of foods and in general are adopting more sedentary lifestyles. Consequently, when lifestyles become more sedentary, caloric intake must be reduced or weight gain is inevitable. Like many public health problems, obesity is complex and multi-factorial in etiology; it has genetic, ethnic and hormonal aspects, and psychological and sociological factors can influence the incidence and progression of becoming overweight (Stare and McWilliams, 1981).

Though seemingly very complex, ultimately obesity is the result of a positive energy balance. An energy-dense diet and lack of exercise have been considered important elements in the etiology of obesity. If energy intake is greater than energy output, positive energy balance exists and excess energy is stored in the body as fat. Conversely, if energy intake is less than output, energy balance is negative and body tissue and fat will be used to make up the difference. That is the intent of weight control. Preventing overweight or obesity in childhood is perhaps the best strategy to ultimately controlling one's weight in the long term. Once an overweight condition exists, it is important to correct it at once. To start combating obesity, adequate nutrient intakes in the context of a relatively low-energy diet are required. It is particularly important to include in the diet foods that contribute a relatively high proportion of nutrients in relation to their energy content. Fortified high-fibre breakfast cereals are among the foods that meet these criteria and thus they may be useful foods to recommend to individuals trying to reduce their body mass (Delargy et al., 1995).

Fortified breakfast cereals are particularly nutrient dense and it has been shown that the consumption of breakfast cereals is associated with significantly higher intakes of micronutrients amongst teenagers (Crawley, 1993). These foods could therefore be a particularly beneficial dietary addition for those reducing their energy intake (Crawley, 1995).

Conclusion

The beneficial effects of fortified breakfast cereals on micronutrient intake and status has been clearly demonstrated, making them an ideal food for today's modern lifestyle. Consumption of breakfast cereals has also been shown to improve the blood folate status and to lower blood homocysteine levels, thereby reducing the risk of NTDs and heart disease (Cuskelly et al., 1995; Tucker et al., 1996). Regular consumption of breakfast cereals has also been shown to result in lower dietary fat intakes and body mass index (Gibson and O'Sullivan, 1995; Kirk et al., 1997). There is even evidence that regular consumption is associated with lower blood cholesterol levels (Resnicow, 1991). The World Bank stated in 1995 'The control of vitamin and mineral deficiencies is one of the most extraordinary development-related scientific advances of recent years. Probably no other technology [food fortification] available today offers as large an opportunity to improve lives and accelerate development at such low cost and in such a short time'.

References

Albertson, A.M. and Tobelmann, R.C. (1993) Impact of ready-to-eat cereal consumption on the diet of children 7–12 years old. *Cereal Foods World*, **38**, 428–434.
Al-Shawi, A.N. (1992) Nutrient intakes of university women in Kuwait. *Journal of the Royal Society of Health*, **112**(3), 114–118.
American Dietetic Association (1994) Positions of the American Dietetic Association: enrichment

and fortification of foods and dietary supplements. *Journal of the American Dietetic Association*, **6**, 661–663.

Amin, E.K. (1980) Bahrain Nutrition Status Survey. UNICEF Gulf Area Office, Abu Dhabi.

Bailey, L. (1995) Folate intake recommendations from a nutritional science perspective. *Cereal Foods World*, **40**, 63–66.

Bailey, L., O'Farrell-Ray, M., Mahan, C. and Dimperio, D. (1983) Vitamin B$_6$, iron and folacin status of pregnant women. *Nutrition Research*, **3**, 783–793.

Bothwell, Th., Charlton, R.W., Cook, J.D. and Finch, C.A. (1979) *Iron Metabolism in Man*, Blackwell, Oxford.

British Nutrition Foundation (1994) *Food Fortification*, British Nutrition Foundation, London.

Butterworth, C.E. (1992) Effect of folate on cervical cancer: synergism among risk factors. *Annals of the New York Academy of Sciences*, **669**, 293–299.

Centers for Disease Control and Prevention (1991) Recommendations for the use of folic acid to reduce the numbers of cases of spina bifida and other neural tube defects. *Morbidity and Mortality Weekly Report*, **41**, 1–7.

Cook, J.D. and Lynch, S.R. (1986) The liabilities of iron deficiency. *Blood*, **68**, 803–809.

Crawley, H. (1993) The role of breakfast cereals in the diets of 16- to 17-year-old teenagers in Britain. *Journal of Human Nutrition and Dietetics*, **6**, 205–215.

Crawley, H. (1995) The nutrient and food intakes of 16–17-year-old female dieters in the UK. *Journal of Human Nutrition and Dietetics*, **8**, 25–34.

Cuskelly, G.J., McNulty, H. and Scott, J.M. (1995) Effect of increasing dietary folate on red cell folate: implications for prevention of neural tube defects. *Lancet*, **347**, 657–659.

Czeizel, E.A. and Dudas, I. (1992) Prevention of the first occurrence of neural tube defects by periconceptional vitamin supplementation. *New England Journal of Medicine*, **327**(26), 1832–1835.

Delargy, H.J., Burley, V.J., O'Sullivan, K., Fletcher, R.J., Blundell, J.E. (1995) Effects of different soluble:insoluble fibre ratios at breakfast on 24-h pattern of dietary intake and satiety. *European Journal of Clinical Nutrition*, **49**, 754–766.

Department of Health (1992) Nutrition of the elderly. Report No. 43, HMSO, London.

Department of Health Expert Advisory Group (1992) *Folic Acid and the Prevention of Neural Tube Defects*, HMSO, London.

Doyle, W., Crawford, M.A., Wynn, A.H.A. and Wynn, S.W. (1990) The association between maternal diet and birth dimensions. *Journal of Nutritional Medicine*, **1**, 9–17.

Gibson, S.A. and O'Sullivan, K.R. (1995) Breakfast cereal consumption patterns and nutrient intakes of British schoolchildren. *Journal of the Royal Society of Health*, **115**, 366–370.

Giovannucci, E., Stampfer, M.J., Colditz, G.A., Rimm, E.B., Trichopoulos, D., Rosner, B.A., Speiter, F.E. and Willett, W.C. (1993) Folate, methionine, and alcohol intake and risk of colorectal adenoma. *Journal of the National Cancer Institute*, **85**, 875–884.

Glass, R.L. and Fleisch, S. (1974) Dental caries incidence and the consumption of ready-to-eat breakfast cereals. *Journal of the American Dental Association*, **88**, 807.

Gregory, J., Foster, K., Tyler, H. and Wiseman, M. (1990) *The Dietary and Nutritional Survey of British Adults*, HMSO, London.

Hallberg, L. (1988) Iron balance in pregnancy, in *Vitamins and Minerals in Pregnancy and Lactation* (ed. H. Berger), Raven Press, New York, pp. 115–127.

Hammond, G.K. (1994) The nutritional role of breakfast in the diets of college students. *Journal of the Canadian Dietetic Association*, **55**, 69–74.

Herceberg, S., Preziosi, P., Galan, P., Yacoub, N., Kara, G. and Deheeger, M. (1996) La consommation du petit dejeuner dans l'etude du Val-de Marne 3. La valeur nutritionnelle du petit dejeuner et ses relations avec l'equilibre nutritionnelle global et le statut mineral et vitaminique. *Cahier Nutrition et Dietetique*, **31** (suppl. 1), 18–25.

Hoppner, K. and Verdier, P. (1984) Contribution of breakfast cereals to the daily intake of folacin, pantothenic acid and biotin. *Canadian Institute of Food Science and Technology*, **17**, 121–124.

Johnson, I., Gordon, H. and Borenstein, B. (1988) Vitamin and mineral fortification of breakfast cereals. *Cereal Foods World*, **33**, 278–283.

Kamel, B.S. and Martinez, O.B. (1984) Food habits and nutrient intake of Kuwaiti males and females. *Ecology of Food and Nutrition*, **15**, 261–272.

Keast, D.R., Cook, A.J. and Olson, B.H. (1997) Folate intakes of women of childbearing years pre- and post-folic acid enrichment of the food supply. Presented at the FASEB Annual Meeting, April 6–9, 1997, New Orleans, LA.

Kirk, T.R., Burkill, S. and Cursiter, M. (1997) Dietary fat reduction achieved by increasing consumption of a starchy food – an intervention study. *European Journal of Clinical Nutrition*, **51**, 1–8.

Lozoff, B. and Brittenham, G.M. (1986) Behavioural aspects of iron deficiency. *Progress in Haematology*, **14**, 23–53.

Martin, L., Hunter, S., Lauve, R. and O'Leary, J. (1995) Severe obesity: expensive to society, frustrating to treat, but important to confront. *Southern Medical Journal*, **88**, 895–902.

McNamara, S. (1995) Food fortification in the United States: a legal and regulatory perspective. *Nutrition Reviews*, **53**, 134–138.

McNulty, H., Eaton-Evans, J., Woulahan, G. and Strain, J.J. (1994) The effect of fortification on daily micronutrient intakes of breakfast cereal consumers in Great Britain. *Proceedings of the Nutrition Society*, **53**, 143A.

McNulty, H., Eaton-Evans, J., Cran, G., Woulahan, G., Boreham, C., Savage, J.M., Fletcher, R. and Strain, J.J. (1996) Nutrient intakes and impact of fortified breakfast cereals in schoolchildren. *Archive of Diseases in Childhood*, **75**, 474–481.

McPartlin, J., Halligan, A., Scott, J.M., Darling, M. and Weir, D.G. (1993) Accelerated folate breakdown in pregnancy. *Lancet*, **341**, 148–149.

Morbidity and Mortality Weekly Report (1992) Recommendations for the use of folic acid to reduce the number of cases of spina bifida and other neural tube defects. *Morbidity and Mortality Weekly*, **41**, 1–7.

Medical Research Council Vitamin Study Research Group (1991) Prevention of neural tube defects: results of the medical research council vitamin study. *Lancet*, **338** (8760), 131–137.

Morgan, K.J. (1986) Breakfast consumption patterns of older Americans. *Journal of Nutrition in the Elderly*, **5**(4), 19–44.

Morgan, K.J. and Zabik, M.E. (1984) The influence of ready-to-eat cereal consumption at breakfast on nutrient intakes of individuals 62 years and older. *Journal of American College of Nutrition*, **3**, 27–44.

Morgan, K.J., Zabik, M.E. and Leveille, G.A. (1981) The role of breakfast in nutrient intake of 5- to 12-year-old children. *Journal of American Clinical Nutrition*, **34**, 1418–1427.

Morgan, K.J., Zabik, M.E. and Stampley, M.S. (1986) Breakfast consumption patterns of US children and adolescents. *Nutrition Research*, **6**, 635–646.

Mostafa, S.A. and Nuwayhed, H.T. (1979) *Gross Pattern of Kuwaiti Children from Birth to 60 Months*. Nutrition Unit, Preventive Health Division, Ministry of Public Health, Kuwait.

Nicklas, T.A., Myers, L. and Berenson, G.S. (1995) Total nutrient intake and ready-to-eat cereal consumption in the Bogalusa Heart Study. *Nutrition Review*, **53**, S39–S45.

Ortega, R.M., Requejo, A.M., Redondo, R., Lopez-Sobaler, A.M., Andres, P., Ortega, A., Gasper, M.J., Quintas, E. and Navia, B. (1996) Influence of the intake of fortified breakfast cereals on dietary habits and nutritional status of Spanish schoolchildren. *Annals of Nutrition and Metabolism*, **40**, 146–156.

Payne, J.A. and Belton, N.R. (1993) Nutrient intake and growth in pre-school children. II Intake of mineral and vitamins. *Journal of Human Nutrition and Dietetics*, **5**, 299–304.

Popkin, B., Haines, P. and Patterson, R. (1992) Dietary changes in older Americans. *American Journal of Clinical Nutrition*, **55**, 823–830.

Resnicow, K. (1991) The relationship between breakfast habits and plasma cholesterol levels in schoolchildren. *Journal of School Health*, **61**, 81–85.

Romano, P., Waitzman, N., Scheffler, R. and Pi, R. (1995) Folic acid fortification of grain: an economic analysis, *American Journal of Public Health*, **85**, 667–676.

Rowe, N.H., Anderson, R.H. and Wanninger, L.A. (1974) Effects of ready-to-eat breakfast cereals on dental caries experience in adolescent children: a three-year study. *Journal of Dental Research*, **53**, 33.

Saldanha, L. (1993) Vitamin and mineral status of Americans. The impact of breakfast. Presented at the XV International Congress of Nutrition, Adelaide, pp. 7–259.

Sawaya, W.N. (1985) *Dietary Survey on Infants and Pre-school Children in Saudi Arabia*, Ministry of Health/Ministry of Agriculture and Water, Saudi Arabia.

Schaller, D.R. and Olson, B.H. (1996) A food industry perspective on folic acid fortification. *Journal of Nutrition*, **126**, 761S–764S.

Schuster, K., Bailey, L. and Mahan, C. (1983) Effect of maternal pyridoxine-HCl supplementation on the vitamin B_6 status of mother and infant and on pregnancy outcome. *Journal of Nutrition*, **113**, 977–988.

Scott, J. and Weir, D. (1996) Homocysteine and cardiovascular disease. *Quarterly Journal of Medicine*, **89**, 561–563.

Sedrani, S.H. (1986) Are Saudis at risk of developing vitamin D deficiency? *Saudi Medical Journal*, **7**(5), 427–433.

Selhub, J., Jacques, P.F., Wilson, P.W., Rush, D. and Rosenberg, I.H. (1993) Vitamin status and intake as primary determinants of homocysteinaemia in an elderly population. *American Medical Association*, **270**, 2693–2698.

Smithells, R.W., Seller, M.J., Harris, R., Fielding, D.W., Schorah, C.J., Nevin, N.C., Sheppard, S., Read, A.P., Walker, S., and Wild, J. (1983) Further experience of vitamin supplementation for prevention of neural tube defects recurrences. *Lancet*, **1**(8332), 1027–1031.

Soemantri, A.G. (1985) Iron deficiency anaemia and educational achievement. *American Journal of Clinical Nutrition*, **42**, 1211–1228.

Sommerville, J. and O'Reagan, M. (1993) The contribution of breakfast to micronutrient adequacy in the Irish diet. *Journal of Human Nutrition and Dietetics*, **6**, 223–228.

Stanek, K. (1990) Diet quality and eating environment of pre-school children. *Journal of the American Dietetic Association*, **90**, 1582–1584.

Stare, F.J. and McWilliams, M. (1981) *Living Nutrition*, John Wiley and Sons, New York.

Tucker, K., Selhub, J., Wilson, P.W.F. and Rosenberg, I.R. (1996) Dietary intake pattern relates to plasma folate and homocysteine concentrations in the Framingham Heart Study. *Journal of Nutrition*, **126**, 3025–3031.

Walter, T., Dallman, P.R., Pizarro, F., Velozo, L., Pena, G., Bartholomew, S.J., Hertramph, E., Olivares, M., Leteilier, A. and Arredondo, M. (1993) Effectiveness of iron-fortified infant cereal in prevention of iron deficiency anemia. *Pediatrics*, **91**, 976–982.

Wang, C.Y., Reilly, C., Patterson, C., Morrison, E. and Tinggi, U. (1992) Contribution of breakfast cereals to Australian intakes of trace elements. *Food Australia*, **44**, 70–72.

Ward, M., McNulty, H., McPartlin, J., Strain, J.J., Weir, D.G. and Scott, J.M. (1997) Plasma homocysteine, a risk factor for cardiovascular disease, is lowered by physiological doses of folic acid. *Quarterly Journal of Medicine*, **90**, 519–524.

Yetley, E. and Raider, J. (1995) Folate fortification of cereal-grain products: FDA policies and actions. *Cereal Foods World*, **40**, 67–71.

5 Nutritional implications of ingesting modified foods

R. JAMES STUBBS

Introduction

In the Western world the vast majority of people are living longer than ever before and dying mainly of non-infectious diseases, primarily cancer, cardiovascular diseases, diabetes and, increasingly, obesity and its complications (World Health Organization, 1990). It is apparent that environmental factors are important in the aetiology of these diseases. This implies that if the population can be protected from the environmental factors that contribute to the onset of certain diseases then the health, well-being and longevity of Western populations will be increased. A major component of the environment that is increasingly implicated in the aetiology of non-infectious diseases is the composition of the diet. For instance, it is estimated that 30% of all adult-onset cancers are dietary related and a substantial proportion of cardiovascular disease has a dietary origin (World Health Organization, 1990).

As individuals we have relatively little direct control over many aspects of the environment that may affect the aetiology of non-infectious disease (e.g. background levels of radionuclides or chemical mutagens). This is not the case with diet. The organizations that produce, make and market food are continually changing food ingredients and means of food production for a variety of reasons. Many changes may be beneficial to health (e.g. decreasing the *trans* fatty acid content of margarine) and some (e.g. feeding animal products to British cattle) may not. It is not therefore surprising that there is now perhaps greater interest and concern about the composition of diet and its effects on the health and well-being of the public at large than at any time this century.

Initial health concerns centred around removing the potentially detrimental effects of certain ingredients in foods. Attention has also focused on maximizing the nutritive value of foods. Foods and their constituents are currently viewed by consumers as potential sources of agents that can actively promote health and well-being and stave off the inevitable encroachment of non-infectious disease. The market economy has recognized the potential in this area and now 'functional foods' and 'nutraceuticals' are available with the promise of increased consumer longevity, health and well-being. At the same time there remains widespread interest and concern about the potentially detrimental role the Western diet plays in the development of a number of major diseases (see above), including the current pandemic of diabetes mellitus and obesity. In many Western countries 35–50% of all adults are classified as either overweight (body mass index, BMI 25–29) or obese (BMI ≥30) (Department of Health, 1995; Seidell, 1995). There is concern that secular changes in the macronutrient composition of the diet may contribute to the increased prevalence of over-weight and obesity in developed and developing countries (Danforth, 1985; Department of Health, 1995). This chapter focuses on the macronutrients fat and carbohydrate (including fibres or unavailable complex carbohydrates), foods that alter dietary fat and carbohydrate availability or content (by various means), and the impact that ingesting these foods can have on appetite, energy balance and the bioavailability of fat-soluble vitamins and minerals. The intention is to discuss current – and therefore usually contentious – issues in relation to fats, carbohydrates, their substitutes and how their inclusion in foods may affect nutritional status. Relationships between the effects of fats, carbohydrates and other macronutrients will only be discussed where appropriate.

Recently, attention has focused on the possible ways in which macronutrients may affect energy balance and other aspects of health (Danforth, 1985; Stubbs, 1995a). Great emphasis has been placed by public health agencies on the need to reduce dietary fat intake and increase carbohydrate intake (especially starch) (Department of Health, 1992, 1995). The effect of sugars on appetite and energy balance remains controversial. Food companies have responded to consumer demand by creating an exponential rise in the number of low- and lower-fat foods available. Low-sugar foods are also available although (with the large exception of dental caries) the health benefits of these are not clearly demon-strated (nor indeed, refuted). There are now a number of fat and carbohydrate substitutes either in commercially available foodstuffs or under development for inclusion in foods. Never before has it been possible to consume foods that look and taste so good yet contain so little energy or so few nutrients. Controversy currently rages as to whether technological refinements to produce foods that provide more pleasure than nutritive value should be promoted. However, it is likely that in the current free-market environment people primarily select foods they like over foods they do not like, and that the health consequences of ingest-ing the selected food are often a secondary factor in food choice. Furthermore, consumers appear to be reluctant to sacrifice the hedonistic quality of their diet in the interest of optimizing nutrient intakes. Under these conditions it could be convincingly argued that chemically modified foods that enable consumers not to select a particularly unhealthy diet may have a role to play in today's market economy. A major problem is that each new process or food component that alters the macronutrient content of the diet needs to be judged objectively on its own individual merits. However, with the intense interest expressed by consumers, pressure groups and producers in major new products and their development, it is unclear whether such objectivity can be obtained. As the food industry produces new foods with components that mimic or alter the nutrient composition of the diet there is a growing need to understand (through rigorous, independent scientific evaluation) the way in which diet composition and associated characteristics (e.g. the taste and texture of food) influence appetite and energy balance. This is necessary in order to improve our understanding of the nutritional consequences of ingesting modified foods.

The impact of low-fat foods on energy intake

The potential role of low-fat foods in promoting consumer health and well-being

As mentioned above current government recommendations in a number of Western countries have strongly suggested that the fat content of the diet should be reduced. The Health of the Nation White Paper (1992) identified, in the area of diet and nutrition, key risk factor targets to be achieved by 2000–2005. As regards dietary fat intake and obesity the relevant targets were:

- to reduce the average percentage of food energy derived by the population from saturated fatty acids by at least 35% by 2005 (to no more than 11% of food energy) (Baseline year, 1990)
- to reduce the average percentage of food energy derived by the population from total fat by at least 12% by 2005 (to no more than about 35% of total food energy) (Baseline year, 1990)
- to reduce the proportion of men and women aged 16–64 who are obese by at least 25% and 33%, respectively, by 2005 (to no more than 6% of men and 8% of women) (Baseline year, 1986/1987).

Associated public health messages have prompted a dramatic increase in the number of low- and lower-fat foods available to consumers. These products are sold and bought on the strong implication that their increased consumption will reduce the health risks associated with greater levels of fat and energy intake. This assumes that such products will lead to lower energy and fat intakes than their full-fat counterparts. In order to fully understand the nutritional implications of ingesting low-fat foods it is important to understand:

- the differences between different types of low-fat foods
- the effects that dietary fat exerts on appetite and energy intake
- the effects that different types of low-fat food have on feeding behaviour
- the effects of low-fat foods on fat-soluble vitamin and mineral bioavailability.

Low-fat foods can be classified as foods that are:

- unmodified, inherently low-fat foods, such as bread, pasta or sugary drinks
- foods that have been physically modified to reduce their fat content (often by technological alterations of the food matrix, such as including more water in the structure of low-fat spreads)
- foods that have been chemically modified to reduce the fat content but maintain the orosensory qualities of full-fat foods (achieved through chemical alterations in fat structure to reduce its metabolizable energy value).

Some low-fat foods are high in protein (e.g. lean meat) but this chapter will largely be restricted to fat, carbohydrate and the relationship between the two.

Types of low-fat foods

Unmodified low-fat, (high-carbohydrate) foods. These foods have always been low in fat and high in carbohydrate. Such foods are not manipulated to reduce their fat content and their composition has remained stable over long periods of time. People will have learned to associate the taste, texture and flavour of such foods with the postingestive consequences of having ingested them. The sensory qualities of these foods reliably inform the subject of the postingestive consequences of ingesting them and conditioned (or learned) appetites for these foods will be stable.

Modified lower- and low-fat foods (reduced-fat foods). Lower- and low-fat foods are new versions of foods that originally have had a relatively high fat content. The availability of these products has grown enormously in recent years. Some low-fat versions of commonly available food products have become so successful that they now dominate market sales. For instance, low-fat milk now accounts for the majority of all milk sold. Various technological approaches have been devised to attempt to maintain the sensory qualities of the original higher fat versions of these foods (e.g. low-fat spreads). However, subjects are usually able to detect, by sensory discrimination, low-fat from the original high-fat versions when they are simultaneously compared. The ability of subjects to correctly identify which version is which is sometimes less reliable.

Foods in which fat has been substituted by a fat substitute (fat mimetic). Due to the fact that dietary fat adds important sensory and textural qualities to foods, the food industry has been prolific in attempting to produce compounds that mimic the qualities of dietary fat (Akoh, 1995). Some of these products are about half as energy dense as dietary fat and are based on a digestible protein or carbohydrate matrix. Recently the US Food and Drug Administration (FDA) has granted permission for the sucrose polyester Olestra to be used as a fat replacer in savoury snack foods. Olestra™ is an acaloric fat mimetic formed by chemically linking fatty acids to a backbone of sucrose molecules. This substance is acaloric because it is not digested and absorbed into the human body (Fallat *et al.*, 1976). Olestra has similar appearance, physical and sensory properties to dietary fat. Unlike several other fat mimetics, Olestra is heat stable and can be used in cooking. Thus Olestra has now added a new dimension to the concept of a low-fat food. This compound mimics the sensory and textural qualities of dietary fat extremely well and thus preserves those aspects of the food matrix that are contributed by real fat (e.g. the crispiness of snacks fried at high temperature). Because it is sensorially so similar to real fat it may act as a useful tool to reduce metabolisable energy intake from fat. However, because it mimics the sensory qualities of dietary fat so well it may, if ingested in significant quantities, actually help maintain sensory preference for dietary fat.

Olestra also has effects on fat-soluble vitamin absorption (Miller and Allgood, 1993; Westrate and van het Hof, 1995). Before considering how low-fat foods may influence appetite and energy balance it is pertinent to consider what is known about the effect dietary fat has on appetite and energy balance.

The effects of dietary fat on appetite and energy balance

In considering the effects that diet composition has on appetite and energy intake there are a number of sources of data that can be referred to.

Epidemiological and diet survey studies

These studies have the advantage of using large numbers of subjects who are going about their everyday activities in their natural setting. The ecological validity of such studies is therefore theoretically high. However, it should be borne in mind that there are a number of methodological problems associated with epidemiological and diet survey studies that must be taken into account and which inevitably weaken the conclusions derived from them. Firstly, the errors in data collection are high and are not necessarily random (e.g. underreporting of energy intake in the obese (Schoeller, 1990; Black et al., 1991; Goldberg et al., 1991)). Secondly, in many studies subjects are not randomly selected and the population is not therefore necessarily totally representative of the general population. Thirdly, many epidemiological studies are cross-sectional and assume that the processes influencing the phenomena under investigation are uniform over time and hence over age groups. Clearly this is not always the case. The results of diet survey and epidemiological studies should therefore be treated with some caution.

Laboratory-based studies

The laboratory setting allows the effects of diet composition on energy intake to be studied with greater control. However, experiments typically use small numbers of non-randomly selected subjects in the artificial environment of the laboratory, employing protocols and techniques that are often unfamiliar to the subject. It is also important to understand the limitations of the laboratory approach when attempting to extrapolate the results of experiments conducted in the laboratory (where the signal-to-noise ratio may be artificially elevated) to everyday life.

Intervention studies

Intervention studies often represent a good compromise between the artificiality of the laboratory and the lack of control over both manipulation and measurement that occurs in epidemiological studies. Typically subjects adhere to a given manipulation (for example consuming *ad libitum* a number of low-fat foods made available by the investigator) but go about their normal lives so that the impact of the manipulation (for example on fat and feeding behaviour) can be assessed.

Because each approach has its advantages and limitations it is important to examine the effect of diet composition on appetite and energy balance in each experimental environment. If broadly similar phenomena are apparent in each of these experimental conditions it is reasonable to accept that the phenomenon under scrutiny is robust and not an artefact of the experimental conditions themselves.

Dietary fat and energy intake

There is now a growing body of evidence derived from most of the recent epidemiological studies on diet and body weight suggesting that macronutrients do exert different effects on the degree of body fatness. A number of studies suggest that fatter people appear to consume a higher proportion of their energy intake from fat rather than from carbohydrate (see Lissner and Heitmann (1995) for a review). It is generally assumed that this implicates high-fat diets in the promotion of excess energy intake. However, BMI has often correlated negatively with energy intake in the same studies. While it can be accepted from validation studies (Black *et al.*, 1991; Schoeller, 1990) that the obese appear to systematically underreport energy intake, it is not clear what the composition of the underreported component is.

Lissner and Heitmann (1995) have scrutinized the epidemiological evidence in relation to dietary fat and obesity. They note that ecological studies describing dietary fat intake and obesity at the population level give mixed results; indeed the extensive cross-European MONICA studies showed negative correlations between fat intake and BMI (see Lissner and Heitmann (1995)). They point out that because of the problems inherent in ecological studies these mixed results are likely to be biased 'by both confounding and unknown data quality factors that differ systematically across the populations studied' (Lissner and Heitmann, 1995). Nevertheless (with some notable exceptions), cross-sectional studies are generally in agreement that the percentage of fat in the diet correlates positively with body fatness (though not always with energy intake). Prospective studies yield mixed results, probably because of the public attention that dietary fat has received and the fact that subjects will often change their behaviour in relation to expectation when they are aware that they are being studied (reverse causality). In other words, the process of actually studying the subjects may make them more health conscious. Thus when Colditz *et al.* (1990) used a combined retrospective and prospective design, they found that fat intake was positively associated with previous but not subsequent weight changes.

Relatively aggressive interventions in well-motivated subjects have led to significant reductions in fat intake with apparently modest effects on indices of energy balance, such as body weight (Raats and Sparks, 1995). One multi-centre trial (the Women's Health Trial) reported that reduction of fat intake from a mean of 39% of energy intake to 20% after six months (Burrows *et al.*, 1993). This was reportedly accompanied by a modest reduction in energy intake. Two less aggressive, but more consumer-relevant, interventions found that the adoption of low-fat versions of commonly eaten foods led to a reduced fat intake but not energy intake (Gatenby *et al.*, 1995; Aaron *et al.*, in press). In one of these studies subjects did exhibit a modest but significant reduction in weight on the reduced-fat regimen, which may not have been detected by the use of diet records over a few days (Gatenby *et al.* ,1995).

Numerous laboratory studies have shown that when humans or animals are allowed to feed *ad libitum* on high-fat energy-dense diets, the subjects consume similar amounts of food but more energy (which is usually accompanied by weight gain) than when they feed *ad libitum* on lower-fat, less energy-dense diets (Duncan *et al.*, 1983; Lissner *et al.*, 1987; Kendall *et al.*, 1991; Stubbs *et al.*, 1995a,b). This subject has recently been reviewed by Warwick and Schiffman (1992) and by Stubbs (1995). Weight losses in the laboratory are typically modest when subjects feed *ad libitum* on low-fat less energy-dense diets and this supports the finding of intervention studies. It is important to note that many of these studies only allow subjects to alter the amount and not the composition of the foods ingested. Blundell (1996) noted that excess energy intakes on high-fat diets occur because subjects eat a similar amount of food as on low-fat diets. The excess energy intake is therefore not characterized by an active drive to eat more food, rather it is a passive failure to compensate for elevations in the energy density of the diet in the form of fat (Blundell, 1996).

When high-fat and high-carbohydrate foods are made isoenergetically dense, this differential influence that carbohydrate and fats exert on feeding (Van Stratum *et al.*, 1978; Stubbs *et al.*, 1996) or motivation to eat (Johnstone *et al.*, 1996) appears less clear cut. Under these conditions carbohydrate appears to exert a more acute, immediate effect in suppressing hunger while fat exerts a more delayed effect (Johnstone *et al.*, 1996). In two studies where subjects have been allowed to feed *ad libitum* on low- or high-fat diets, which were isoenergetically dense, there was no difference in energy intake over two weeks (Van Stratum *et al.*, 1978; Stubbs *et al.*, 1996).

Fat also exerts less feedback at the postabsorptive level since controlled parenteral nutrient infusions show lipids to invoke the least degree of caloric compensation in rodents (Walls and Koopmans, 1992) and in humans (Gil *et al.*, 1991).

It has been suggested from theoretical considerations that when ingested in excess, dietary fat is more efficiently stored as body fat than either carbohydrate or protein (Flatt, 1978). This is because in order to store large dietary excesses of protein or carbohydrate these substances must be converted to fat. The metabolic pathways involved in converting these nutrients to fat are relatively expensive. It should, however, be borne in mind that carbohydrate intakes have to be quite considerable before *de novo* lipogenesis occurs (Acheson and Jequier, 1982). These considerations led the WHO report on diet, nutrition and the prevention of chronic diseases to state that 'There is increasing evidence from experimental animal studies, human physiological measures of energy metabolism, and bioenergetic considerations, that dietary fat is particularly conducive to weight gain' (World Health Organization, 1990). Having considered the effect of dietary fat on energy intake or indices thereof, it is important to ask whether low-fat foods affect feeding behaviour in a manner that is consistent with what is currently known about the effect of dietary fat on appetite and energy balance.

Low fat-foods and feeding behaviour

There is evidence that consumption of low-fat foods decreases the risks of over-consumption, partly because of their (usually) lower energy density and the fact that carbohydrates may operate as a more rapid physiological cue for satiety (Johnson *et al.*, 1995; Raben *et al.*, 1995). Furthermore high-carbohydrate, low-fat foods will exert a greater osmotic load than fats do, which may increase fluid consumption. This in turn may assist in preventing excess food intake, although excess energy intake is possible when subjects feed *ad libitum* on covertly modified, energy-dense, high-carbohydrate diets (Stubbs *et al.*, in press). The question remains, however, of whether free-living subjects achieve excess energy intakes when feeding on commonly available high-carbohydrate foods. There is little evidence that increasing consumption of low-fat foods will lead to spontaneous weight loss. If people increase their consumption of low-fat foods and if the energy density of the newly selected diet is lower than that of the diet they previously selected (Mela, 1997), they may experience modest weight loss, which plateaus relatively quickly. Nevertheless, such a change in food selection would be likely to decrease the risk of excess energy intake.

Recently, studies have examined the effects of attempting to increase consumption of modified low-fat foods on fat and energy intake. A large multi-centre trial (the MSFAT trial) in The Netherlands examined how increasing the consumption of low-fat food products affected energy and nutrient intakes in a large group of Dutch consumers (Zimmermanns *et al.*, undated). The major finding of this study was that increased consumption of low-fat food products decreased total fat intake in line with government recommendations. However, average energy intakes were similar to pre-study levels, suggesting that the increased consumption of low-fat foods decreases fat but not energy intake. These results confirm those of an earlier intervention in which a group of subjects was encouraged to increase consumption of low-fat food products, compared to a control group (Aaron *et al.*, in press). Mela (1997) provides a comprehensive review of these effects. Furthermore, detailed analysis of this data set showed that fat intake was significantly reduced only in subjects who consumed above 35% of energy intake from fat at the outset of the study. The intervention had little effect on the fat intake of people who were low-fat consumers at the beginning of the study. These data may help to explain why increased consumption of modified low-fat foods appears to have had little impact in reversing the trend of increased overweight and obesity in Western society. While it is often noted that the explosion in the low-fat food market has not been paralleled by a decrease in the prevalence of obesity, it is difficult to ascertain quantitatively what the effects on the prevalence of obesity would have been in the absence of these developments. Indeed, in the absence of increasing public interest in obesity, its prevalence may have increased at a faster rate than at present. Furthermore, the growth of the low-fat food market also paves the way for further developments such as the proposed 'small steps' argument whereby a small reduction in fat content of many foods could significantly reduce total fat intake and hence energy intake, while maintaining the technical functionality and the consumer acceptability of food products.

Selection of dietary fat by Western consumers

The above studies have examined the effects of eating low-fat foods on appetite and/or energy intake and body weight. These studies assume that people will actually select lower-fat foods if they are made available to them. This is not necessarily the case. Mela (1995) notes that 'the populations of North America and western Europe, with economic and market access to a diet of virtually any possible composition, consume 37–42% of their food energy as fat'. Despite public health information advising consumers to reduce dietary fat intakes, Western countries are remarkably resistant to the dietary change. A number of factors appear to mitigate against reducing the fat content of the diet we select. A brief examination of the literature gives some indications that (a) these reasons are complex and (b) there do appear to be a number of recurring factors that oppose dietary change. Firstly, it appears that the population is not sufficiently aware of the composition of the diet they actually consume and many people do not feel a need to change their diet. For example, Mela (1993) asked 293 UK consumers to estimate the fat content of 24 common foods. While the relative positioning of foods with regard to fat content was generally correct, there was a consistent tendency to overestimate the fat content of low-fat foods and to underestimate the fat content of high-fat foods. The majority of people surveyed in one study felt that their diet was healthy and not too high in fat, regardless of actual fat intake (Lloyd *et al.*, 1993). Consumers therefore fail to recognize what actually comprises effective dietary change.

Lloyd *et al.* (1995) examined the barriers to dietary change that have been identified by consumers themselves. They found that 'one of the most consistently reported problems was that of reduction in taste quality of the diet'. Other studies found that over 40% of subjects had difficulty in adopting low-fat diets on the basis of taste (Pierce *et al.*, 1984; Terry *et al.*, 1991; Kristal *et al.*, 1992). Kristal *et al.* suggest that 'the largest decrease in fat intake will be accomplished through interventions that reduce the reliance on fats as a food flavour'. Other problems included an increase in cost, a decrease in convenience, the lack of family support for certain changes and an inability to judge the fat content of foods. Urban *et al.* (1992) found that the maintenance of low-fat diets in the follow-up period after the Women's Health Trial was primarily influenced by 'the time and money costs associated with meal planning and preparation' while interventions that induce a feeling of deprivation appear to counteract the success of adopting low-fat diets. In the Women's Health Trial increasing the intakes of complex carbohydrates (fruits, vegetables and grains) was the most difficult dietary change for the women to make. This was also apparent in other studies (Gorder *et al.*, 1986; Buzzard *et al.*, 1990; Burrows *et al.*, 1993). Thus a barrier to increasing consumption of complex carbohydrates can contribute to the barrier in decreasing fat intake.

The long-term maintenance of low-fat intakes appears to be facilitated by the development of distaste for dietary fat during the intervention period. This reinforces the avoidance of high-fat foods and the selection of low-fat foods. In the Women's Health Trial over half of the women studied reported that while on the low-fat diet they developed a distaste for dietary fat: 56% disliked the taste and 60% felt physically uncomfortable after eating high-fat foods. These findings are consistent with the data which suggest that preference for dietary fat increases with BMI (Drenowski *et al.*, 1985; Mela and Sacchetti, 1991) and that dietary fat intake appears to be higher as BMI increases (Lissner and Hietman, 1995). Thus while the dietary changes that need to be made are relatively clear, the factors that facilitate reduction of dietary fat intake are more complex and difficult to bring into effect. Because one of the major obstacles to behavioural change to reduce fat intake is taste, the food industry has been active in developing constituents that mimic the taste characteristics of dietary fat but decrease the amount of fat in the food or its bioavailability. Recently the sucrose polyester Olestra has been licensed for use in snack foods. What then is the likely effect of ingesting fat mimetics on appetite and energy intake in humans? A consideration of the literature relating to the effects of Olestra on feeding behaviour sheds light on these issues.

The effects of decreasing the energy density of the diet by substituting real fat with Olestra

In 12 published studies that examined the effects of Olestra-based foods on energy intake, relative to full-fat foods, adults showed very poor compensation for a decrease in the energy density of the diet by replacement of natural fat with Olestra. The compensation for the energy deficit produced by the Olestra-based foods did not exceed 30%. This was the case when subjects were allowed to select from a variety of familiar food items subsequent to ingesting Olestra (e.g. Cotton *et al.*, 1993; Hulshof *et al.*, 1994a,b and c; Johnson *et al.*, 1995; Miller *et al.*, 1995), and where subjects were fed *ad libitum* on systematically manipulated diets of a fixed composition that was either full fat or had 30% of real fat replaced with Olestra (Bray *et al.*, 1995; Sparti *et al.*, 1995). This effect appears to be fairly robust in both lean and obese adults over the time periods of the studies concerned. There is some indication that the fat-mimicking properties of Olestra may be important in producing poor compensation in these experiments. This is because in two short-term replications by Hulshof (1994a,b and c) a series of manipulations was made that used fat/water, fat/Olestra and Olestra/water mixtures in the manipulated foods. Interestingly, while compensation was not significant when fat was replaced by Olestra, men compensated by 66% for the energy deficit when fat was substituted by water. This suggests that Olestra may have a greater capacity to 'deceive' the appetite system in the short to medium term (two days to two weeks) than when fat is simply substituted with water.

In two further studies lean young men compensated almost perfectly for the energy deficit when real fat was substituted with Olestra at breakfast (Burley and Blundell, 1991; Rolls *et al.*, 1992). In these two studies fat, but not energy intake was decreased by the manipulation. It may be that manipulation at breakfast affords the maximum time for caloric deficits to be detected and for compensation to occur before the end of the day. Indeed Hulshof (1994a,b and c) showed that there was a tendency for compensation to be greater after a breakfast substitution than when the substitution occurred at lunch-time or during mid afternoon. In addition, a further study has been conducted by Rolls' group in which 96 male and female snackers were given Olestra-based or full-fat chips. The effect was studied in two conditions: 'informed' and 'uninformed'. The Olestra chips reduced energy and fat intakes in the 'uninformed' group, while they reduced fat but not energy intake in the 'informed' group (Miller *et al.*, 1995).

Only one study has been conducted in children. They responded to a covert substitution of Olestra for fat by compensating for 80% of the energy progressively over two days. It is likely that children will compensate better for caloric dilution of the diet because their energy requirements are higher than those of adults, per kilogram of body weight (Birch *et al.*, 1993). However, it is perhaps also worth mentioning that Lissner and Heitmann warn that it is presently unclear at what age a person should adopt a lower-fat diet since one intervention study among Finnish children (Vartianinen *et al.* 1986) 'gave some suggestion that height velocity may have been suppressed during the low-fat intervention period, along with weight'.

Thus different types of low-fat food have different effects on appetite and energy balance depending on (i) whether they are modified or not, (ii) whether the modification leads to a reduction in the energy density of that food and (iii) the extent to which the changes in the fat content of the modified food are sensorially distinct. In addition to the effects that low-fat foods exert on feeding behaviour, they may also influence nutrient bioavailability.

The effects of low-fat foods on fat-soluble vitamin bioavailability

The major effects that unmodified low-fat foods are likely to have on fat-soluble vitamin bioavailability are (i) decreased intakes of lipid sources that contain fat-soluble vitamins as the result of a decreasing total daily fat energy intake and (ii) the effects that unavailable complex carbohydrates contained in unmodified low-fat foods may have in decreasing the metabolizable energy available from fat. Neither of these effects is likely to pose any threat to fat-soluble vitamin status in relation to published recommended dietary allowances. Modified lower-fat and low-fat foods that use digestible fat replacers or variations in the water–lipid matrix to lower the fat content are likely to exert similar effects.

Low-fat foods that decrease the metabolizable energy available from fat by using non-absorbable fat-based compounds or by binding dietary fat in the intestine will increase the fat content of undigested foods entering the colon. Since the fat phase of the digesta will be increased, the concentration of fat-soluble vitamins contained therein will also increase. Indeed a number of studies have shown how faecal excretion of fat-soluble vitamins is increased when Olestra is ingested (Miller and Allgood, 1993). For example, Westrate and van het Hof (1995) examined the effects of Olestra inclusion in the diet (12.4 g/day) on plasma concentrations of five different carotenoids and vitamin E in 21 volunteers. They also examined the effects of ingesting 3 g/day of Olestra in 53 healthy volunteers. 12.5 g/day of Olestra significantly reduced plasma beta-carotene concentrations by 34% and of plasma lycopene by 52%. Smaller but significant reductions were found in the plasma concentrations of beta-cryptoxanthin, lutein, zeaxanthin and vitamin E. Daily doses of 3 g/day reduced plasma concentrations of beta-carotene by 20% and lycopene by 38%. Olestra-based snack foods are supplemented by a number of fat-soluble vitamins in an attempt to offset this effect. Any compound or preparation that decreases the digestion and absorption of dietary fat from the gut will effectively maintain a lipophilic pool within the gut that will tend to hold fat-soluble micronutrients, decreasing their bioavailability. Increasing the carbohydrate (especially the unavailable complex carbohydrate) content of the diet can affect the digestibility of fat (Blaxter, 1989). Carbohydrates (and their substitutes) can also influence energy balance through their influence on appetite and feeding behaviour.

The impact of carbohydrate-rich and aspartame-based foods on energy intake

Carbohydrates and metabolizable energy intake

Carbohydrates in foods can affect energy intake through changes in appetite and (unlike most dietary fats) the metabolizable energy available from the diet by influencing the overall digestibility of the diet (metabolizable energy is the difference between the gross energy of the food ingested and that which is voided in faeces and other routes and represents the energy available to an organism). The assumption that each of the dietary macronutrients is completely digested has been questioned in numerous metabolic balance studies in farm animals and subsequently in man (Rubner, 1885; Atwater, 1902, 1910). More recently Paul and Southgate (1978) reassessed these values based on on-going theoretical considerations and practical results. Furthermore, the assumed constancy of metabolizable energy factors for the dietary macronutrients is probably erroneous. For example, certain unavailable complex carbohydrates decrease the apparent digestion of fat (Blaxter, 1989). Carbohydrates vary in their digestibility and hence in their metabolizable energy values. There is considerable confusion in the literature relating to the functional terminology of carbohydrate fractions that are digested in the small intestine and those that are not (Livesey, 1990). Livesey notes that variation in the availability of dietary energy is largely due to the occurrence, utilization and effects of those dietary carbohydrates that escape small intestinal digestion (Livesey, 1992); these are the so-called unavailable complex carbohydrates. Previous estimates gave a value of zero for this undigested component of the diet (Paul and Southgate, 1978). Recent extensive analyses by Livesey (1990, 1992) and others (British Nutrition Foundation, 1990) have, however, suggested that 50% of the energy in unavailable complex carbohydrates is available to humans after the processes of fermentation and short-chain fatty acid absorption (Livesey, 1990, 1992). Other factors, such as microwave cooking (which will increase the number of beta-linkages), can affect the digestibility of available complex carbohydrates (Cummings, personal communication). Carbohydrates may also influence energy balance through their effects on feeding behaviour.

Carbohydrates and appetite

Carbohydrates appear to be efficient inhibitors of appetite in the short term. The effectiveness of carbohydrates in suppressing appetite includes the effects of sugars and longer chain oligosaccharides such as maltodextrin and polysaccharides. In studies where subjects have recorded their food intakes using food diaries, carbohydrate was found to be less well associated with a suppression of subsequent intake than energetically similar amounts of protein. It was also more strongly associated with suppression of subsequent intake than fat

(DeCastro, 1987). Under these naturalistic conditions dietary fat contributes around 2.2 to 2.3 times more to energy density than carbohydrate or protein. The relationship between the composition of the diet ingested and hunger revealed similar patterns under these experimental conditions, namely carbohydrate contributed less to suppression of hunger than protein and more than energetically similar amounts of fat (DeCastro and Elmore, 1988).

When nutrient loads in excess of 1 MJ are given to subjects in the laboratory similar patterns emerge. Hill and Blundell (1986) found that a high-protein meal produced a greater sensation of fullness and a decreased desire to eat, relative to a high-carbohydrate meal of the same energy content. Hill and Blundell (1990) also found that both obese and normal-weight subjects reduced their subsequent meal intakes by 19 and 22%, respectively after a high-protein meal compared to a high-carbohydrate meal. Barkeling *et al.* (1990) found that energy intake during the evening was depressed by 12% after consumption of a high-protein meal at lunch-time, compared to when a high-carbohydrate meal was given at lunch-time. Carbohydrates have been found to be more satiating than dietary fat when fat contributes more to the energy density of the diet. Under these conditions high-fat foods lead to higher energy intakes than high-carbohydrate foods (Lissner *et al.*, 1987; Tremblay *et al.*, 1991; Stubbs *et al.*, 1995a,b).

Carbohydrates and excess energy intake

Fat is not the only nutrient that can give rise to overconsumption. There is evidence that high-carbohydrate diets can also generate a high energy intake, as for example in the Guru Walla phenomenon, where a culturally prescribed over-feeding regime, using high-carbohydrate diets, leads to considerable weight gain (Pasquet and Apfelbaum, 1994). It has been shown that six men over-ate and gained weight on high-carbohydrate energy-dense diets compared to less energy-dense diets of the same nutrient ratios and similar sensory characteristics (Stubbs *et al.,* in press). Subjects were able to detect the differences in hunger when this was achieved primarily by using carbohydrates (Stubbs *et al.,* 1997) but not when the energy density of the diet was altered by increasing its fat content (Stubbs *et al.,* 1995). There is no theoretical reason why it is not possible to over-eat on high-carbohydrate diets. The key issue is whether it is probable that high-carbohydrate, energy-dense diets will produce excess energy intakes in real life. Furthermore the form in which carbohydrates are ingested may be important.

Types of carbohydrate and appetite

A number of studies have compared the satiating effects of preloads containing different hexoses and found relatively few differences between them in terms of appetite responses. However, it is unclear whether this uniform response relates to the constraints of the preloading method or whether the monosaccharides simply have similar satiating efficiencies. This lack of a detectable differential effect of carbohydrate-type on appetite may relate to the fact that studies of sufficient duration and/or sensitivity have not yet been conducted. There is some evidence that starches produce a more blunted, yet prolonged, influence on satiety than mono- and disaccharides (see above). However, these effects seem relatively modest and to date there is little published data to suggest that sugars and starches exert large differential effects on intake. Postingestive satiety also appears to be influenced by the structure of starch as indicated by the difference between high amylose and amylopectin foods (Van Amelsvoort and Weststrate, 1992). These differences in the satiating effects of different starches may be due to differences in their rates of absorption and utilization (Holt *et al.*, 1992). The quantitative importance of these differences for energy intake is currently unknown. Most work on the effects of different carbohydrates on energy intake has been done with unavailable complex carbohydrates, which have received much attention in the past as dietary constituents that may assist in achieving weight loss.

Dietary fibre and energy intake

The idea that unavailable complex carbohydrates act as bulking agents in the gut and decrease rates of digestion and hence passage time (the so-called 'time–energy displacement' concept) has been used suggest that the addition of unavailable complex carbohydrates to the diet enhances satiation and limits meal size. At least one commercial weight-reducing diet has been marketed on the basis of this mechanism. Indeed the phenomenon has been used to limit weight gain in farm animals on single feeds (Forbes, 1995). Unfortunately, Western consumers have access to more than a single 'feed'. In all, over 50 studies have been conducted that have examined the effects of dietary unavailable complex carbohydrate on food intake and body weight (Levine and Billington, 1994). These have been extensively covered in four reviews to which the reader is referred for a detailed discussion of this issue (Stevens, 1988; Blundell and Burley, 1987; Burley and Blundell, 1990; Levine and Billington, 1994;). In summary, various loads of unavailable complex carbohydrate at one meal have been shown to decrease both hunger and energy intake at the next meal, but the effects are relatively modest. Twenty-six long-term studies have examined the effects of increased unavailable complex carbohydrate ingestion on body weight (Levine and Billington, 1994). This seemingly large number of trials has produced differing results because the methods employed differed from study to study. Nevertheless it can be generally concluded that supplementing the diet with tolerable levels of extracted unavailable complex carbohydrate appears to have, at best, modest effects in decreasing body weight over several months or more. However, unavailable complex carbohydrate-rich bulky diets of low energy density may have a considerable effect in preventing excess energy intake (by lowering the energy density of the diet) and are also believed to have other health benefits (see Spiller (1992) for a detailed treatment). The postingestive effects of unavailable complex carbohydrate will also depend on the amount and type ingested and are likely to be influenced by the proportions of soluble and insoluble unavailable complex carbohydrate, which will have different effects on gastro-intestinal processing. It is becoming increasingly apparent that fermentable carbohydrates produce significant quantities of short-chain fatty acids. The absorption and metabolism of acetate, propionate and butyrate may exert influences on satiety. The complex effects that unavailable complex carbohydrate exert in gastro-intestinal processing may also influence energy and nutrient balance through their effects on fat and micronutrient absorption.

The impact of consuming high unavailable complex carbohydrate diets on mineral bioavailability and nutrient absorption

Unavailable complex carbohydrate and mineral absorption

There has been some concern as to whether the ingestion of high levels of dietary unavailable complex carbohydrates decreases mineral absorption. Detailed reviews of this area include Cummings (1978), Hallberg (1981), Kelsay (1982), Forbes and Erdman (1983), Harland and Morris (1985) and Spiller, 1992). These texts give a detailed consideration of this complex area that cannot be achieved within the scope of the present chapter. What follows is a summary of the main points.

It is possible that under some circumstances unavailable complex carbohydrates could decrease the bioavailability of trace elements by interfering with their absorption. This in turn could precipitate marginal trace element deficiencies. The exact effects of different forms of unavailable complex carbohydrates on mineral bioavailability are unclear because of the complexities of nutrient interactions in the small intestine and the role that colonic bacteria may play in salvaging bound minerals when unavailable complex carbohydrates are fermented in the large intestine. Harland and Morris (1985) note that unavailable complex carbohydrate/phytate/mineral interactions are influenced by the various physical and chemical conditions that occur in the gut. On balance it would appear that ingestion of high levels of dietary unavailable complex carbohydrate decrease the apparent absorption of the minerals zinc, calcium, magnesium, iron and copper. The extent to which this occurs for each metal varies from study to study. Frolich (1984) reviewed 55 studies conducted between 1942 and 1984, which examined mineral bioavailability from cereals. Increased cereal and grain ingestion led to negative mineral balances in 35 studies, unaltered balances in two and positive balances in 18. The review also suggested that certain foods ingested along with cereals increased mineral bioavailability. A number of studies show sizeable percentage effects (20–50% decreased absorption relative to control) under relatively extreme conditions, i.e. where doses of unavailable complex carbohydrates considerably exceeded the average unavailable complex carbohydrate intake of the population (e.g. Van Dokkum, 1982). Others have found relatively little effect of unavailable complex carbohydrate on mineral bioavailability when phytate intake was controlled (e.g. Andersson et al., 1983). Phytate also binds minerals and occurs in most high unavailable complex carbohydrate fruits, vegetables and whole grains (Munoz and Harland, 1992). It is believed that the presence of phytate in high unavailable complex carbohydrate foods is largely responsible for the mineral binding that occurs in the gut when these foods are ingested (Harland and Morris, 1985). The higher the phytate:mineral molar ratio, the greater the risk there is of high levels of mineral binding. Thus ingestion of mineral-rich foods can lower this ratio and decrease the risk of marginal trace element deficiencies. Thus studies tend to show equivocal effects of unavailable complex carbohydrate ingestion on mineral bioavailability at low to moderate doses of unavailable complex carbohydrates and phytate, with the reliability of decreased bioavailability increasing as the dose of unavailable complex carbohydrate increases. On balance the data at present suggest that moderate increases in unavailable complex carbohydrate intake are unlikely to precipitate significant subclinical trace element deficiencies that would compromise the health of individuals who are not already deficient in trace elements and who regularly ingest a variety of mineral-rich foods. It should again be remembered that moderate increases in unavailable complex carbohydrate intake are likely to be attended by a number of other potential health benefits.

Unavailable complex carbohydrate and lipid absorption

Increased dietary unavailable complex carbohydrate intake increases the faecal volume and lipid content of faeces (Southgate and Durnin, 1970; Losowsky, 1978; Southgate, 1982; Cassidy and Calvert, 1992). The increased faecal fat could arise from poorly digested lipids in the unavailable complex carbohydrate itself, ingested lipid (due to unavailable complex carbohydrate decreasing fat absorption) or other endogenous sources (Cassidy and Calvert, 1992). Cassidy and Calvert summarized the available evidence relating to the effects of dietary unavailable complex carbohydrate on lipid absorption and note that unavailable complex carbohydrate supplements do appear to modify the rates of absorption of fatty acids and cholesterol. This is possibly because unavailable complex carbohydrate sequestrates bile acids, and so disrupts the micellar solubility of lipids in the intestinal tract, or because it interferes with the diffusion of lipids across the intestinal epithelium. Cassidy and Calvert (1992) also note that prolonged elevated unavailable complex carbohydrate intakes may result in adaptive changes in the morphology of the small intestine that may interfere with triglyceride digestion, interfere with absorption of unesterified fatty acids and decrease cholesterol absorption. It is, however, difficult to quantify these effects at present since, to date, human studies have provided inconsistent results. However, Livesey (1990, 1992) estimated that the digestibility of Western diets would be altered by no more than 5% as a result of the effects of moderate increases in unavailable complex carbohydrate intake, although theoretically, this value could be greater for diets containing extreme amounts of unavailable complex carbohydrates. Furthermore, the long-term effects of a 5% alteration in energy balance would be cumulatively significant.

The amount and type of dietary unavailable complex carbohydrate can also influence carbohydrate and protein absorption and utilization. The glycemic index of a food will affect the rate of absorption and utilization of carbohydrates, which in turn will influence the contribution of other metabolic fuels to energy expenditure. Fermentation of complex carbohydrates in the colon also produces short-chain fatty acids which, on absorption, influence carbohydrate and fat metabolism (Wolever and Jenkins, 1992). Increased ingestion of unavailable complex carbohydrate rich food sources also significantly decreases the apparent and true digestibility of protein in animals, by several per cent, in what appears to be a dose-dependent manner. This effect is apparent in a number of species, including man (Gallaher and Schneeman, 1992).

The effects of dietary unavailable complex carbohydrate on vitamin absorption

If dietary unavailable complex carbohydrate decreases fat absorption and increases fat excretion it is likely that the absorption of fat-soluble vitamins contained in foods may also be decreased. Studies examining the effects of increased unavailable complex carbohydrate intake on vitamin A status have proved equivocal (Kasper, 1992). Kasper notes that several findings suggest that a high intake of unavailable complex carbohydrate from unleavened wholemeal bread may be responsible for rickets in certain Asian communities, because of its effect in decreasing vitamin D_3 absorption. Relationships between dietary unavailable complex carbohydrate intake and vitamins E and K status remain unclear. The effects of other agents (e.g. fat mimetics and novel dietary unavailable complex carbohydrates) that influence lipid absorption and vitamin status are discussed elsewhere in this chapter.

In summary, the conclusions of Munoz and Harland (1992) should be borne in mind: 'The possibility that the chelating effects of dietary unavailable complex carbohydrate may produce deficiencies of minerals, vitamins and trace elements has been extensively investigated in both animals and humans. Available studies permit no final conclusions. Most are short term and poorly controlled, and similar studies conducted by different investigators often produce different results'. It would appear probable that the chelating effects of dietary unavailable complex carbohydrate are most likely to precipitate subclinical or even clinical deficiencies in minerals, vitamins and trace elements under conditions of marginal intakes of micronutrients coupled with large intakes of dietary unavailable complex carbohydrate (Frolich, 1992).

A novel unavailable complex carbohydrate: chitosan

Chitin and chitosan are nitrogenous polysaccharides occurring in fungi, many invertebrates and some brown algae. Chitin is usually obtained from the cuticles of sea animals. Chitin is similar in structure to cellulose but is composed of units of 2-acetyl amino-2-deoxy-D-glucopyranose, linked by 1,4 glycosidic bonds. Most amino groups of chitin are acetylated while most amino groups of chitosan are deacetylated.

There has been considerable interest in chitosan for a number of industrial and biotechnological purposes (e.g. Thacharidi and Rao, 1995, Ishii *et al.*, 1995). Because it has the ability to bind certain lipid-based materials, interest has focused on chitosan as a potential antihypercholesterolemic and antihyperlipidemic agent. Nauss (1983) examined the lipid-binding capacity of chitosan with respect to micellar solutions, e.g. bile salts, dodecyl sulphate, natural ox bile and artificial mixed emulsion. They found that under optimal conditions chitosan could co-precipitate with 4 to 5 times its weight with all the lipid aggregates tested (Nauss, 1983). While the binding process appears to be quite complex, the primary driving force appears to be determined by ionic interactions.

In 1980 Sugano *et al.* reported that in Wistar rats fed a high-cholesterol diet for 20 days, addition of 2–5% (w/w) of chitosan to the diet resulted in a significant (25–30%) decrease in plasma cholesterol without influencing food intake and growth. Chitosan levels of 10% (w/w) in the diet tended to decrease food intake and significantly reduce weight gain compared to a control group (Sugano *et al.*, 1980).

Maezaki *et al.* (1993) tested the hypocholesterolemic effect of chitosan in adult men. 3–6 g chitosan a day, in the form of biscuits, was given to eight healthy men for 14 days (7 days at 3 g/day followed by 7 days at 6 g/day). Chitosan ingestion led to a significant increase in the faecal excretion of primary bile acids, cholic acid and cenodeoxycholic acid. Serum cholesterol was also significantly decreased (Maezaki *et al.*, 1993). During the test period *ad libitum* food intake was not affected.

The lipid-binding properties of chitosan have also led to interest in it as a tool that can be used to assist in weight control in humans. While no reliable human trials have been published to assess the efficacy of chitosan in this context, a number of studies have been conducted in rodents using somewhat high doses of this compound. Deuchi *et al.* (1994) compared the effect of 23 different forms of unavailable complex carbohydrate on apparent fat digestibility in Sprague-Dawley rats by adding 5 g chitosan per 100 g food to an *ad libitum* diet for two weeks per treatment. Chitosan markedly increased faecal lipid excretion (by 9.3 times that of control) and reduced the apparent fat digestibility to 53% of control values. Protein digestibility was only affected to a minor degree. The weight of faeces in the chitosan-containing diet was 184% that for the control diet (5 g cellulose per 100 g food). Body-weight gain in the rats fed on the chitosan-based diet was significantly reduced.

Kanauchi *et al.* (1994) found that excretion of dietary fat in faeces appears to be further increased when rats are fed a mixture of chitosan and ascorbic acid, and suggested that chitosan complexes with fat in the acid environment of the stomach (emulsification mediated by ascorbic acid). On entry into the alkaline small intestine the complex forms a gelled matrix that reduces digestion and absorption of the complexed fat (Kanauchi *et al.*, 1994). This proposed mechanism appears to be largely lipid specific. In studies of rodents, chitosan appears to be most effective at reducing fat absorption when there is more fat in the diet, around 20% (w/w), and when chitosan was included at between 5–10% (w/w). It is currently unclear whether these dramatic effects are likely to occur in human subjects, particularly since the doses of chitosan administered in the rodent studies were too large to be realistically administered to human subjects. These data are interesting because they illustrate the dramatic effects that certain naturally occurring dietary constituents can have on metabolizable energy availability from the diet.

There are potential concerns about the effects of fat-binding agents in the gut. It is to be expected that fat-binding agents such as chitosan may bind other nutrients and certain trace elements. Indeed one study has reported that continuous and massive intake of chitosan affects mineral and fat-soluble vitamin status in rats fed a high-fat (20% w/w) diet. Deuchie *et al.* (1995) reported that it was necessary to double the calcium content of the diet to prevent decreased calcium absorption and decreased bone mineral content. In this study chitosan also produced a marked and rapid decrease in serum vitamin E levels (Deuchi *et al.*, 1995).

While unavailable complex carbohydrates only account for a small proportion of dietary energy intake in the Western diet (no more than 1–3% energy intake), a considerable proportion of carbohydrate energy ingested in the Western diet is derived from sugar. Sugar is particularly interesting to the present discussion because a number of intense sweeteners are used extensively to add sweetness to foods without the attendant energy that is derived from sugars. In order to understand the effects of sugars and intense sweeteners on appetite and energy balance it is important to understand how sugars, sweetness and artificial sweeteners influence feeding behaviour.

Sweetness, sugars and intense sweeteners

For the last decade there has been a heated debate about the effects of sweetness, sucrose and artificial sweeteners on energy balance (Booth *et al.* 1988; Clydesdale, 1995). The key issue relates to what effects sweetness, plus or minus carbohydrate energy, has on appetite and energy balance. There are three main hypotheses:

(i) adding sweetness without calories to foods leads to lower levels of energy intake than when sweetness with calories is added

(ii) sweetness without calories leads to a cephalic phase stimulation to eat

(iii) ingestion of sugars (sweetness with calories) correlates with thinness and lowers fat intake, which is itself the reason for the lower body weight.

Clearly these hypotheses have enormous implications for appetite and energy balance control in consumers at large.

Sweetness is a factor favouring the selection and subsequent ingestion of sweet foods. Most animals display a preference for sweetness at a very early age and (until the advent of intense sweeteners) sweetness was a reliable sensory cue that a food was a source of readily available energy in the form of sugars. Conversely, different people exhibit markedly different preferences for sweetness intensities and so simply adding sweetness to foods will not stimulate everyone to eat. Assuming that sweetness does in general stimulate the selection and consumption of foods, it is pertinent to enquire whether sweetness with or without calories differentially affects appetite and energy intake.

Does sweetness without calories lead to lower levels of energy intake and body weight than sweetness with calories?

Despite the common assumption that replacing dietary sugars with intense sweeteners will promote a more negative energy balance, there is a remarkable paucity of data to demonstrate this effect. The work of Porikos and Van Itallie (1984) is unusual because subjects were already in a positive energy balance on the control diet (probably due to the sumptuous mode of food presentation) and were then in approximate energy balance on the low-energy density, aspartame-enriched foods. There is certainly little epidemiological evidence to suggest that artificial sweetener consumption correlates with lower BMIs or that increased artificial sweetener consumption in the population has contributed to any reduction in the prevalence of obesity. According to Mela (1997) this may account for the fact that artificial sweeteners tend not to be used so much as a substitute for sugar but are added to foods to enhance their appeal.

The majority of studies that examine the effect of sweetness, sugars and artificial sweeteners are short term and therefore do not address the issue of energy balance (see Anderson, in Clydesdale, 1995).

Does sweetness without calories lead to a cephalic-phase stimulation to eat?

Most authors seem to agree that the purely postingestive effects of aspartame do not stimulate intake. Blundell and Rogers (1994) initially reported that artificially sweetened drinks can actually stimulate appetite. They suggested that sweetness without calories provides a sensory cue for carbohydrate calories that leads to cephalic-phase physiological changes that anticipate energy intake (Blundell and Rogers, 1994). They note that intense sweeteners have only been found to stimulate intake when a food has been sweetened with intense sweeteners or when a less sweet food has been compared with an isoenergetically equivalent food to which sweetness has been added (the 'additive principle') and not when two foods of differing energy density but the same level of sweetness are compared. This they call the 'substitutive principle'. This is especially important as Mela argues that most intense sweeteners are employed in an 'additive' rather than a 'substitutive' manner (Mela, 1997). Again this area is bedevilled by methodological controversies, such as the appropriate drink vehicle for the sweetener (water or a familiar soft drink), the time-course of the experiment and the subjects used. Blundell and Rogers (1994) argue that the strongest experimental designs contain tests of both the additive and substitutive principle. No long-term studies that address energy balance have yet achieved this dual testing. Black and Anderson (1994) reported that the use of aspartame-sweetened water leads to an acute short-term increase in subjective appetite in lean men but that aspartame-sweetened carbonated soft drinks induce a transient suppression of appetite in similar subjects over a similar time-frame. The issue is complicated by the fact that satiety can be transiently conditioned by starch-containing drinks that are paired with a given sensory cue such as flavour (see Booth et al., 1988). Once conditioned, similar levels of satiation can be transiently induced by the conditioning stimulus alone. Therefore the effects of prior conditioning could influence the outcome of short-term studies using vehicles that mimic the sensory properties of familiar foods.

In summary, there is little evidence that artificial sweeteners reliably decrease appetite or reduce energy intake, but they could perhaps prevent any excess energy intake that would otherwise occur when calories were provided as drinks. There are conditions where artificially sweetened drinks have been found to stimulate appetite and less often energy intake, but there is little evidence to suggest that sweeteners reduce intake. Understanding the applicability of these findings to free-living humans is an important area yet to be resolved. It is also important to bear in mind that many of the experiments examining these issues have used drinks and not solid foods and there is evidence that energy derived from solid foods or drinks may exert different effects on feeding behaviour. Calories contained in drinks appear to be poorly compensated for. Mattes (1996) conducted a meta-analysis of feeding responses to either liquid or solid manipulations of the nutrient and energy content of the diet. The analysis suggests that the physical state of ingested carbohydrates may be important in influencing subsequent caloric compensation. The reasons for this are at present unclear but may relate to the rate, timing and density at which the energy is ingested. There may be a threshold in these parameters below which energy is poorly detected.

The effect on energy intake of sweetness with calories

It is now generally accepted that the views of the early 1970s are wrong, i.e. that sweetness provided in the form of calories stimulated energy intake and contributed in a major way to increases in obesity. Indeed epidemiological data suggest that consumption of sugars, i.e. sweetness with calories, is associated with thinness. Yet the same studies tend to show that as sugar intake increases so does energy intake. This suggests that more physically active people select more sugars and therefore does not necessarily imply that increased sugar intake spontaneously promotes thinness. When considering these data, the limitations of epidemiological studies must therefore be taken into account and there are very few interventions of sufficient duration to affect energy balance. It is pertinent to note that (i) increasing the energy density of the diet with maltodextrins can lead to excess *ad libitum* energy intakes and (ii) energy-containing drinks are poorly compensated for. Nevertheless fat intake under naturalistic conditions does appear to be more of a risk factor for weight gain. This does not, of course, mean that increasing the energy density of the diet with sweet carbohydrates will never increase energy intakes. While there is evidence of some reciprocity in the population between carbohydrates and sugar intake on the one hand and fat intake on the other, this probably reflects the fact that people eat to defend against energy deficits, rather than implying that there is some active process whereby increased sugar intake promotes dietary fat avoidance. The intervention studies conducted by Mela's group found that increased use of reduced-fat foods did not lead to any directional change in sucrose intake in any group or subgroup (Mela, 1997). It was also found that when high-sucrose consumers increase their intake of reduced-sugar foods they increase their fat intake, presumably because of non-macronutrient specific increases in energy intake. There is little or no evidence that increasing sugar intake promotes a negative energy balance and weight loss. Indeed, there is evidence to suggest that physically active people (e.g. athletes) actively supplement their energy intakes using drinks rich in short-chain carbohydrates. Presumably such drinks facilitate higher energy intakes. Their effects on energy intake in more sedentary consumers, who constitute the majority of the population, are presently unclear. At the time of writing the critical experiments examining the effects of titrating sugars, fats and starches into the diet on subsequent macronutrient selection have not been conducted.

References

Aaron, J.I., Gatenby, S.J., Jack, V. and Mela, D.J. (in press) Effect of reduced fat and reduced sugar food use on diet and weight control status of free-living consumers. *Proceedings of the Nutrition Society*.

Acheson, K.J. and Jequier, E. (1982) Glycogen synthesis versus lipogenesis after a 500 gram carbohydrate meal in man. *Metabolism*, **31**, 1234–1240.

Akoh, C.C. (1995) Lipid based fat substitutes. *Critical Reviews in Food Science and Nutrition*, **35**, 405–430.

Andersson, H., Navert, B., Bingham, S.A., Englyst, H.N. and Cummings, J.H. (1983) The effects of breads containing similar amounts of phytate but differing amounts of wheat bran on calcium, zinc and iron balance in man. *British Journal of Nutrition*, **50**, 503–510.

Atwater, W.O. (1902) *On the Digestibility and Availability of Food Materials*, Agricultural Experiment Station 14th Annual Report, Storrs, Connecticut.

Atwater, W.O. (1910). *Principles of Nutrition and Nutritive Value of Foods*, Farmer's Bulletin No. 142, US Department of Agriculture, Washington, DC.

Barkeling, B., Rossner, S. and Bjorvell, H. (1990) Efficiency of a high-protein meal (meat) and a high carbohydrate meal (vegetarian) on satiety measured by automated computerised monitoring of subsequent food intake, motivation to eat and food preferences. *International Journal of Obesity*, **14**, 743–751.

Birch, L.L., Johnson, S.L., Jones, M.B. and Peters, J.C. (1993) Effects of a non energy fat substitute on children's energy and macronutrient intake. *American Journal of Clinical Nutrition*, **58**, 326–333.

Black, R.M. and Anderson, G.H. (1994) Sweeteners, food intake and selection, in *Appetite and Body Weight Regulation: Sugar, Fat and Macronutrient Substitutes* (eds J.D. Fernstrom and G.D. Miller), CRC Press, Florida, USA.

Black, A.E., Goldberg, G.R., Jebb, S.A., Livingstone, M.B.E., Cole, T.J. and Prentice, A.M. (1991) Critical evaluation of energy intake data using fundamental principles of energy physiology. 2. Evaluating the results of published surveys. *European Journal of Clinical Nutrition*, **45**, 583–599.

Blaxter, K. (1989) *Energy Metabolism in Animals and Man,* Cambridge University Press, Cambridge, UK.

Blundell, J.E. (1996) Food intake and body weight regulation, in *Regulation of Body Weight: Biological and Behavioural Mechanisms*, (eds C. Bouchard and G. Bray), Dahlem Workshop Reports, Life Sciences Research Report 57, John Wiley and Sons Ltd., Chichester, England.

Blundell, J.E. and Burley, V.J. (1987) Satiation, satiety and the action of fibre on food intake. *International Journal of Obesity*, **11** (suppl. 1), 9.

Blundell, J.E. and Rogers, P.J. (1994) Sweet carbohydrate substitutes (intense sweeteners) and the control of appetite: scientific issues, in *Appetite and Body Weight Regulation: Sugar, Fat and Macronutrient Substitutes* (eds J.D. Fernstrom and G.D. Miller), CRC Press, Florida, USA.

Booth, D.A., Rodin, J. and Blackburn, G.L. (eds) (1988) *Sweeteners, Appetite and Obesity.* Proceedings of the workshop on 'The effect of sweeteners on food intake' held by the North American Association for the Study of Obesity, Boston, Massachusetts, 14th October, 1987, Appetite **11** (Suppl. 1).

Bray, G.A., Sparti, A., Windhauser, M.M. and York, D.A. (1995) Effect of two weeks fat replacement by Olestra on food intake and energy metabolism. *FASEB*, **9**(3), p. A439.

British Nutrition Foundation (1990) *Complex Carbohydrates in Foods*, the report of the British Nutrition Foundation's Taskforce, Chapman & Hall, London.

Burley, V.J. and Blundell, J.E. (1990) Action of dietary fibre on the satiety cascade in *Dietary Fibre: Chemistry, Physiology and Health Effects* (eds D. Kritchevsky, C. Bonfield and J.W. Anderson), Plenum Press, New York.

Burley, V.J. and Blundell, J.E. (1991) Evaluation of the action of a non-absorbable fat on appetite and energy intake in lean, healthy males in obesity in Europe: 63–65 (ch 11).

Burrows, E.R., Henry, H.J., Bowen, B.J. and Henderson, M.M. (1993) Nutritional applications of a clinical low fat dietary intervention to public health. *Journal of Nutrition Education*, **25**, 167–175.

Bursztein, S., Elwyn, D.H., Askanazi, J. and Kinney, J.M. (1989) *Energy Metabolism, Indirect Calorimetry and Nutrition*, Williams and Wilkins, Baltimore, Maryland.

Buzzard, I.M., Asp, E.H., Chlebowski, R.T., Boyar, A.P., Jeffrey, R.W., Nixon, D.W., Blackburn, G.L., Jochimsen, P.R., Scanlon, E.F., Insull, R.M., Elashoff, R.M., Butrum, R. and Wynder, E.L. (1990) Diet intervention methods to reduce fat intake nutrient and food group composition of self selected low fat diets. *Journal of the American Dietetic Association*, **90**, 42–50.

Cassidy, M.M. and Calvert, R.J. (1992) Effects of dietary fibre on intestinal absorption of lipids, in *CRC Handbook of Dietary Fibre in Human Nutrition* (ed. G.A. Spiller), CRC Press, Inc., Boca Raton, California, pp. 153–262.

Clydesdale, F.M. (ed) (1995) Nutritional and health aspects of sugars. *American Journal of Clinical Nutrition*, **62** (suppl. 1).

Colditz, G.A., Willet, W.C., Stampfer, M.J., London, S.J., Segal, M.R. and Speizer, F.E. (1990) Patterns of weight change and their relation to diet in a cohort of healthy women. *American Journal of Clinical Nutrition*, **51**, 1100–1105.

Cotton, J.R., Burley, V.J. and Blundell, J.E. (1993) Effect on appetite of replacing natural fat with sucrose polyester in meals or snacks across one whole day. *International Journal of Obesity*, **17** (suppl. 2), 47.

Cummings, J.H. (1978) Nutritional implications of dietary fibre. *American Journal of Clinical Nutrition*, **31**, 521–529.

108 NUTRITIONAL ASPECTS OF FOOD PROCESSING

Danforth, E. (1985) Diet and obesity. *American Journal of Clinical Nutrition*, **41**,1132–1145.

DeCastro, J.M. (1987) Macronutrient relationships with meal patterns and mood in the spontaneous feeding behaviour of humans. *Physiology and Behaviour*, **39**, 561–569.

DeCastro, J.M. and Elmore, D.K. (1988) Subjective hunger relationships with meal patterns in the spontaneous feeding behaviour of humans: evidence for a causal connection. *Physiology and Behaviour*, **43**, 159–165.

Department of Health (1992) *The Health of the Nation: A Strategy for Health in England*, HMSO, London.

Department of Health (1995) Obesity: reversing the Increasing Problem of Obesity in England, Report from the Nutrition and Physical Activity Task Forces, Department of Health, London.

Deuchi, K., Kanuchi, O., Imasato, Y. and Kobayashi, E. (1994) Decreasing effect of chitosan on the apparent fat digestibility by rats fed on a high-fat diet. *Bioscience, Biotechnology and Biochemistry*, **58**, 1613–1616.

Deuchi, K., Kanuchi, O., Shizukuishi, M. and Kobayashi, E. (1995) Continuous and massive intake of chitosan affects mineral and fat-soluble vitamin status in rats fed on a high-fat diet. *Bioscience, Biotechnology and Biochemistry*, **59**, 1211–1216.

Drenowski, A., Brunzell, J., Sande, K., Iverius, P.H. and Greenwood, M.R.C. (1985) Sweet tooth reconsidered: taste responsiveness in human obesity. *Physiology and Behaviour*, **35**, 617–622.

Duncan, K.H., Bacon, J.A. and Weinsier, R.L. (1983) The effects of high and low energy density diets on satiety, energy intake, and eating time of obese and non obese subjects. *American Journal of Clinical Nutrition*, **37**, 763–767.

Fallat, R.W., Gluek, C.J., Lutmer, R. and Mattson, F.H. (1976) Short-term study of sucrose poly-ester: a nonabsorbable fat-like material as a dietary agent for lowering plasma cholesterol. *American Journal of Clinical Nutrition*, **29**, 1204–1215.

Flatt, J.P. (1978) The biochemistry of energy expenditure, in *Recent Advances in Obesity Research*, vol. II (ed. G.D. Bray), Newman Publishing, London, pp. 211–228.

Forbes, J.M. (1995) *Voluntary Food Intake and Diet Selection in Farm Animals*, CAB International, Oxon.

Forbes, R.M. and Erdman, J.W. (1983) Bioavailability of trace mineral elements. *Annual Review of Nutrition*, **3**, 213–231.

Frolich, W. (1984) *Bioavailability of minerals from unrefined cereal products: in vitro and in vivo studies*. Department of Food Chemistry, Chemistry Centre, University of Lund, Lund.

Frolich, W. (1992) Bioavailability of minerals from cereals, in *CRC Handbook of Dietary Fibre in Human Nutrition* (ed. G.A. Spiller), CRC Press, Inc., Boca Raton, California, pp. 209–243.

Gallaher, D.D. and Schneeman, B.O. (1992) Effect of dietary fibre on protein digestibility and utilisation, in *CRC Handbook of Dietary Fibre in Human Nutrition* (ed. G.A. Spiller), CRC Press, Inc., Boca Raton, California, pp. 179–208.

Gatenby, S.J., Aaron, G., Morton, G. and Mela, D.J. (1995) Nutritional implications of reduced-fat food use by free-living consumers. *Appetite*, **25**, 241–252.

Gil, K., Skeie, B., Kvetan, V., Askanazi, J. and Friedman, M.I. (1991) Parenteral nutrition and oral intake: effect of glucose and fat infusion. *Journal of Parenteral and Enteral Nutrition* **15**, 426–432.

Goldberg, G.R., Black, A., Jebb, S.A., Cole, T.J., Murgatroyd, P.R., Coward, W.A. and Prentice, A.M. (1991) Critical evaluation of energy intake using fundamental principles of energy physiology. 1. Derivation of cut-off limits to identify under recording. *European Journal of Clinical Nutrition*, **45**, 569–581.

Gorder, D.D., Dolecek, T.A., Coleman, G.G., Tillotson, J.L., Brown, H.B., Lenz-Litzow, K., Bartsch, G.E. and Grandits, G. (1986) Dietary intake in the Multiple Risk Factor Intervention Trial (MRFIT): nutrient and food group changes over 6 years. *Journal of the American Dietetic Association*, **86**, 744–751.

Hallberg, L. (1981) Bioavailability of dietary iron in man. *Annual Review of Nutrition*, **1**, 123–147.

Harland, B.F. and Morris, E.R. (1985) Fibre and mineral absorption, in *Dietary Fibre Perspectives: Reviews and Bibliography 1* (ed. A.R. Leeds), John Libbey and Co Ltd., London, pp. 72–82.

Hill, A.J. and Blundell, J.E. (1986) Macronutrients and satiety: the effects of a high-protein or high-carbohydrate meal on subjective motivation to eat and food preferences. *Nutrition and Behaviour*, **3**, 133–144.

Hill, A.J. and Blundell, J.E. (1990) Comparison of the action of macronutrients on the expression of appetite in lean and obese humans. *Annals of the New York Academy of Sciences*, **575**, 529–530.

Holt, S., Brand, J., Soveny, C., and Hansky, J. (1992) Relationship of satiety to postprandial glycemic, insulin and cholecystokinin responses. *Appetite*, **18**, 129–141.

Hulshof, T., de Graaf, C. and Westrate, J.A. (1994a) Short-term satiating effect of the fat replacer sucrose polyester (SPE) in man. Study 2, in *Fat and Non-absorbable Fat in the Regulation of Food Intake* Hulshof T., PhD thesis, Wageningen, pp. 101–127 (ch. 6).

Hulshof, T., de Graaf, C. and Westrate, J.A. (1994b) Short-term satiating effect of the fat replacer sucrose polyester (SPE) in man. Study 1, in *Fat And Non-Absorbable Fat In The Regulation Of Food Intake In.* Hulshof T., PhD thesis, Wageningen, pp. 101–127 (ch. 6).

Hulshof, T., de Graaf, C. and Westrate, J.A. (1994c) The effects of covert changes in the amount of fat and a non-absorbable fat (sucrose polyester) in croissants, on food intake and appetite, in *Fat And Non-Absorbable Fat In The Regulation Of Food Intake In* Hulshof T., PhD thesis, Wageningen, pp. 59–80 (ch. 4).

Ishii, H., Minegishi, M., Lavitpichayawong, B., and Mitani, T. (1995) Synthesis of chitosan-amino acid conjugates and their use in heavy metal uptake. *International Journal of Biological Macromolecularity*, **17**, 21–23.

Johnson, S.L., Cooper, D.A., Stone, M., Seagle, H., Smith, S., Wyatt, F., Riccardi, K., Tran, Z., Peters, J.C. and Hill, J.O. (1995) Effects of covert substitution of Olestra on self-selected food intake. *FASEB*, **10**(3), 3166.

Johnstone, A.M, Stubbs, R.J. and Harbron, C.G. (1996) Effect of overfeeding macronutrients on day-to-day food intake in man. *European Journal of Clinical Nutrition*, **50**, 418–430.

Kanauchi, O., Deuchi, K., Imasato, Y. and Kobayashi, E. (1994) Increasing effect of a chitosan and ascorbic acid mixture on fecal dietary fat excretion. *Bioscience, Biotechnology and Biochemistry*, **58**, 1617–1620.

Kasper, H. (1992) Effects of dietary fibre on vitamin metabolism, in *CRC Handbook of Dietary Fibre in Human Nutrition* (ed. G.A. Spiller), CRC Press, Inc., Boca Raton, California, pp. 253–262.

Kelsay, J.L. (1981) Effect of diet fibre level on bowel function and trace mineral balances of human subjects. *Cereal Chemistry*, **58**, 2–5.

Kelsay, J.L. (1982) Effects of fibre on vitamin and mineral bioavailability, in *Dietary Fibre in Health and Disease* (eds G.V. Vahouny and D. Kritchevsky), Plenum Press, New York, pp. 91–103.

Kendall, A., Levitsky, D.A., Strupp, B.J. and Lissner, L. (1991) Weight-loss on a low fat diet: consequence of the impression of the control of food intake in humans. *American Journal of Clinical Nutrition*, **53**, 1124–1129.

Kristal, A.R., White, E., Shattuck, A.L., Curry, S., Anderson, G.L., Fowler, A. and Urban, N. (1992) Long term maintenance of a low-fat diet: durability of fat-related dietary habits in the women's health trial. *Journal of the American Dietetic Association*, **92**, 553–559.

Levine, A.S. and Billington, C.J. (1994) Dietary fibre: does it affect food intake and body weight in *Appetite and Body Weight Regulation: Sugar, Fat and Macronutrient Substitutes* (eds J.D. Fernstrom and G.D. Miller), CRC Press, Florida, pp. 191–200.

Lissner, L. and Heitmann, B.L. (1995) Dietary fat and obesity: evidence from epidemiology. *European Journal of Clinical Nutrition*, **49**, 79–90.

Lissner L., Levitsky D.A., Strupp B.J., Kalkwarf H.J. and Roe D.A. (1987) Dietary fat and the regulation of energy intake in human subjects. *American Journal of Clinical Nutrition*, **46**, 886–892.

Livesey, G. (1990) Energy values of unavailable carbohydrate and diets: an inquiry and analysis. *American Journal of Clinical Nutrition*, **51**, 617–637.

Livesey, G. (1992) The energy values of dietary fibre and sugar alcohols in man. *Nutrition Research Reviews* **5**, 61–84.

Lloyd, H.M., Paisley, C.M. and Mela, D.J. (1993) Changing to a low fat diet: attitudes and beliefs in UK consumers. *European Journal of Clinical Nutrition*, **47**, 361–373.

Lloyd, H.M., Paisley, C.M. and Mela, D.J. (1995) Barriers to the adoption of reduced-fat diets in a UK population. *Journal of the American Dietetic Association*, **95**, 316–322.

Losowsky, M.S. (1978) Effects of dietary fibre on intestinal absorption, in *Dietary Fibre, Current Development of Importance to Health* (ed. K.W. Heaton), John Libbey, London, 129.

Maezaki, Y., Tsuji, K., Nakagawa, Y., Akimoto, M., Tsugita, T., Takekawa, W., Terada, A. and Mitsuoka, T. (1993) Hypocholesterolemic effect of chitosan in adult males. *Bioscience, Biotechnology and Biochemistry*, **57**, 1439–1444.

Mattes, R.D. (1996) Dietary compensation by humans for supplemental energy provided as ethanol or carbohydrate in fluids. *Physiology and Behaviour*, **59**, 179–187.

Mela, D.J. (1993) Consumer estimates of the percentage of energy from fat in common foods. *European Journal of Clinical Nutrition*, **47**, 735–740.

Mela, D.J. (1995) Understanding fat preference and consumption: applications of behavioural sciences to a nutritional problem. *Proceedings of the Nutrition Society*, **54**, 453–464.

Mela, D.J. (1997) Impact of macronutrient-substituted foods on food choice and dietary intake. *Annals of the New York Academy of Sciences*, **819**, 96–107.

Mela, D.J. and Sacchetti, D.A. (1991) Sensory preferences for fats: relationship with diet and body composition. *American Journal of Clinical Nutrition*, **53**, 908–915.

Miller, K.W. and Allgood, G.S. (1993). Nutritional assessment of Olestra, a non-caloric fat substitute. *International Journal of Food Sciences and Nutrition*, **44** (suppl. 1), S77–S82.

Miller, D.L., Hammer, V.A., Peters, J.C. and Rolls, B.J. (1995) Effects of substituting fat-free (Olestra) potato chips on 24 hour fat and energy intake. *FASEB* Apr 1995 (Part 1): A190, Abstract No. 1110.

Munoz, J.M. and Harland, B.F. (1992) Overview of the effects of dietary fibre on the utilisation of minerals and trace elements, in *CRC Handbook of Dietary Fibre in Human Nutrition* (ed. Spiller, G.A.), CRC Press, Inc., Boca Raton, California, pp. 245–254.

Naismith, D.J. and Rhodes, C. (1995) Adjustment in energy intake following the covert removal of sugar from the diet. *Journal of Human Nutrition and Dietetics*, **8**, 167–175.

Nauss, J.L. (1983) The binding of micellar lipids to chitosan. *Lipids*, **18**: 714–719.

Pasquet, P. and Apfelbaum, M. (1994) Recovery of initial body weight and composition after long-term massive overfeeding in men. *American Journal of Clinical Nutrition*, **60**, 861–863.

Paul, A.A. and Southgate, D.A. (eds McCance and Widdowson), (1978) *The Composition of Foods*, 4th edn, HMSO, London.

Pierce, D.K., Conner, S.L., Sexton, G., Calvin, L., Connor, W.E. and Matarazzo, J.D. (1984) Knowledge and attitudes towards coronary heart disease and nutrition in Oregon families. *Preventative Medicine*, **13**, 390–395.

Porikos, K.P. and Van Itallie, T.B. (1984) Efficacy of low-calorie sweeteners in reducing food intake, in *Aspartame: Physiology and Biochemistry* (ed. L.D. Stegink), Marcel Dekker Inc., New York, pp. 273–286

Raats, M.M. and Sparks, P. (1995) Unrealistic optimism about diet-related risks: implications for interventions. *Proceedings of the Nutrition Society*, **54**, 737–745.

Raben, A. (1995) *Appetite and Carbohydrate Metabolism*, PhD thesis, Royal Veterinary and Agricultural University, Copenhagen.

Rolls, B.J., Pirragha, P.A., Jones, M.B. and Peters, J.C. (1992) Effects of Olestra on non caloric fat substitute on daily energy and fat intakes. *American Journal of Clinical Nutrition*, **56**, 84–92.

Royal College of Physicians (1993) Obesity report. *Journal of the Royal College of Physicians London*, **17**, 3–58.

Rubner, M. (1885) Calorimetrische untersuchungen. *Zeitschrift fur Biologie*, **19**, 535–562.

Schoeller, A.D. (1990) How accurate is self-reported dietary energy intake? *Nutrition Reviews*, **48**, 373–379.

Seidell, J. (1995) Obesity in Europe: scaling an epidemic. *International Journal of Obesity*, **19** (suppl. 3), S1–S4.

Southgate, D.A.T. (1982) *Dietary Fibre in Health and Disease* (eds G.V. Vahouny and D. Kritchevsky), Plenum Press, New York.

Southgate, D.A.T. and Durnin, J.V.G.A. (1970) Calorie conversion factors: an experimental re-assessment of the factors used in the calculation of energy value of human diets. *British Journal of Nutrition*, **24**, 517–535.

Sparti, A., Windhauser, M., Lovejoy, J. and Bray, G. (1995) Subjects eat for carbohydrate not calories after dietary fat replacement with Olestra. American Journal of Clinical Nutrition, 61(4), 902.

Spiller, G.A. (ed) (1992) *CRC Handbook of Dietary Fibre in Human Nutrition*, CRC Press, Inc., Boca Raton, California.

Stevens, J. (1988) Does dietary fibre affect food intake and body weight? *Journal of the American Dietetic Association*, **88**, 939.

Stubbs, R.J. (1995) Macronutrients effects on appetite. *International Journal of Obesity Related Metabolism and Disorders*, **19**(5), S11–S19.

Stubbs, R.J., Harbron, C.G., Murgatroyd, P.R. and Prentice, A.M. (1995) Covert manipulation of dietary fat and energy density: effect on substrate flux and food intake in men feeding *ad libitum*. *American Journal of Clinical Nutrition*, **62**(2), 316–330.

Stubbs, R.J., Ritz, P., Coward, W.A. and Prentice, A. M. (1995) Covert manipulation of the ratio of dietary fat to energy density: effect on food intake and energy balance in free-living men feeding *ad libitum*. *American Journal of Clinical Nutrition*, **62**(2), 330–338.

Stubbs, R.J., Harbron, C.G. and Prentice, A.M. (1996) The effect of covertly manipulating the dietary fat to carbohydrate ratio of isoenergetically dense diets on *ad libitum* food intake in free-living humans. *International Journal of Obesity*, **20**, 651–660.

Stubbs, R.J., Johnstone, A.M. and Harbron, C.G. (1997) The effect of covertly manipulating the energy density of high-carbohydrate diets on *ad libitum* food intake in 'pseudo free-living' humans. *Proceedings of the Nutrition Society*.

Sugano, M., Fujikawa, T., Hiratsuji, Y., Nakashima, K., Fukuda, N. and Hasegawa, A. (1980) Novel use of chitosan as a hypocholesterolemic agent in rats. *American Journal of Clinical Nutrition*, **33**, 787–793.

Terry, R.D., Oakland, M.J. and Ankeny, K. (1991) Factors associated with adoption of dietary behaviour to reduce heart disease risk among males. *Journal of Nutrition Education*, **23**, 154–159.

Thacharidi, D. and Rao, K.P. (1995) Development and *in vitro* evaluation of chitosan based transdermal drug delivery systems for the controlled delivery of propanolol hydrochloride. *Biomaterials*, **16**, 145–148.

Tremblay, A., Lavallee, N., Almeras, N., Allard, L., Despres, J.P. and Bouchard, C. (1991) Nutritional determinants of the increase in energy intake associated with a high-fat diet. *American Journal of Clinical Nutrition*, **53**, 1134–1137.

Urban, N., White, E., Anderson, G.L., Curry, S. and Kristal, A.R. (1992) Correlates of maintenance of a low-fat diet among women in the women's health trial. *Preventative Medicine*, **21**, 279–291.

Van Amelsvoort, J.M.M. and Weststrate, J.A. (1992) Amylose-amylopectin ratio in a meal affects postprandial variables in male volunteers. *American Journal of Clinical Nutrition*, **55**, 712–718.

Van Dokkum, W., Wesstra, A. and Schippers, F.A. (1982) Physiological effects of fibre rich types of bread 1. The effect of dietary fibre from bread on the mineral balance of young men. *British Journal of Nutrition*, **47**, 451–460.

Van Stratum, P., Lussenburg, R.N., van Wezel, L.A., Vergroesen, A.J. and Cremer, H.D. (1978) The effect of dietary carbohydrate:fat ratio on energy intake by adult women. *American Journal of Clinical Nutrition*, **31**, 206–212.

Vartianinen, E., Puska, P., Pietinen, P., Nissinen, A., Leino, U. and Uusitalo, U. (1986) Effects of dietary fat modification on serum lipids and blood pressure in children. *Acta Paediatrica Scandinavica*, **75**, 396–401.

Walls, E.K. and Koopmans, H.S. (1992) Differential effects of intravenous glucose, amino acids and lipid on daily food intake in rats. *American Journal of Physiology*, **262**, R225–R234.

Warwick, Z.S. and Schiffman, S.S. (1992) Role of dietary fat in calorie intake and weight gain. *Neuroscience and Biobehavioural Reviews*, **16**, 585–596.

Westrate, J.A. and van het Hof, K.H. (1995) Sucrose polyester and plasma carotenoid concentrations in healthy subjects. *American Journal of Clinical Nutrition*, **62**, 591–597.

Wolever, T.M.S. and Jenkins, D.J.A. (1992) Effect of dietary fibre and foods on carbohydrate metabolism, in *CRC Handbook of Dietary Fibre in Human Nutrition* (ed. G.A. Spiller), CRC Press, Inc., Boca Raton, California, pp. 111–152.

World Health Organisation (1990) *Nutrition and the Prevention of Chronic Diseases,* WHO Technical Report Series No 797.

Zimmermanns, N. and van het Hof, K. *The Effect of Light Products on Food Intake and Indicators of Health* (undated pamphlet), Unilever Research Laboritorium, Vlaadingen, The Netherlands.

6 Nutrition and genetically engineered foods

CLAIRE DOMONEY, PHIL MULLINEAUX and
ROD CASEY

Introduction

Biotechnology is a science that has been employed throughout the history of
mankind to improve food production, and the impact of centuries of developments in plant and animal breeding and domestication, and in brewing, fermentation and bread-making skills, is clear. Modern gene biotechnology, or genetic
engineering, is a relatively recent development of this science that has occurred
over the past decade and the application of this to food production has resulted
in a wave of new food products that are beginning to enter the market-place.
Although there are now 16 approvals in the UK for the use of genetically modified organisms, or material derived from them, in food, only two of these have
so far been put on sale in supermarkets. These two products are a paste made
from genetically modified tomatoes and a cheese made from chymosin that has
been isolated from a microbe modified to produce this protein. About 80% of
the current research in plant biotechnology is directed towards the improvement
of food plants and it is likely therefore that there will be a large increase in the
number of food products derived from genetically modified organisms available
in supermarkets. The impact of plant biotechnology is likely to be even greater
in the future with an ever-increasing vegetarian population and the continuing
search by food manufacturers for novel, palatable and nutritious plant-derived
meat replacers. This chapter concentrates on aspects of food plant genetic modification, or manipulation, and its nutritional implications, together with the difficulties associated with the aims and objectives of this work. Since there is only
one example of a commercial food product made from a genetically modified
higher plant, this chapter will focus necessarily on general aspects of such work
and speculate on the likely outcome of the underpinning work currently in
progress.

The broad aims of plant genetic manipulation

The principal aim of all research directed at food plant manipulation is the
improvement of quality characteristics. These characteristics may be defined by
food manufacturers, consumers, growers or breeders. Food manufacturers and
consumers will define quality in terms of characteristics apparent in the end
product, whereas growers and breeders consider plant quality in relation to

whole plant response to the environment and its ability to perform under adverse conditions, such as drought and extremes of temperature, and to withstand attack by microorganisms and insects. In many cases, the two definitions of quality will be at variance with each other and, indeed, may result in completely opposing objectives. For example, a protein that gives a plant resistance to attack by insects may be one that is defined as an antinutrient by the food industry and the protein is at once both desirable and undesirable. There are many examples of this dilemma and some of these will be referred to later.

Any group of broad general targets decided on for genetic manipulation may be subdivided by considering the complexity of the biological process leading to a quality characteristic. For example, production of a protein may be achieved by introducing a copy of a gene for the desired protein into the target plant or, if removal of the protein is required, by expression of an antisense, or back-to-front, copy of the gene to interfere with its normal expression. Surprisingly, introducing an additional sense copy of a gene into plants can lead to inactivation of both the introduced and the resident genes, a process referred to as sense gene suppression. Sense suppression of the enzyme polygalacturonase is the basis for the genetically modified tomato with improved rates of ripening and resistance to splitting, now marketed by the foodstore chains Safeway and J. Sainsbury as a purée (Grierson, 1996). Although there are many problems associated with these gene manipulation approaches, in their simplest form expression of one gene is sufficient to achieve the desired result. On the other hand, manipulation of characteristics such as taste or antioxidant content (pages 120 and 124) demands dissection of complex pathways, elucidation of the steps responsible for control of those pathways and intelligent approaches to alteration of the enzymes responsible for these steps. A main concern of these manipulations in food plants, from the viewpoint of a nutritionist or a plant biologist/pathologist, is the possible inadvertent and unintended alteration of other processes. In many situations, an unintended alteration may be an end result that could not have been predicted using available knowledge and, indeed, could have been learned only by performing the manipulations. In other situations, however, a sound basic knowledge of the target genes, their activities during plant development and the proteins they encode can greatly assist rational manipulation with desired consequences. A great deal of knowledge has already been accrued through the study of naturally occurring mutant forms of particular genes and these studies have highlighted the links and relationships between different pathways in plants.

The science of genetics is based on Mendel's observations of characteristics, including a wrinkled-seeded mutation, in peas. Peas carrying this mutation have been used by the fresh food industry for a long time, because their seeds are sweeter. However, it is only in recent years that the biochemical basis for this mutation has been understood. It is now clear that a defect in a starch-synthesizing enzyme is the primary determinant of seed wrinkling in these peas (Bhattacharyya et al., 1990). However, the defect affects not only the type and quantity of starch that is made but results in a cascade effect, ultimately affecting the type and amount of seed protein and oil, the sugar and water contents of the seed and eventually the seed shape (Wang and Hedley, 1993). It is the basic knowledge acquired from studies such as this, and from related studies in other plants, that allows certain predictions to be made about the consequences of manipulating the activities of other starch-synthesizing genes for specific purposes.

Tools required for plant genetic manipulation

In considering the likelihood of achieving a desired end product with or without undesired secondary effects, it is necessary also to consider the tools and specific knowledge that are required for a particular genetic manipulation. First, the desired gene should be identified and its expression in its original home as fully understood as possible. The expression of this gene may be mimicked in another plant by the introduction of this gene, together with all its control sequences, into the second plant. Gene control sequences, or promoters, have been widely studied and most information about important regulatory control elements has come from studies in which promoters and marker genes have been introduced into other plants where their activities have been monitored and dissected. If a more widespread expression of a gene is required than is observed in its parent plant, then a different promoter will be required. In many cases, constitutive or semi-constitutive promoters have been used for general expression. This may be desirable, for example, in expressing proteins that give a plant resistance to a disease but the chances of secondary effects are much greater here, where interference with other plant processes may result from constitutive promoter control, and widespread expression, of a foreign gene. One illustration of this lies in experiments designed to retard tomato fruit ripening by interfering with the synthesis of the fruit-ripening hormone. A general interference with the synthesis of S-adenosyl methionine (SAM), a precursor of the hormone, resulted in plants that were very stunted and sick. However, by restricting the interference in SAM metabolism to late stages of fruit development, through the use of appropriate control sequences, other plant processes were unaffected and the desired result was achieved (Good *et al.*, 1994).

The techniques used for the introduction of novel genes into plants, plant transformation, are still relatively inefficient and the small number of transformed plants that contain the gene of interest must be segregated from untransformed ones. This is currently achieved by co-transformation with a herbicide or antibiotic-resistance gene. If the plant can grow in the presence of the herbicide or antibiotic, then it contains a resistance gene and is also likely to contain the gene of interest. These transformation procedures, in their present form, necessarily result in plants expressing not only the primary target gene but also an additional resistance gene. Any effects resulting from the latter also need to be considered in the experimental design and planning stage, but it is considered that these resistance genes are unlikely to be active following any cooking or processing of food and, in any case, are likely to be destroyed by digestion. Nonetheless, concerns over resistance genes resulted in the initial limitation, in the UK, to marketing of genetically modified tomatoes as a processed, heat-treated paste. Research efforts continue to seek alternative methods to introduce the desired genes only into food plants. In this connection, it should be emphasized that, with conventional plant breeding, linked genes are transferred along with a gene specifying a desired character and, although the proportion of the former is reduced by backcrossing, residual linked genes remain whose identities and effects are uncharacterized. In this respect, genetic manipulation differs from conventional plant breeding in that it allows species barriers to be crossed for gene transfer and it also allows the introduction of known and characterized genetic material.

Specific targets for the genetic manipulation of food plants

Quality characteristics, as defined by food manufacturers and consumers, include parameters as diverse as crop composition (protein, sugar, starch, oil, antinutrient, allergen and antioxidant content and composition), taste, aroma and shelf-life of the food products. As mentioned earlier, definition of these characteristics alone may result in diametrically opposed objectives and targets. This chapter cannot provide an in-depth analysis of current research in all the above areas. It seeks, however, to highlight aspects of research in some of these areas in relation to knowledge that has been gained and the likely value of this to nutrition and food.

Manipulation of storage products

Plant storage products make a very important contribution to the dietary intake of energy and protein in animals, including humans. In the human diet, this contribution can be direct from the plant or indirect through the consumption of meat derived from animals fed on the plant products. As a result of this utilization of plant storage reserves by food and feed industries, a lot of attention has focused on the properties of these major compounds and on the possibilities that exist for their manipulation. Plant storage organs accumulate reserves of proteins, oils and carbohydrates, including starches, and any manipulation of these is theoretically possible, provided there is no ensuing detrimental effect on the biological function of the storage organ and there is a capacity within the organ for any intended overproduction of target compounds in terms of supply of key building blocks.

Nutritional compounds. Storage compounds such as starch are already widely used by the food industry. Starch is used, for example, in sauces, yoghurts and as a thickening agent. At present, much of the demand for different types of starch is satisfied through their chemical interconversion. This is not only expensive but is also undesirable in that it uses chemicals and generates waste. Genetically modified plants that store starches with different composition and functional properties are therefore viewed as a cleaner option in food production. Clearly the pathways leading to starch are complex and are interlinked with other pathways, so predicting the outcome of any given alteration in a starch-synthesizing enzyme is not straightforward. However, as mentioned earlier, much has been learned from studies of naturally occurring mutants, such as the wrinkled-seeded pea.

Apart from their advantages in food processing technology, plants with genetically modified starches have direct nutritional and health implications. Variation in the extent of digestibility of different starches can have important implications for health and a high proportion of starch that is resistant to digestion is considered to be beneficial in the human diet (Liljeberg, 1995), where energy is not of primary consideration. In developing countries, however, a higher content of digestible starch would be considered desirable. The quantitative contribution to energy metabolism of different carbohydrate sources is a matter of debate (Livesey and Elia, 1995) and current studies using sources of mutant starches can be expected to yield much information.

Based on observations of naturally occurring mutants, directed alterations in starch synthesis can be expected to have an impact on pathways to other storage products, for example oil and protein. Desirable changes in oil composition could, therefore, be derived either as a secondary effect of another modification (Wang and Hedley, 1993) or as a result of expressing an introduced gene encoding a fatty acid modifying enzyme. The latter approach has been adopted for oil-rich crops and is aimed at redirecting the profile of fatty acids that are synthesized, research that is aimed partly at generating healthier oils (Murphy, 1994).

Protein is a storage compound that is of great importance in animal and human nutrition since animals have specific requirements for ten essential amino acids, in addition to a general need for dietary protein. Proteins from different plants are deficient in one or more of the ten essential amino acids. Although these deficiencies can be very much reduced by a diet composed of protein from different plant sources, thereby overcoming the deficiency associated with any particular one, there has long been an interest in obtaining a nutritionally complete plant protein source (de Lumen, 1992). This would have great impact in developing nations and would also be relevant to the animal feed industry where, to overcome deficiencies in sulphur-containing amino acids in legume seed protein, methionine is often added to animal feed formulas, a practice that is both expensive and inconvenient. Legume seeds are a rich source of protein and in order to obtain a nutritionally balanced legume protein the characterization and genetic manipulation of relevant genes in these species has been undertaken. This is work that also has a clear benefit in the further development of products aimed at the growing vegetarian market.

Early experiments to introduce extra sulphur-containing amino acids into legume proteins met with limited practical success, although much was learned from the exercise in terms of protein functionality and the feasibility of altering particular domains of proteins (Saalbach *et al.*, 1995a). Several drawbacks to engineering existing seed proteins, besides that of interfering with their functionality, have been highlighted (Müntz *et al.*, 1997). An alternative approach has been to introduce genes encoding sulphur amino-acid-rich proteins from other species into legumes. Two candidate protein genes have been identified, one in Brazil nut (Altenbach *et al.*, 1987) and the other in sunflower (Kortt *et al.*, 1991). A gene encoding the methionine-rich Brazil nut albumin protein has been introduced into the narbon bean (a Mediterranean grain legume that is closely related to the broad bean) and into soybean (Saalbach *et al.*, 1994; Townsend and Thomas, 1994; Saalbach *et al.*, 1995b). Transformed narbon beans expressing the novel protein at up to 5% of extractable seed protein have been reported and this has been reflected in a doubling of the total methionine content of seed flour (Saalbach *et al.*, 1995b). Soybean lines expressing the novel protein as 10% of extractable seed protein showed, however, only a 26% increase in methionine content (Townsend and Thomas, 1994; Müntz *et al.*, 1997). Further analyses of these transformed plants have shown that the metabolic demands imposed by expressing high levels of a sulphur amino-acid-rich protein have caused competition for the formation of sulphur-containing compounds. In the narbon bean, although the methionine content of transgenic seeds was higher as a result of expression of the foreign protein, the total sulphur content was unchanged as a result of a proportional decrease in the formation of a sulphur-rich dipeptide, γ-glutamyl-S-ethenyl-cysteine (GEC) (Müntz *et al.*, 1997). In soybean, the unexpectedly small increase in methionine content of transformed lines was found to be due to a suppression of the synthesis of other methionine-containing proteins, including a protease inhibitor protein (see later) (Müntz *et al.*, 1997).

These experiments have demonstrated the feasibility of engineering the sulphur-containing amino acid content of the seed protein of economically important grain legumes. However, the secondary changes that were observed were unexpected and have highlighted a lack of knowledge in these plants of sulphur supply, the control of pathways of sulphur metabolism, the mechanism by which amino acids can be channelled from one synthetic pathway to another and the control of gene expression by amino acid supply. Early experiments on the effects of sulphur starvation on protein synthesis in peas provide some answers to the last of these questions (Beach *et al.*, 1985). It should be noted that, in the case of transgenic narbon bean and soybean expressing a novel protein, at least some of the secondary effects, although unplanned, were in fact beneficial. The dipeptide GEC is an unpalatable constituent of animal fodder, preventing more widespread use of narbon bean (Müntz *et al.*, 1997). Protease inhibitors are equally considered to be undesirable constituents of food and decreasing their amount is an objective that has been pursued by other means (see later). In reality, however, any further use of the Brazil nut albumin gene for genetic engineering experiments will be limited since this albumin has been shown to be the major allergen of Brazil nut (Nordlee *et al.*, 1996). Similar allergenicity testing will have to be performed on other candidate proteins for food plant transformation. Furthermore, possibilities for identifying and removing domains of proteins that are responsible for allergic responses in animals need to be investigated.

Antinutritional compounds. Several diverse groups of antinutritional compounds have been identified in plants and these differ in relative importance among species. Derivatives of sugars, oligosaccharides, are classified as antinutritional compounds because of their association with the generation of flatulence and despite the evidence that suggests that these compounds play a positive role in animals in maintaining beneficial gut microflora (Morgan *et al.*, 1992). Genetic manipulation of oligosaccharides to reduce antinutritional effects, while retaining effects that are beneficial to animal health, may be possible but will require greater understanding of pathways in plants to these compounds than is currently available. It should also be considered that oligosaccharides perform beneficial roles in plants, such as providing protection against frost damage and possibly having a role during seed desiccation (de Lumen, 1992), and because of this only limited alterations to these compounds may be practical. A class of oligosaccharides abundant in grain legumes, the raffinose oligosaccharides, has been shown to be affected by mutations in starch-synthesizing enzymes (Frias *et al.*, 1996) and once again desirable changes may be effected as an indirect consequence of an alteration in a distinct pathway.

Several plant compounds have been shown to interfere with digestion in animals and these have been targets for removal or modification in order to improve the quality of food plant products. Phytates, for example, are present in many plant seeds, represent an unavailable source of phosphorus in plant ingredients and can bind cations that are necessary for the action of many enzymes. The potential for expressing in plants a microbial enzyme, phytase, which can degrade phytates, has been explored (Pen *et al.*, 1993). Addition of transgenic tobacco seeds, containing microbial phytase, to a phosphorus-deficient diet was shown to be very effective in improving the performance of broilers (Pen *et al.*, 1993). This approach may be extended ultimately to the problems caused by other antinutritional compounds, including allergens.

Although several other plant compounds have the potential to interfere with animal digestive processes, enzyme inhibitors are generally considered to be these plant proteins that irreversibly bind to and inhibit animal digestive enzymes. The primary action of protease inhibitor proteins, and the secondary effects on the pancreas and the synthesis of digestive enzymes, which have been clearly demonstrated in small animals (Liener and Kakade, 1980), have resulted in these inhibitors being the focus of much attention in nutritional consideration of plant food products. Legumes are particularly rich sources of protease inhibitor proteins and many legume products are processed by a combination of heat and pelleting in order to denature and inactivate inhibitors. This processing, besides being considered to be inadequate for complete inactivation in some cases, results necessarily in a compromise product, since negative nutritional effects on, for example, amino acid bioavailability can be caused by the treatment (Classen et al., 1993). Genetic manipulation of inhibitors offers the possibility of providing a raw material that may be processed both more cheaply and in such a way as to cause less damage to the nutrients present. It is clear, however, that there are many different types of inhibitor proteins present in plants. These have been grouped into at least 12 classes (Richardson, 1991) and so generalizations as to their nutritional effects cannot be made, even for inhibitors of the same class. The exact antinutritional status of many inhibitor proteins requires clarification because, in many cases, antinutritional effects in whole animals are inferred from assays using purified enzymes or from studies using different inhibitors (Al-Wesali et al., 1995). These proteins provide a good example of those that pose a problem in quality definition: whereas they are regarded as antinutritional by food and feed industries, transfer to and expression of some inhibitor genes in other plants have been shown to improve plant performance by preventing attack by insects (Hilder et al., 1990). The identification of wild species of soybeans lacking some of the major protease inhibitor proteins that are present in soybean cultivars (Domagalski et al., 1992) suggests that not all inhibitor proteins are essential for plant function and that at least some of those present in seeds may be candidates for removal by genetic manipulation in other species. Much groundwork is required, therefore, to establish the precise roles of individual inhibitors and the scope for interfering with their expression.

The possible positive role that plant inhibitors may play in the prevention of animal tumorigenesis should also be considered in their genetic manipulation. Protease inhibitors from soybean, field bean and amaranth have been implicated as effective chemoprotectors against carcinogenesis (Le Guen and Birk, 1993; Fernandes and Banerji, 1995) and, as such, increases in their concentration may be a desired objective.

Investigation and characterization of the inhibitor proteins that are present in pea seeds have shown how proteins of different inhibitory potency are derived from two very similar closely linked genes (Domoney et al., 1994, 1995). Experimental data such as these allow methods to be devised for suppression of inhibitor gene expression in seeds without interfering with expression of the same or related genes in other plant parts in response to attack by pests. However, much of the information about the dispensability or otherwise of these and other genes in plants will come ultimately from transgenic plants in which gene activities have been suppressed through antisense gene technology (see earlier). The demonstration of inhibitor gene activity in other plant parts under normal growing conditions, for example in alfalfa roots in response to microbes in the soil (McGurl *et al.*, 1995), validates a selective approach to manipulation of these genes. With continuing improvements in transformation procedures for economically important crops, the information base on which rational gene manipulation can proceed will grow exponentially.

Manipulation of taste and aroma

The manipulation of taste and aroma in food plants involves consideration of a plethora of compounds whose roles in plants may not be understood and may be very complex to dissect. An example of such a group of compounds is the glucosinolate family, which is associated with undesirable sulphurous smells and flavours or an astringent taste in many *Brassica* species, including oilseed rape. Removal of these glucosinolates from oilseed rape would greatly increase the value of the seed protein-rich meal residue, after oil extraction, for animal feed and vegetarian food products (Murphy, 1996). However, in light of the fact that other glucosinolates and their derivatives can protect animals from chemically induced cancers (Tawfiq *et al.*, 1995), manipulation of genes encoding enzymes on the pathways to these compounds needs to be selective. Furthermore, the plant leaf glucosinolate pattern must also be considered as this is very important in plant defence responses in *Brassica* and certain other cruciferous genera. Leaf glucosinolates reduce the palatability of leaf tissue to generalist herbivores, such as pigeons, slugs, snails and insects, but also attract and stimulate feeding and egg-laying by specialist insects, such as flea beetles. Genetic, seasonal and environmental differences both in total glucosinolate and in the ratio of individual glucosinolates have been examined (Mithen *et al.*, 1995) and both parameters have been shown to be important in mediating plant–herbivore interactions, with overall increases in glucosinolate content reducing the extent of grazing by pigeons and slugs but increasing in particular types of aliphatic glucosinolates associated with increases in flea beetle feeding (Giamoustaris and Mithen, 1995). Studies such as these have led to the conclusion that optimal glucosinolate profiles will depend on prevalence of pests in particular geographical areas and other methods of control (Giamoustaris and Mithen, 1995) and serve to illustrate the complexities associated with manipulation of a single family of compounds in plants.

Many of the volatile aroma compounds of tomatoes (Buttery *et al.*, 1987), bananas (Tressl and Drawert, 1973), cucumbers (Galliard and Phillips, 1976) and many other fruits and vegetables have been attributed to lipoxygenase (LOX)-associated lipid oxidation pathways (Figure 6.1). LOX enzyme activity is present in probably every part of all plants, increasing in amounts under stress conditions to play a role in plant defence reactions, but is also present in large amounts in unstressed parts of certain plants. Potato tubers and soybean seeds, for example, both contain high levels of LOX activity (Pinsky *et al.*, 1971), far beyond that which is essential; it appears to be possible to remove the activity from soybean seeds without detriment to the plant (Pfeiffer *et al.*, 1992).

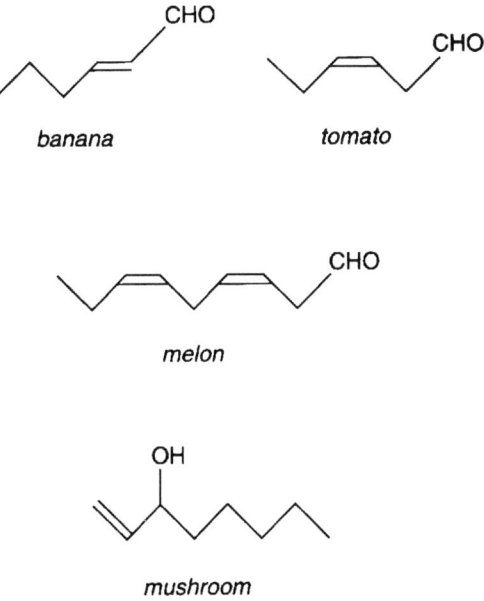

banana   tomato

melon

mushroom

Figure 6.1 Some fruit and vegetable taste and aroma compounds thought to be derived from lipoxy-genase-associated lipid oxidation.

Although it is not obvious why large amounts of LOX should have evolved in these two particular examples, it is clear from many studies that different LOXs have different specificities and play different physiological roles.

All LOXs catalyse the same reaction, incorporating molecular oxygen into polyunsaturated fatty acids (PUFAs) to form the corresponding *cis–trans* conjugated hydroperoxides (HPOs). Linoleic and linolenic acids are the most common PUFAs in plant organs. The reaction is important in the context of food quality because it destroys important essential PUFAs. It also forms highly reactive, toxic chemicals (the HPOs) that must be detoxified by the plant before they cause damage. Plant cells have two ways of carrying out such detoxification. The first is the scission of the carbon chain, at the point of oxygen insertion, by hydroperoxide lyase. Such splitting of, for example, the 13HPO of linoleic acid will produce a 12-carbon compound that can be converted into the so-called 'wound hormone' traumatin (Zimmerman and Caudron, 1979) and a volatile 6-carbon aldehyde, *n*-hexanal. The 13HPO of linolenic acid will give rise to hexenals, including *cis*-3-hexenal, *trans*-3- hexenal and *trans*-2-hexenal. The last is an effective bacteriocide and thus the lipid oxidation pathway plays a role in plants' defence strategies (Croft *et al.*, 1993). Short-chain unsaturated aldehydes, and alcohols derived from them, are also important and desirable components of the tastes and flavours of many fruits and vegetables, whereas *n*-hexanal is primarily responsible for the undesirable 'grassy–beany' flavour of soybean and other legume seed protein products (Fujimaki *et al.*, 1965). LOXs are therefore both desirable and undesirable components of plant organs in the context of taste and flavour generation.

Manipulation of the amounts of LOX in particular plant parts might be expected to have a significant effect on the generation of tastes and flavour compounds, and this has proved to be the case in soybean and pea seeds. Removal of LOX isoform 2 (LOX-2) from soybean seeds (which normally contain three LOX isoforms) through conventional mutant identification and breeding results in improved consumer acceptability of full-fat soy flour and unblanched soymilk preparations from the seeds that lack LOX-2 (Davies *et al.*, 1987). This improvement, perceived in taste trials as lower scores for beany, rancid and oily flavour and aroma attributes, was correlated with a decrease in lipid oxidation and seems to be a consequence of decreased *n*-hexanal and *n*-hexenal production (Matoba *et al.*, 1985; Davies *et al.*, 1987). Similar experiments with peas have shown that genetic removal of LOX-2 also leads to reduced production of 13HPO from linoleic acid and, consequently, reduced *n*-hexanal formation (Wu *et al.*, 1995; Casey *et al.*, 1995). This has implications for the processing of frozen peas, which are routinely blanched before freezing to inactivate enzymes and reduce off-flavour formation on storage. Genetic removal of enzymes that form off-flavours might obviate the need for blanching.

The second detoxification system in plant cells, specific to the 13HPO of linolenic acid, is the initial formation of an allene oxide (Vick and Zimmerman, 1987) that is converted to jasmonate (Vick and Zimmerman, 1984), an important plant growth regulator that activates plant defence genes under stress conditions. The pathway to jasmonate, often referred to as the octadecanoid signalling pathway (Farmer and Ryan, 1992), is activated when, for instance, a tomato or potato plant is wounded by insect damage, with the subsequent jasmonate-mediated stimulation of protease inhibitor genes (see above). The protease inhibitors are then formed throughout the plant and act as an anti-insect protection system. It follows from this that any attempts to manipulate the amounts of LOX in plants, to improve food quality, must take into account the implications for plant stress physiology. Genetic variation has been used successfully to manipulate LOX amounts, as illustrated by peas and soybeans above, and genetic variants with altered amounts of LOX activity may generally have the potential for manipulating flavour volatile profiles, but their usefulness is difficult to assess in widely differing genetic backgrounds. For this reason, genetic engineering has been considered as a strategy to modify the spectrum of aroma compounds, through an increase or decrease in a particular LOX activity; it is, for instance, possible to reduce the amount of LOX in a given plant organ by antisense technology (page 113) and to evaluate the consequences of this for flavour production. For this to be practical, expression of a LOX antisense gene should be limited to the appropriate plant organ, in order to minimize any potentially deleterious effects on whole plant stress responses. Bell *et al.* (1995) have significantly reduced chloroplastic LOX in *Arabidopsis* by genetic engineering and shown that this greatly reduces both the wound-induced production of jasmonate and the activation of jasmonate-responsive genes. Increases in LOX activity and subsequent HPO production could also have adverse effects on the antioxidant status (page 124) of the affected plant organ. Such manipulation therefore requires a thorough understanding of individual LOX species in relation to plant biology. The work of Eiben and Slusarenko (1994) provides an excellent example of the level of understanding that is required to effect directed manipulation without compromising plant health.

Recombinant DNA technology has provided opportunities for the production of industrial enzymes by fermentation. Some of these have been used in foods; probably the best-known example is bovine chymosin (rennin) for cheese-making, which is produced in yeast, fungi or bacteria (*Escherichia coli*), instead of extracting it from calf stomach (page 112). In principle a wide range of enzymes may be produced by fermentation and used either as food additives or as biocatalysts in the formation of food ingredients. LOXs have been produced in *E. coli* using DNA sequences from a number of plant sources, including, for example, soybean (Kramer *et al.*, 1994), rice (Ohta *et al.*, 1992) and potato (Geerts *et al.*, 1994), and different LOX enzymes have been shown to convert PUFAs into different HPOs. These in turn can be used as feedstocks for the production of chirally pure aldehydes, alcohols and other volatile flavour compounds for use as food additives. The major advantage of such an enzyme-based system is the control of stereochemistry.

Manipulation of bread-making quality

In addition to catalysing the formation of hydroperoxides, LOXs can also cause oxidation of other biological compounds, notably proteins and pigments, in a reaction referred to as co-oxidation. The chemistry of LOX-mediated co-oxidation is poorly understood (see Robinson *et al.*, 1995) but it is very significant to nutrition as it modifies the properties of proteins and destroys pigments. Pigment destruction has implications for the colour and antioxidant status of foods (see Whitaker, 1991 and page 124), and products of co-oxidation may possess taste and aroma properties. Protein co-oxidation is most significant, in terms of food, to the bread-making industry.

It is normal practice in bread-making to add soybean flour to wheat flour, the former acting as an enzyme-active bread 'improver'. It improves dough rheology, in particular providing tolerance to over-mixing (Frazier, 1979), and produces a whiter crumb through co-oxidative bleaching of wheat pigments. Other oxidative enzymes can have similar effects on dough rheology, but the important component in enzyme-active soyflour is most likely to be LOX. Wheat has endogenous LOX activity (Shiiba *et al.*, 1991) but it either is present in insufficient quantity, and/or has insufficient co-oxidizing potential, to play the same role as soybean LOX in bread-making. Although the molecular basis of LOX action in bread-making is not clear, it is likely to include the formation of intermolecular disulphide bridges between the high-molecular-weight (HMW) glutenin polypeptides of wheat endosperm. The importance of these polypeptides to bread-making has been clearly demonstrated (Flavell *et al.*, 1989; Shewry *et al.*, 1995a). Their structure (Shewry *et al.*, 1995b) provides a basis for the viscoelastic behaviour of wheat seed protein (see below). LOX may enhance this behaviour by catalysing, through co-oxidation, increased formation of intermolecular disulphide bonds and a stronger viscoelastic network.

There are alternatives to the addition of soybean flour to obtain the benefits of LOX activity. Large amounts of LOX can be produced by microbial fermentation (see above). For this to be practical, and acceptable as a food additive, the yields of enzyme activity will need to be high, the enzyme must have a good co-oxidative capacity, it should be identical to that from natural sources and should not compromise bread quality through the production of objectionable off-flavours. This requires a thorough knowledge of the properties of individual LOX isoforms; it is, for example, well established that only one of the two pea seed LOX isoforms has the ability to co-oxidize pigments and to produce carbonyl compounds (Yoon and Klein, 1979). Such information is essential if particular LOXs are to be produced by fermentation for use as food additives.

Another alternative to the use of soybean flour in bread-making is to genetically engineer wheat to produce a co-oxidizing legume LOX in its seeds. The recent capability to genetically transform wheat (see Shewry *et al.*, 1995b and Christou, 1996) will enable production of new wheat varieties in which protein quality has been enhanced by the expression of transgenes in developing seeds. Such transgenes will include those encoding the HMW glutenins, proteins in which central repeat motifs may form a loose β-spiral with inherent elasticity and terminal cysteinyl residues will provide thiol groups for intermolecular disulphide bond formation. These proteins, which are largely responsible for the elasticity of bread dough, form a polymeric, elastic network that is stabilized by interchain disulphide bonds. Increases in the amount of HMW glutenin protein, achieved by standard plant breeding, are correlated with increased bread-making quality. These findings suggest that it should be possible in the future to genetically engineer bread wheat for improved quality by the introduction and expression of additional copies of HMW glutenin genes. This approach can be coupled with qualitative alterations in the structures of the individual proteins, based on an understanding of their biophysical and functional properties. Initial targets will be the modification of the numbers and distribution of disulphide bonds, the length of the central repetitive domain and the strength of the β-spiral formed by this central region. Details of the approaches and likely future trends in the manipulation of bread-making quality are described in Shewry *et al.* (1995b).

Prospects for manipulation of antioxidant content in plants

Plants synthesize several classes of antioxidants, including ascorbic acid (vitamin C), phenylpropanoids (principally flavonoid pigments), carotenoids, tocopherols (principally α-tocopherol (vitamin E)) and glutathione. All except the last are regarded as important components of our diet. Antioxidants represent a major class of compounds which, in plants, are implicated in protection from a wide range of environmental stresses and in the delay and control of senescence processes in leaves and fruits. Thus the manipulation of antioxidants in plants has the triple prospect of impacting on human nutrition, on the performance of the crop plant during its growing season and on the postharvest performance of the crop product.

This section assesses the prospects and the strategies that have been or could be employed for increasing the content of one or more antioxidants in crop plant species by genetic manipulation. The species of transgenic plants in which the first experiments were carried out were not, for the most part, food plants and the principal aim of such experiments was not to improve antioxidant content for dietary reasons but to promote plant tolerance to oxidative stress caused by adverse environmental conditions, to manipulate flower colour or simply to gain a better understanding of the biochemistry of the antioxidant in question. Nevertheless, such experiments can be used to assess the prospects for manipulating antioxidants in food crop species with a view to influencing the nutritional or postharvest performance of crop products.

Although the basic requirements and materials for plant genetic manipulation have already been described (page 114), additional conditions have to be met before the biosynthesis or turnover of a metabolic product, such as an antioxidant, can become a subject for genetic manipulation. First, there should be some strong indication of which reactions regulate the biosynthesis and turnover of the antioxidant in question. Second, DNA sequences encoding enzymes that catalyze these reactions in the metabolism of the antioxidant must be isolated or available. A useful alternative tool would be the availability of DNA encoding a regulatory protein capable of co-ordinately controlling the expression of several steps in the metabolism of that antioxidant.

Several approaches have been successful so far in enhancing the content of specific antioxidants. These are:

1. The overproduction of an enzyme catalysing a reaction that is perceived to be a key step in the biosynthesis of the antioxidant. In principle, genetic manipulation techniques can permit the use of a DNA sequence encoding the enzyme from any organism.
2. Overproduction of an enzyme involved in maintaining the pool of an antioxidant in the reduced state. Active antioxidant compounds also have their oxidized counterparts and enzymes have been identified that can recycle the latter to their active reduced states. For example, monodehydroascorbate can be reduced to ascorbic acid by the action of the enzyme monodehydroascorbate reductase (MDAR). Biochemical evidence is now available to support the idea that increasing the capacity of plants to recycle antioxidants to their reduced forms results somehow in an increase in the total pool size of that antioxidant (see below).

3. Manipulation of the expression of a regulatory gene which coordinately controls the expression of genes encoding several steps in a biosynthetic pathway. The advantage of this approach is that one could achieve a measure of control over quite complex metabolic pathways and networks even if no key single reaction has been recognised as a target for manipulation.
4. Successful enhancement of the level of one antioxidant, by manipulation of a key enzyme activity, that leads to a parallel enhancement of the pool size of another antioxidant which is not the immediate subject of genetic manipulation.

Examples of all of the above exist and will be illustrated below for specific antioxidants. However, in some cases unexpected problems emerge with transgenic plants containing altered capacity for antioxidant metabolism. Such experiences serve to illustrate the complexity of the systems being dealt with and the often inadequate state of knowledge of antioxidant biochemistry in plants.

Glutathione (γ-L-glutamylcysteinylglycine, GSH) is not a dietary antioxidant but is nevertheless considered to be a key component in the defence of both plants and animals against oxidative stress (Mannervik *et al.,* 1989; Creissen *et al.,* 1994). It is included for discussion here because of the effects that manipulation of the glutathione pool may have on the ascorbate pool and also because there is some understanding of the biosynthesis of glutathione and the reduction–oxidation (redox) cycles in which it participates. DNA sequences encoding glutathione reductase (GR), which catalyses the reduction of oxidized glutathione (GSSG) to its reduced form (GSH), and γ-glutamylcysteine (γ-EC) synthetase and GSH synthetase, which catalyse the two-step glutathione biosynthetic pathway, are available from plant, animal and bacterial sources.

In order to understand the role of glutathione in the protection of chloroplasts from photo-oxidative stress, tobacco plants were transformed with either the *gshI* or *gshII* genes from *E. coli* that encode γ-EC and GSH synthetases, respectively. These chimaeric genes were constructed to target the enzymes to tobacco chloroplasts. Overproduction of GSH synthetase did not increase the foliar glutathione content but transgenic plants expressing γ-EC synthetase contained up to seven-fold higher concentrations of foliar glutathione. Paradoxically, the latter group of plants showed oxidative stress symptoms (increased hydrogen peroxide amounts, severe necrotic and chlorotic lesions, impaired photosynthetic performance and increased steady-state amounts of messenger RNA for the cytosolic Cu/Zn superoxide dismutase enzyme). These symptoms may be due to the accumulation of γ-EC, the metabolic intermediate in the biosynthesis of glutathione, since tobacco plants containing both transgenes showed almost complete amelioration of the oxidative stress symptoms associated with a decline in amounts of γ-EC and a further rise in amounts of glutathione (Creissen *et al.,* 1996). These data suggest that, provided there is a co-elevation of both steps in the biosynthesis of glutathione, thereby preventing the accumulation of a toxic metabolic intermediate, it is possible to enhance substantially the tissue concentrations of this key antioxidant. If such experiments can be reproduced in crop species, this will allow the effects of enhanced glutathione content on both crop product quality and nutritional value to be determined.

Enhancing GR activity, in one or more of the cytosol, chloroplasts and mitochondria, can lead to improved oxidative stress tolerance in some lines of transgenic tobacco or poplar (Broadbent et al., 1995; Creissen et al., 1995; Foyer et al., 1995). In both plant species, enhancement of GR activity unexpectedly led to an increase in the total foliar concentration of glutathione. The basis for this linkage between an enhanced capacity of a plant tissue to reduce the oxidized form of an antioxidant and the total pool size of that compound remains obscure but may also apply to antioxidants other than glutathione, including ascorbate.

Further work suggests that the amount of MDAR activity may have an influence on the steady-state pool size of ascorbate (Smirnoff and Palanca,1996). Depletion of ascorbate in barley leaves was achieved either by treating them with different concentrations of a herbicide or by subjecting them to various light intensities. Measurement of the activities of ascorbate peroxidase (APX), dehydroascorbate reductase (DHAR) and MDAR revealed a close correlation between MDAR activity and the foliar ascorbate concentration. All of these enzymes collectively shuttle ascorbate back and forth between its oxidized and reduced forms. Sufficient information on MDAR is available for the construction of MDAR transgenes (Grantz et al., 1995; Sano and Asada, 1994) and attempts could be made, therefore, to enhance ascorbate levels in transgenic plant tissues by elevating their amounts of MDAR. However, some authors have cast doubt on this approach because an inverse correlation between the amounts of messenger RNA for MDAR and prevailing ascorbate levels has been observed in several different organs of tomato (Grantz et al., 1995). Overproducing MDAR in transgenic plants of several species may resolve these uncertainties.

Foliar ascorbate content was more than two-fold higher in transgenic poplar plants, overexpressing GR in the chloroplast, than in control plants (Foyer et al., 1995). This is the first example of how manipulating the amount of an enzyme involved in the metabolism of one antioxidant can influence the pool size of another, chemically unrelated, antioxidant. The linkage between glutathione and ascorbate may be through the ascorbate–glutathione cycle, proposed to operate, in its simplest form, as a succession of enzyme-catalysed reactions that link the scavenging of oxyradicals and active oxygen species to the oxidation of ascorbate, reduced in turn by glutathione, which is regenerated by GR (Foyer and Halliwell, 1976).

At present, alternatives to the direct manipulation of the biosynthetic pathway of ascorbate are necessary because not all the steps in this pathway have been deduced. There has been little advance in the knowledge of the biosynthesis of ascorbate since the work of Loewus (1988). Therefore, there is no immediate prospect for manipulating ascorbate levels in plants by directly elevating the activities of key enzymes in the ascorbate biosynthetic pathway.

Phenylalanine is the precursor of the large class of phenolic compounds known collectively as the phenylpropanoids, which include the precursors of the flavonoid pigments, tannins and lignin (Hahlbrock and Grisebach, 1979). Many of these phenolic compounds have been shown to be powerful antioxidants *in vitro* and are now thought to be important dietary constituents that may help to prevent the onset of serious diseases such as cancer (Rice-Evans and Miller, 1995).

The biochemical interconversions in plant phenylpropanoid metabolism are well known, an array of mutants blocked in parts of the pathway to flavonoid pigments has been studied and DNA sequences encoding most of the key steps in pigment biosynthesis and the early steps in the phenylpropanoid biosynthesis are available. Several of the strategies discussed above have been applied to parts of phenylpropanoid metabolism. Overexpression of a bean phenylalanine ammonia-lyase (PAL) gene in transgenic tobacco led to a stimulation of phenyl-propanoid synthesis, although the plants have been of value primarily for study-ing aspects of PAL gene regulation (Lamb *et al.*, 1992).

The successes achieved in the genetic manipulation of flower colour have indicated how flavonoid pigments such as quercitin, considered to be a potent antioxidant (Rice-Evans and Miller, 1995), might be manipulated. Pelargonidin is normally missing from *Petunia* but transformation of a chimaeric gene coding for maize dihydroflavonol 4-reductase (DFR) into this species gave rise to trans-genic plants that had salmon-pink to brick-red coloured flowers resulting from pelargonidin formation (Meyer *et al.*,1987; Folkmann,1993). DFR exists natu-rally in *Petunia* but its substrate specificity differs from that of the maize enzyme in such a way that it does not form pelargonidin.

The highly species-specific nature of many of the biosynthetic steps in flavonoid biosynthesis illustrates the potential difficulties in applying this strat-egy to a spectrum of crop plants. The interrelatedness of the flavonoid classes of pigments makes it almost impossible to predict the outcome of overexpressing any one enzyme in a pathway (Folkmann, 1993). Furthermore, detailed studies on the inheritance of flower colour in transgenic *Petunia* have shown that the expression of a transgene can be highly perturbed in progeny arising from crosses between transgenic and wild-type plants and between different trans-genic lines. This instability was exacerbated by environmental factors such as light intensity, temperature and the age of the plant (Napoli *et al.*, 1990; Folkmann, 1993).

In maize, the regulatory genes *R* and *C1*, control the expression of enzymes catalysing several steps in the biosynthesis of the important flavonoid pigment anthocyanin. The problems of species specificity in manipulating single steps in the biosynthetic networks that give rise to the diversity of flavonoid pigments (see above) should be contrasted with studies on overexpression in transgenic tobacco and *Arabidopsis* of the maize *R* gene product, which is a transcription factor (Folkmann, 1993; Lloyd *et al.*, 1992). In both cases, substantially enhanced anthocyanin production was observed. Additionally, normally unpigmented organs, such as roots, became heavily pigmented in these transgenic plants. The use of a regulatory gene controlling anthocyanin biosynthesis from one species to manipulate the biosynthesis of the same compound in another very different species suggests that a large degree of commonality exists in the regulation of pigmentation in widely different plant species. This could allow for generic approaches to the enhanced production of flavonoid pigments with superior antioxidative activity. However, these approaches may not be straightforward. Further work on overexpression of a transcription factor gene resulted in a severe oxidative stress phenotype. Inhibition of the biosynthesis of phenolic compounds required for cell wall formation resulted and the oxidative stress phenotype may have been a consequence of the depletion of the phenolic compounds, which also act as antioxidants (C. Martin, personal communication). In other words, overexpression of a regulatory gene for a biosynthetic pathway may not have the desirable effect of increasing the concentration of the end product of that pathway.

The tomato fruit is a source of dietary carotenoids (Rice-Evans and Miller, 1995) and a first attempt at manipulating this class of compounds has been reported (Fray *et al.*, 1995). This is the only example so far of the manipulation of a compound with antioxidant properties in a major food crop species. Phytoene synthase is the enzyme responsible for the first committed step in the carotenoid biosynthetic pathway. A general overproduction of the tomato fruit enzyme in transgenic tomatoes resulted in alterations in both the types and quantities of carotenoids in a variety of organs, such as the seed coat, cotyledons, fruit and abscission zones, a pattern of expression that was associated with a dwarf stature; the highest levels of phytoene synthase gene expression gave the most severe stunting. This stunting was associated, in these plants, with a large reduction in amounts of gibberellin A_1 (GA), a plant hormone required for development of normal stature. The dwarfing of the transgenic tomato plants was explained by the diversion of geranylgeranyldiphosphate (GGDP), a key common precursor in the biosynthesis of GA and carotenoids, from GA biosynthesis into carotenoid biosynthesis. While it was apparent that overproduction of phytoene synthase could lead to enhanced synthesis of carotenoids (especially lycopene), it was also clear that several problems will have to be overcome before this strategy can be applied successfully to many plant species. These problems include the diversion of precursors such as GGDP from the biosynthesis of GA and cytokinin (another phytohormone), and the possible undesirable channelling of carotenoid compounds into the biosynthetic pathways for abscisic acid and the xanthophylls. Nevertheless, this work is an important step in the manipulation of plant carotenoid concentrations and in the future it should prove possible to restrict overexpression of phytoene synthase to the tomato fruit, thereby minimizing the described negative effects, as earlier outlined for SAM metabolism (page 114) (Good *et al.*, 1994).

Although the biosynthetic pathways for the tocopherols have been known for some time from isotopic tracer studies (Fryer, 1992), the prospects for the manipulation of vitamin E levels remain poor because of the intractability of isolating and studying the enzymes concerned. The availability of tools (an antibody to, or amino acid sequence information from, an enzyme on the α-tocopherol biosynthetic pathway) would greatly facilitate the direct manipulation of this antioxidant.

The first steps have been taken towards increasing plant concentrations of flavonoids, glutathione, ascorbate and carotenoids, using a genetic engineering approach, but in almost all cases overproduction of the antioxidant has caused problems for the plant. No effort was made in these studies, however, to limit the expression of the transgenes to organs where enhanced antioxidants may do the most good, or no harm, to the plant. As outlined earlier (page 114), the availability of an ever-increasing choice of tissue, organ and inducible promoters allows expression of transgenes to be limited and suggests that the deleterious effects of general antioxidant overproduction in plants can be overcome. The end-use of the crop product will dictate the most desirable ways in which this should be done, for example in the case of tomatoes by limiting the expression of transgenes to the fruit.

From all of the strategies considered, the most promising approach is likely to be the manipulation of regulatory genes that control all, or part, of antioxidant metabolism (Martin, 1996). If ways can be devised for isolating mutants blocked in the biosynthesis of a particular antioxidant, then the rapid advances being made in gene isolation technology will ultimately provide regulatory gene sequences for the future enhancement of the antioxidant content of food plants by genetic manipulation.

Conclusions

The successful genetic manipulation of ripening genes in tomatoes has opened the door to the improvement of many other so-called quality characteristics of food plants using biotechnology. The problems associated with manipulation of many of these characteristics are often linked to a fundamental lack of understanding of the complexity of the relationships among compounds and pathways in plants. Where these relationships and pathways have not been clearly defined previously, using naturally occurring mutants, transgenic plants expressing products of single genes have provided, and will continue to provide, much information that will greatly facilitate the refinement of future experiments. Genetic engineering experiments so far undertaken have demonstrated limitations, for example to the improvement of the sulphur amino acid content of legume seed protein as a result of competition among pathways for sulphur-containing amino acids, to the reduction of particular LOX enzymes without interfering with beneficial plant functions and to increasing the antioxidant content of particular plant organs without deleterious consequences for the plant. Nonetheless, with the knowledge of gene promoter functions and specificities gained from transgenic plants, genes can now be constructed whose activities are restricted in time and space to achieve maximum beneficial effect both for a desired end product and for a healthy plant.

Compromises between plant health and a desired characteristic will often be necessary in the proposed removal or modification of, for example, so-called antinutritional compounds, where beneficial roles in plant development may be suspected. Where such compounds are proteins, a knowledge of protein structure, function and stability can aid in the experimental design for their manipulation. For example, lectins are proteins involved in essential symbiotic functions in legume roots, while being classified as antinutritional compounds in seeds of many legume species. Protein engineering experiments have demonstrated how the normal plant function of modified lectins can be maintained under normal growing conditions while decreasing the stability of such proteins at animal body temperature and hence reducing their antinutritional effects (Hoedemaeker *et al.*, 1993). These experiments serve to illustrate the level of knowledge that will be required for future manipulation of many components of essential plant machinery.

Acknowledgements

We acknowledge the support of MAFF and the BBSRC for research carried out in the Department of Applied Genetics, John Innes Centre. We are grateful to Professor Klaus Müntz, Institute of Plant Genetics and Crop Plant Research, Gatersleben, Germany, for providing information in advance of publication. We thank Tarn Dalzell and Nicola Cooke for their patience in processing this chapter.

References

Altenbach, S.B., Pearson, K.W., Leung, F.W. and Sun, S.S.M. (1987) Cloning and sequence analysis of a cDNA encoding a Brazil nut protein exceptionally rich in methionine. *Plant Molecular Biology*, **8**, 239–250.

Al-Wesali, M., Lambert, N., Welham, T. and Domoney, C. (1995) The influence of pea seed trypsin inhibitors on the *in vitro* digestibility of casein. *Journal of the Science of Food and Agriculture*, **68**, 431–437.

Beach, L.R., Spencer, D., Randall, P.J. and Higgins, T.J.V. (1985) Transcriptional and post-transcriptional regulation of storage protein gene expression in sulfur-deficient pea seeds. *Nucleic Acids Research*, **13**, 999–1013.

Bell, E., Creelman, R.A. and Mullett, J.E. (1995) A chloroplast lipoxygenase is required for wound-induced jasmonic acid accumulation in *Arabidopsis*. *Proceedings of the National Academy of Sciences, USA*, **92**, 9675–9679.

Bhattacharyya, M.K., Smith, A.M., Ellis, T.H.N., Hedley, C. and Martin, C. (1990) The wrinkled-seed character of pea described by Mendel is caused by a transposon-like insertion in a gene encoding starch-branching enzyme. *Cell*, **60**, 115–122.

Broadbent, P., Creissen, G.P., Kular, B., Wellburn, A.R. and Mullineaux, P.M. (1995) Oxidative stress responses in transgenic tobacco containing altered levels of glutathione reductase activity. *Plant Journal*, **8**, 247–255.

Buttery, R.G., Teranishi, R. and Ling, L.C. (1987) Fresh tomato volatiles: a quantitative study. *Journal of Agricultural and Food Chemistry*, **35**, 540–544.

Casey, R., Afzal, N., Domoney, C., Forster, C., Logan, H., O'Neill, M., Wu, Z. and Robinson, D.S. (1995) Pea seed lipoxygenases: Biochemistry, genetics and significance, in *Proceedings of the Second European Conference on Grain Legumes: Improving Production and Utilization of Grain Legumes,* Association Européenne de recherche sur les Protéagineaux, Copenhagen, pp. 406–407.

Christou, P. (1996) Transformation technology. *Trends in Plant Science*, **1**, 423–431.

Classen, H.L., Balnave, D. and Bedford, M.R. (1993) Reduction of legume antinutritional factors using biotechnological techniques, in *Recent Advances of Research in Antinutritional Factors in Legume Seeds*, (eds A.F.B. van der Poel, J. Huisman and H.S. Saini), Wageningen Pers, Wageningen, pp. 501–516.

Creissen, G., Edwards, A. and Mullineaux, P. (1994) Glutathione reductase and ascorbate peroxidase, in *Causes of Photooxidative Stress and Amelioration of Defense Systems in Plants*, (eds C.H. Foyer and P.M. Mullineaux), CRC Press, Boca Raton, pp. 343–364.

Creissen, G.P., Reynolds, H., Xue, Y. and Mullineaux, P. (1995) Simultaneous targeting of pea glutathione reductase and of a bacterial fusion protein to chloroplasts and mitochondria in transgenic tobacco. *Plant Journal*, **8**, 167–175.

Creissen, G.P., Broadbent, P., Stevens, R., Wellburn, A.R. and Mullineaux, P. (1996) Manipulation of glutathione metabolism in transgenic plants. *Biochemical Society Transactions*, **24**, 465–469.

Croft, K.P.C., Jüttner, F. and Slusarenko, A.J. (1993) Volatile products of the lipoxygenase pathway evolved from *Phaseolus vulgaris* (L.) leaves inoculated with *Pseudomonas syringae* pv *phaseolicola*. *Plant Physiology*, **101**, 13–24.

Davies, C.S., Nielsen, S.S. and Nielsen, N.C. (1987) Flavor improvement of soybean preparations by genetic removal of lipoxygenase – 2. *Journal of the American Oil Chemists' Society*, **64**, 1428–1433.

de Lumen, B.O. (1992) Molecular strategies to improve protein quality and reduce flatulence in legumes: a review. *Food Structure*, **11**, 33–46.

Domagalski, J.M., Kollipara, K.P., Bates, A.H., Brandon, D.L., Friedman, M. and Hymowitz, T. (1992) Nulls for the major soybean Bowman–Birk protease inhibitor in the genus *Glycine*. *Crop Science*, **32**, 1502–1505.

Domoney, C., Welham, T., Ellis, N. and Hellens, R. (1994) Inheritance of qualitative and quantitative trypsin inhibitor variants in *Pisum*. *Theoretical and Applied Genetics*, **89**, 387–391.

Domoney, C., Welham, T., Sidebottom, C. and Firmin, J.L. (1995) Multiple isoforms of *Pisum* trypsin inhibitors result from modification of two primary gene products. *FEBS Letters*, **360**, 15–20.

Eiben, H.G. and Slusarenko, A.J. (1994) Complex spatial and temporal expression of lipoxygenase genes during *Phaseolus vulgaris* (L.) development. *Plant Journal*, **5**, 125–135.

Farmer, E.E. and Ryan, C.A. (1992) Octadecanoid precursors of jasmonic acid activate the synthesis of wound-inducible proteinase inhibitors. *The Plant Cell*, **4**, 129–134.

Fernandes, A.O. and Banerji, A.P. (1995) Inhibition of benzopyrene-induced forestomach tumors by field bean protease inhibitor(s). *Carcinogenesis*, **16**, 1843–1846.

Flavell, R.B., Goldsbrough, A.P., Robert, L.S., Schnick, D. and Thompson, R.D. (1989) Genetic variation in wheat HMW glutenin subunits and the molecular basis of bread-making quality. *Bio/Technology*, **7**, 1281–1285.

Folkmann , G. (1993) Control of pigmentation in natural and transgenic plants. *Current Opinions in Biotechnology*, **4**, 159–165.

Foyer, C.H. and Halliwell, B. (1976) The presence of glutathione and glutathione reductase in chloroplasts: a proposed role in ascorbate metabolism. *Planta*, **133**, 21–25.

Foyer, C.H., Souriau, N., Perret, S., Lelandais, M., Kunert, K.-J., Pruvost, C. and Jouanin, L. (1995) Overexpression of glutathione reductase but not glutathione synthetase leads to increases in antioxidant capacity and resistance to photoinhibition in poplars. *Plant Physiology*, **109**, 1047–1057.

Fray, R.G., Wallace, A., Fraser, P.D., Valero, D., Hedden, P., Bramley, P.D. and Grierson, D. (1995) Constitutive expression of a fruit phytoene synthase gene in transgenic tomatoes causes dwarfism by redirecting metabolites from the gibberellin pathway. *Plant Journal*, **8**, 693–701.

Frazier, P.J. (1979) Lipoxygenase action and lipid binding in breadmaking. *Bakers' Digest*, **53**, 8–29.

Frias, J., Fenwick, G.R., Hedley, C.L., Price, K.R., Sørensen, H. and Vidal-Valverde, C. (1996) Improved method for the analysis of α-galactosides in pea by capillary zone electrophoresis (CZE). Comparison with high performance liquid chromatography (HPAC-PAD). *Journal of Chromatography* A, **719**, 213–219.

Fryer, M.J. (1992) The antioxidant effects of thylakoid vitamin E (α-tocopherol). *Plant Cell and Environment*, **15**, 381–392.

Fujimaki, M., Arai, S., Kirigaya, N. and Sakurai, Y. (1965) Studies of flavour compounds in soybean. Part 1. Aliphatic carbonyl compounds. *Agricultural and Biological Chemistry*, **29**, 855–858.

Galliard, T. and Phillips, D.R. (1976) The enzymic cleavage of linoleic acid to C_9 carbonyl fragments in extracts of cucumber (*Cucumis sativus*) fruit and the possible role of lipoxygenase. *Biochimica et Biophysica Acta*, **431**, 278–287.

Geerts, A., Feltkamp, D. and Rosahl, S. (1994) Expression of lipoxygenase in wounded tubers of *Solanum tuberosum* L. *Plant Physiology*, **105**, 269–277.

Giamoustaris, A. and Mithen, R. (1995) The effect of modifying the glucosinolate content of leaves of oilseed rape (*Brassica napus* ssp. *oleifera*) on its interaction with specialist and generalist pests. *Annals of Applied Biology*, **126**, 347–363.

Good, X., Kellogg, J.A., Wagoner, W., Langhoff, D., Matsumura, W. and Bestwick, R.K. (1994) Reduced ethylene synthesis by transgenic tomatoes expressing *S*-adenosylmethionine hydrolase. *Plant Molecular Biology*, **26**, 781–790.

Grantz, A.A., Brummell, D.D. and Bennett, A.B. (1995) Ascorbate free radical reductase mRNA levels are induced by wounding. *Plant Physiology*, **108**, 411–418.

Grierson, D. (1996) Silent genes and everlasting fruits and vegetables? *Nature Biotechnology*, **14**, 828–829.

Hahlbrock, K. and Grisebach, H. (1979) Enzymatic control in the biosynthesis of lignin and flavonoids. *Annual Review of Plant Physiology*, **30**, 105–130.

Hilder, V.A., Gatehouse, A.M.R. and Boulter, D. (1990) Genetic engineering of crops for insect resistance using genes of plant origin, in *Genetic Engineering of Crop Plants* (eds D. Grierson and G. Lycett), Butterworths, London, pp. 51–66.

Hoedemaeker, F.J., van Eijsden, R.R., Díaz, C.L., de Pater, B.S. and Kijne, J.W. (1993) Destabilization of pea lectin by substitution of a single amino acid in a surface loop. *Plant Molecular Biology*, **22**, 1039–1046.

Kortt, A.A., Caldwell, J.B., Lilley, G.G. and Higgins, T.J.V. (1991) Amino acid and cDNA sequences of a methionine-rich 2S protein from sunflower seed (*Helianthus annuus* L.). *European Journal of Biochemistry*, **195**, 329–334.

Kramer, J.A., Johnson, K.R., Dunham, W.R., Sands, R.H. and Funk, M.O. Jr. (1994) Position 713 is critical for catalysis but not for iron binding in soybean lipoxygenase 3. *Biochemistry*, **33**, 15017–15022.

Lamb, C.J., Ryals, J.A., Ward, E.R. and Dixon, R.A. (1992) Emerging strategies for enhancing crop resistance to microbial pathogens. *Bio/Technology*, **10**, 1436–1445.

Le Guen, M.P. and Birk, Y. (1993) Protein protease inhibitors from legume seeds: nutritional effects, mode of action and structure-function relationship, in *Recent Advances of Research in Antinutritional Factors in Legume Seeds* (eds A.F.B. van der Poel, J. Huisman and H.S. Saini), Wageningen Pers, Wageningen, pp. 157–171.

Liener, I.E. and Kakade, N.L. (1980) Protease inhibitors, in *Toxic Constituents of Foodstuffs*, 2nd edn (ed. I.E. Liener), Academic Press, New York, pp. 7–71.

Liljeberg, H. (1995) Nutritional properties of starch in bread: impact of the choice of raw material and/or processing conditions. Ph.D. thesis, Lund University, Sweden.

Livesey, G. and Elia, M. (1995) Short-chain fatty acids as an energy source in the colon: metabolism and clinical implications, in *Physiological and Clinical Aspects of Short-chain Fatty Acids* (eds J.H. Cummings, J.L. Rombeau and T. Sakata), Cambridge University Press, Cambridge, pp. 427–481.

Lloyd, A.M., Walbot, V. and Davis, R.W. (1992) *Arabidopsis* and *Nicotiana* anthocyanin production activated by maize regulators *R* and *C1. Science*, **258**, 1773–1775.

Loewus, F.A. (1988) Ascorbic acid and its metabolic products, in *The Biochemistry of Plants*, vol. 14 (ed J. Preiss) Academic Press, London, pp. 85–107.

Mannervik, B., Carlberg, I. and Larson, K. (1989) Glutathione: General review of mechanism of action, in *Glutathione. Chemical, Biochemical and Medical Aspects*, vol. III: Coenzymes and

Cofactors (eds D. Dolphin, R. Poulson and O. Aramovic), part A, John Wiley & Sons, New York, pp. 187–242.

Martin, C. (1996) Transcription factors and the manipulation of plant traits. *Current Opinion in Biotechnology*, **7**, 130–138.

Matoba, T., Hidaka, H., Narita, H., Kitamura, K., Kaizuma, N. and Kito, M. (1985) Lipoxygenase-2 isoenzyme is responsible for generation of hexanal in soybean homogenate. *Journal of Agricultural and Food Chemistry*, **33**, 852–855.

McGurl, B., Mukherjee, S., Kahn, M. and Ryan, C.A. (1995) Characterization of two proteinase inhibitor (ATI) cDNAs from alfalfa leaves (*Medicago sativa* var. Vernema): the expression of ATI genes in response to wounding and soil microorganisms. *Plant Molecular Biology*, **27**, 995–1001.

Meyer, P., Heidmann, I., Folkmann, G. and Saedler, H. (1987) A new petunia flower colour generated by transformation of a mutant with a maize gene. *Nature*, **330**, 677–678.

Mithen, R., Raybould, A.F. and Giamoustaris, A. (1995) Divergent selection for secondary metabolites between wild populations of *Brassica oleracea* and its implications for plant–herbivore interactions. *Heredity*, **75**, 472–484.

Morgan, A.J., Mul, A.J., Beldman, G. and Voragen, A.G.J. (1992) Dietary oligosaccharides – new insights. *Agro-Food-Industry Hi-Tech*, **3** (6), 35–38.

Müntz, K., Christov, V., Jung, R., Saalbach, G., Saalbach, I., Waddell, D., Pickardt, T. and Schieder, O. (1997) Genetic engineering of high methionine proteins in grain legumes, in *Sulphur Metabolism in Higher Plants. Molecular, Ecophysiological and Nutritional Aspects* (eds W. J. Cram, L.J. De Kok, I. Stulen, C. Brunold and H. Rennenberg), Backhuys Publishers, Leiden, pp. 71–86.

Murphy, D.J. (1994) Transgenic plants – a future source of novel edible and industrial oils. *Lipid Technology*, **6**, 84–91.

Murphy, D.J. (1996) Engineering oil production in rapeseed and other oil crops. *Trends in Biotechnology*, **14**, 206–213.

Napoli, C., Lemieux, C. and Jorgensen, R. (1990) Introduction of a chimaeric chalcone synthase gene into petunia results in reversible co-suppression of homologous genes in *trans*. *The Plant Cell*, **2**, 279–289.

Nordlee, J.A., Taylor, S.L., Townsend, J.A., Thomas, L.A. and Beach, L.R. (1996) Transgenic soybeans containing Brazil nut 2S storage protein. Issues regarding allergenicity, in *Food Allergies and Intolerances* (eds G. Eisenbrand, H. Aulepp, D.D. Dayan, P.S. Elias, W. Grunow, J. Ring and J. Schlatter), VCH Verlagsgesellschaft mbH, Weinheim, pp. 196–202.

Ohta, H., Shirano, Y., Tanaka, K., Morita, Y. and Shibata, D. (1992) cDNA cloning of rice lipoxygenase L-2 and characterization using an active enzyme expressed from the cDNA in *Escherichia coli*. *European Journal of Biochemistry*, **206**, 331–336.

Pen, J., Verwoerd, T.C., van Paridon, P.A., Beudeker, R.F., van den Elzen, P.J.M., Geerse, K., van der Klis, J.D., Versteegh, H.A.J., van Ooyen, A.J.J. and Hoekema, A. (1993) Phytase-containing transgenic seeds as a novel feed additive for improved phosphorus utilization. *Bio/Technology*, **11**, 811–814.

Pfeiffer, T.W., Hildebrand, D.F. and Tekrony, D.M. (1992) Agronomic performance of soybean lipoxygenase isolines. *Crop Science*, **32**, 357–262.

Pinsky, A., Grossman, S. and Trop, M. (1971) Lipoxygenase content and antioxidant activity of some fruits and vegetables. *Journal of Food Science*, **36**, 571–572.

Rice-Evans, C. and Miller, N.J. (1995) Antioxidants – the case for fruit and vegetables in the diet. *British Food Journal*, **97**, 35–40.

Richardson, M. (1991) Seed storage proteins: the enzyme inhibitors. *Methods in Plant Biochemistry*, **5**, 259–305.

Robinson, D.S., Wu, Z., Domoney, C. and Casey, R. (1995) Lipoxygenases and the quality of foods. *Food Chemistry*, **54**, 33–43.

Saalbach, I., Pickardt, T., Machemehl, F., Saalbach, G., Schieder, O. and Müntz, K. (1994) A chimeric gene encoding the methionine-rich 2S albumin of the Brazil nut (*Bertholletia excelsa* H.B.K.) is stably expressed and inherited in transgenic grain legumes. *Molecular and General Genetics*, **242**, 226–236.

Saalbach, G., Christov, V., Jung, R., Saalbach, I., Manteuffel, R., Kunze, G., Brambarov, K. and Müntz, K. (1995a) Stable expression of vicilin from *Vicia faba* with eight additional single methionine residues but failure of accumulation of legumin with an attached peptide segment in tobacco seeds. *Molecular Breeding*, **1**, 245–258.

Saalbach, I., Waddell, D., Pickardt, T., Schieder, O. and Müntz, K. (1995b) Stable expression of the sulphur-rich 2S albumin gene in transgenic *Vicia narbonensis* increases the methionine content of seeds. *Journal of Plant Physiology*, **145**, 674–681.

Sano, S. and Asada, K. (1994) cDNA cloning of monodehydroascorbate radical reductase from cucumber: a high degree of homology in terms of amino acid sequence between this enzyme and bacterial flavoenzymes. *Plant and Cell Physiology*, **35**, 425–437.

Shewry, P.R., Napier, J.A. and Tatham, A.S. (1995a) Seed storage proteins: structures and biosynthesis. *The Plant Cell*, **7**, 945–956.

Shewry, P.R., Tatham, A.S., Barro, F., Barcelo, P. and Lazzeri, P. (1995b) Biotechnology of breadmaking: unraveling and manipulating the multi-protein gluten complex. *Bio/Technology*, **13**, 1185–1190.

Shiiba, K., Negishi, Y., Okada, K. and Nagao, S. (1991) Purification and characterization of lipoxygenase isozymes from wheat germ. *Cereal Chemistry*, **68**, 115–122.

Smirnoff, N. and Palanca, J.E. (1996) Ascorbate metabolism in relation to oxidative stress. *Biochemical Society Transactions*, **24**, 472–478.

Tawfiq, N., Heaney, R.K., Plumb, J.A., Fenwick, G.R., Musk, S.R.R. and Williamson, G. (1995) Dietary glucosinolates as blocking agents against carcinogenesis: glucosinolate breakdown products assessed by induction of quinone reductase activity in murine hepa 1C1C7 cells. *Carcinogenesis*, **16**, 1191–1194.

Townsend, J.A. and Thomas, L.A. (1994) Factors which influence the *Agrobacterium*-mediated transformation of soybean. *Journal of Cell Biochemistry* (suppl.), **18A**, Abstract X1–014.

Tressl, R. and Drawert, F. (1973) Biogenesis of banana volatiles. *Journal of Agricultural and Food Chemistry*, **21**, 560–565.

Vick, B.A. and Zimmerman, D.C. (1984) Biosynthesis of jasmonic acid by several plant species. *Plant Physiology*, **75**, 458–461.

Vick, B.A. and Zimmerman, D.C. (1987) Pathways of fatty acid hydroperoxide metabolism in spinach leaf chloroplasts. *Plant Physiology*, **85**, 1073–1078.

Wang, T.L. and Hedley, C.L. (1993) Genetic and developmental analysis of the seed, in *Peas: Genetics, Molecular Biology and Biotechnology* (eds R. Casey and D. R. Davies), CAB International, Wallingford, Oxon, pp. 83–120.

Whitaker, J.R. (1991) Lipoxygenases, in *Oxidative Enzymes in Foods* (eds D.S. Robinson and N.A.M. Eskin), Elsevier Applied Science, London and New York, pp. 175–215.

Wu, Z., Robinson, D.S., Domoney, C. and Casey, R. (1995) High performance liquid chromatographic analysis of the products of linoleic acid oxidation catalyzed by pea (*Pisum sativum*) seed lipoxygenases. *Journal of Agricultural and Food Chemistry*, **43**, 337–342.

Yoon, S. and Klein, B.P. (1979) Some properties of pea lipoxygenase isoenzymes. *Journal of Agricultural and Food Chemistry*, **27**, 958–962.

Zimmerman, D.C. and Caudron, C.A. (1979) Identification of traumatin, a wound hormone, as 12-oxo-trans-10-dodecanoic acid. *Plant Physiology*, **63**, 536–541.

7 Use of food ingredients to reduce degenerative diseases

IAN JOHNSON

Introduction

Leaving aside war and natural disasters, the major causes of death in most human populations are infant mortality, which has a variety of causes, infectious diseases and the degenerative diseases of later life. In modern industrialized societies a combination of medical technology and improved public hygiene has reduced infant mortality to levels undreamed of before the twentieth century. Mortality from infectious diseases has also fallen dramatically, although progress in this area is under constant threat from drug-resistant organisms and emerging pathogens. As mortality in early life is reduced, more individuals will inevitably succumb to degenerative diseases – principally cancer and cardiovascular diseases – in later life. There are obvious advantages to be gained from preserving health in the middle-aged and elderly, both from the point of view of individuals who wish to lead long active lives and for the state, which strives always to avoid the costs of prolonged medical care. For medical scientists and formulators of public policy, the challenge for the next century is to minimize the rate of onset of mortality from degenerative diseases during middle age. This chapter seeks to explore the role of food production and processing in the achievement of that goal.

Post-war affluence and the development of highly efficient agricultural and food manufacturing industries have solved most of the problems of nutrient supply that were still prevalent in Western industrialized countries during the first half of the twentieth century. These improvements have undoubtedly made a major contribution to the decline in infant mortality and the reduced incidence of infectious diseases. On the other hand, Western diets are now widely regarded as at least partially responsible for the relatively high prevalance of ischaemic heart disease, stroke and many cancers in the West. The evidence for this is based on a combination of epidemiological studies and biomedical research that has begun to unlock the complex pathophysiology of degenerative disease. For example, Keys' classic studies on the relationships between cardiovascular disease and diet, culminating in the Seven Countries Study (Keys, 1980), drew attention to the adverse consequences of over-consumption of saturated fat. Similarly Doll and Peto (1981) showed from comparative studies of populations across the world that between 30 and 70% of cancers in the West were probably caused by diet, although the mechanisms remain unclear.

Despite frequent allegations in the popular media that scientists cannot agree on the basic characteristics of a prudent healthy diet, a remarkable degree of consensus has in fact emerged over the last two decades (Cannon, 1992). The current dietary reference values for the UK (Department of Health, 1991) include recommendations for the control of total and saturated fat intake at levels significantly lower than current consumption. In contrast, an increase in the consumption of complex carbohydrates, including non-starch polysaccharides (dietary fibre), is recommended. There is also an increasing recognition that fruit and vegetable intake is inversely related to the risk of cardiovascular disease and cancer, and this has led to public health campaigns designed to increase consumption substantially. The food production industries have been quick to recognize the developing public interest in the relationship between diet and the risk of degenerative diseases and this has led to the introduction of a variety of products designed to assist consumers to comply with official dietary recommendations or to take advantage of less well established models of diet and health. So-called 'functional foods', 'vitafoods' and 'nutraceuticals' are the latest manifestations of this commercial trend. Broadly speaking there are two approaches to the development of 'healthy' food products. The first is a deliberate reduction in the level of components that are regarded as having an adverse effect, notably total energy, total fat and saturated fat. The alternative strategy is to enrich the product with supposedly beneficial constituents thought to be lacking in conventional Western diets. This chapter is concerned with the logic and consequences of the second approach.

An inadequate diet?

Given the sheer abundance and variety of Western diets it seems perverse to suggest that they may be in any way deficient in nutrients or other essential constituents. However, there is a good case to be made for the possibility that social, agricultural and commercial pressures have, even in times of plenty, favoured the development of diets that are less than optimal for the preservation of health. Throughout most of the evolutionary history of the species, human beings were hunter-gatherers, dependent on, and presumably adapted to, the foods available in their immediate environment. Modern estimates suggest that the principal components of such a diet would have been fruit, leaves, seed pods and roots (Peters and O'Brien, 1981). Because fruit and leaves have a low energy density, around 5 kg of food would be needed to provide 2000 kcal per day. Under these circumstances consumption of some meat, which is a concentrated source of protein and energy, would have obvious advantages but it is realistic to assume that human beings are adapted to a diet containing rather more plant material and less meat and animal fat than is commonly consumed in the industrialized West.

Another striking aspect of the hunter-gatherer diet is the potentially huge variety of foods that it can provide. The study of Peters and O'Brien (1981) suggested that edible materials from as many as 333 different plant genera would have been available to early human beings. One effect of a shift to a settled agricultural existence is that the variety of plant foods consumed falls dramatically. Diets based on cultivated foods have been available for only about 10 000 years or so, which is about 1% of human history. It is unlikely that human beings have lost their biological adaptation to a complex variety of plant foods during so short a period. Thus the obvious advantages of abundant energy and protein derived from cultivated cereals and domesticated animals may have been paid for by a reduction in the intake of beneficial plant components of various kinds including fibre, micronutrients and biologically active secondary plant metabolites.

There is abundant epidemiological evidence to support the general hypothesis that plant materials exert protective effects against the development of degenerative diseases. Block *et al.* (1992) analysed nearly 200 studies on the relationship between fruit and vegetable intake and the risk of cancer in humans, and concluded that statistically significant evidence for a protective effect had been obtained in 128 out of 156 studies in which a quantitative estimate of relative risk could be made. These protective effects extended to almost all the most important sites of cancer in humans, but particularly strong evidence was obtained for cancers of the alimentary tract, lung, breast and female reproductive organs. Because of the difficulty of analysing the fine detail of human food intake with any precision, it is much more difficult to obtain evidence for a protective effect of any particular type of fruit or vegetable. However, Steinmetz and Potter (1991) examined this issue in some detail by analysing a selection of published reports. Drawing on 115 case-control studies, they examined 12 classes of fruits and vegetables for evidence of a negative, zero or positive association with risk of cancer. There was strong evidence for a negative relationship between risk of cancer and consumption of leafy green vegetables, carrots and fruit. The implications of such findings are of potentially great socio-economic importance. For example, in most of the studies reviewed by Block *et al.* (1992) individuals with the lowest intake of fruit and vegetables experienced a risk of developing cancer that was about twice that of those with the highest intake, and the fraction of the population exposed to differences in risk of this magnitude was typically between 20 and 33%.

Protective constituents of plant foods

The sheer volume and variety of the putative hunter-gatherer diet is probably impossible to reproduce in the context of the industrialized West but some approximation to it is perhaps achieved by vegetarians and near-vegetarians in western Europe and America who minimize their intake of meat and other animal products. In keeping with the epidemiological findings obtained from the study of omnivorous populations with differing levels of fruit and vegetable consumption, there is good evidence that vegetarians experience a reduced risk of degenerative disease compared to that of omnivores living in the same industrialized environment. For example, Thorogood *et al.* (1994) studied approximately 6000 British vegetarians and 5000 meat-eating controls in a prospective study designed to compare mortality in the two groups over 12 years. The vegetarians experienced reduced mortality from all causes, coronary heart disease (CHD) and cancer, although the reduction in death from CHD was not statistically significant. The relatively lower mortality amongst the vegetarians could not be attributed to any difference in other lifestyle factors. However, it was not clear whether it was meat consumption that was deleterious or the high consumption of plant foods that was beneficial. This is a crucial question. Some might argue that meat consumption is directly damaging to health. For example, in a recent review Barnard *et al.* (1995) estimated that the extra health-care costs attributable to meat consumption in the USA is between US $28.6 billion and US $61.4 billion per annum because of excess risks of hypertension, coronary heart disease, cancer, gallbladder disease, food poisoning and musculo-skeletal disorders associated with obesity in meat eaters. However, if plant foods are themselves actively beneficial, rather than simply displacing meat from the diet, then dietary supplementation with the putative protective factors in plant foods is an obvious strategy for protecting the health of meat eaters. Such an approach holds attractions for the food industry, who can use it to develop new products, and for most governments, who for a variety of political and philosophical reasons would prefer not to discourage meat consumption.

The growing interest in the possible protective effects of plant constituents has prompted several important growth areas in nutrition research over the last few decades. The first and most widely accepted hypothesis was the concept of dietary fibre as a protective factor against cancer and metabolic disorders. More recently, interest in the adverse biological effects of free radicals has encouraged research on the antioxidant vitamins and on other constituents of plants that can act as antioxidants in the body. A third emerging topic is concerned with anticarcinogenic secondary plant metabolites. In the remainder of this chapter the opportunities and challenges posed by these various issues will be considered.

Dietary fibre

Plant cell walls are complex structures containing a variety of β-linked polysaccharides that are resistant to hydrolysis by the endogenous digestive enzymes of the alimentary tract. The ability of those substances to exert a mild laxative effect has long been recognized and the virtues of wholemeal cereals were stressed by early advocates of vegetarianism, including Sylvester Graham and John Harvey Kellogg. More recently Surgeon Captain Cleave developed the concept of the 'saccharine disease', a complex syndrome of metabolic and degenerative disorders that he attributed to over-consumption of refined carbohydrate (Cleave *et al.*, 1969). The term 'dietary fibre' was first used in a clinical context by Hipsley (1953) in a paper on toxaemia in pregnancy. The term came into common use in the 1970s with the development of a more general 'dietary fibre hypothesis' for the aetiology of certain metabolic and gastrointestinal disorders in Western industrialized societies. The physician and epidemiologist Hugh Trowell first defined dietary fibre as the 'remnants of plant cell walls resistant to hydrolysis (digestion) by the alimentary enzymes of man' (Trowell, 1972). The concept was later redefined more precisely as 'The sum of lignin and the plant polysaccharides that are not digested by the endogenous secretions of the mammalian digestive tract' (Trowell et al., 1976). This definition encompasses all of the polysaccharide components of cell walls, together with closely associated phenolic substances. It excludes non-digestible sugars and protein, but it is criticised by some on the grounds that it does not exclude so-called 'resistant starch', a component of dietary starch that also escapes digestion in the small bowel, largely because of the retrogradation of amylose or the encapsulation of starch within robust plant cell walls. The more restrictive term 'non-starch polysaccharides' is used to define cell wall polysaccharides that have been rendered free of starch by carefully controlled analytical procedures (Englyst et al., 1992).

Even modern diets contain a relatively large number of different plant tissues from a variety of species (Selvendran et al., 1987). Cell walls perform a host of different physiological and mechanical functions in the living plant and they tend to retain their properties in the alimentary tract. The soft tissues of fruits and leaves contain parenchymatous cells with relatively thin walls. A combination of mechanical stiffness and hydrostatic pressure determines the characteristic texture of many plant foods. Such cell walls contain a mixture of insoluble cellulose fibrils and xylans, uronic acid rich polysaccharides (pectins) and soluble arabinogalactans. The vascular tissues of plant stems and leaves are specialized to retain an open tubular structure and rigidity is maintained by secondary thickening and deposition of lignin.

Although seeds have probably always formed an important part of the human diet, large quantities of non-digestible polysaccharides from cereal grains would not have been available prior to the domestication of cereals about 10 000 years ago. Seeds contain starch as a storage polysaccharide enclosed within a tough outer coat of lignified tissue, rich in arabinoxylans, which helps to prevent desiccation and invasion by fungi and predatory invertebrates. Bran is the outer highly lignified layers of wheat grains, which are removed to a varying degree during the milling of flour. Some cereal grains, including oats, barley and rye, also contain β-glucans, which are water soluble during digestion. Hence oat gum is the principal source of soluble dietary fibre in the human diet and is largely responsible for the nutritional properties of oat bran, which have attracted much medical and commercial interest in recent years.

Legume seeds are rich sources of storage polysaccharides and oils. These important sources of digestible energy are enclosed within cell walls that have greater strength and thickness than those of cereal grains. Legumes like the guar bean, and the carob or locust bean, contain resistant storage polysaccharides with β-linked mannose polymers containing short galactose side chains. Such polymers are soluble in water but the side chains cause loose intermolecular entanglements, whilst preventing aggregation of the polymers. As a result of these interactions the polysaccharides form viscous dispersions, which can be used to modify the rheology of food systems. The outer surfaces of tubers such as the potato contain waxy lipids called suberins, which protect the tissue against desiccation and decay. Strictly speaking suberin does not conform to the definition of dietary fibre and little is known of its physiological effects.

Physiological effects

The rate of digestion and absorption of foods is the first rate-limiting step determining the biological availability of nutrients. The gut therefore influences many aspects of nutrient metabolism. The large bowel is also a major site of cancer and other degenerative conditions; all these aspects of gastro-intestinal physiology are thought to be influenced by the level and type of fibre in the diet. The basic premise of the dietary fibre hypothesis as formulated by Burkitt and Trowell and their successors is that the populations of Western industrialized societies suffer from chronic fibre deprivation caused by the low level and over-refinement of plant foods in their diets (Trowell *et al.*, 1985). This proposal has generated an enormous amount of research and commercial activity but it has been extremely difficult to test the dietary fibre hypothesis directly; hence no protective role has been firmly established for fibre against any disease. This is partly because the development of cancer, heart disease and diabetes occurs over many years, and partly because of the difficulty of controlling or measuring the dietary habits of large numbers of people for long periods of time. Nevertheless a combination of epidemiological evidence and experimental physiology has provided a wealth of supportive evidence for the fibre hypothesis and recommended levels of fibre intake are now included in the dietary guidelines of all developed nations.

The small intestine. The small bowel, which is the principal site of nutrient absorption, is the longest of the digestive organs and has the greatest surface area. Initial hydrolysis of proteins, triglycerides and most starch takes place within the duodenum and upper jejunum, under the influence of pancreatic enzymes. The final stages of hydrolysis occur at the mucosal surface and the products are absorbed into the circulation via the specialized epithelial cells of the intestinal mucosa. In adult humans the first fermentable residues from a meal enter the colon approximately four and a half hours after ingestion. As assimilation of nutrients progresses the resistant polysaccharides of the cell wall remain behind and the physical and chemical properties of the digesta are modified by the presence of cell wall fragments and dispersed polysaccharides. These effects can modify the functions of the intestine to a degree that may have important implications for health.

The presence of solid food residues slows transit, probably by delaying gastric emptying and perhaps also by increasing the viscosity of the chyme so that it tends to resist the peristaltic flow. Highly viscous polysaccharides, such as guar gum and pectin, increase the mouth to caecum transit time still further. The susceptibility of cell walls to physical disruption during their passage through the alimentary tract varies considerably from one type of food to another, but any intact cell walls that do survive the early stages of digestion will tend to restrict the access of digestive enzymes to their substrates. Even when enzymes and their substrates do come into contact, the presence of cell wall polysaccharides may slow the diffusion of hydrolytic products through the partially digested matrix in the gut lumen.

These effects of plant cell walls and isolated components of dietary fibre on the motility and digestive functions of the small intestine provide a rationale for the long-postulated protective effects of dietary fibre against metabolic disorders such as hypercholesterolaemia and diabetes mellitus. The 'glycaemic index' is a measure of the quantity of glucose appearing in the blood stream after ingestion of a complex food (Jenkins *et al.*, 1981). It was developed as a means of predicting the effect of foods on blood glucose level, as an aid in the formulation of diabetic diets. The glycaemic index is expressed as the ratio of the area under the blood-glucose curve following a test meal to that produced by an equal quantity of some reference food such as glucose or white bread. When glucose is used as a reference, complex starchy foods tend to have glycaemic indices lower than 100%. Many of the foods with very low values are pulses, probably because legume seeds have thick cell walls that resist destruction during processing and cooking, and serve as a barrier that protects their constituent starch granules from rapid hydrolysis in the duodenum. Unfortunately this type of effect is very difficult to predict from simple analytical values for dietary fibre because it reflects structure, rather than the absolute quantity of cell wall polysaccharides within the food. It is also difficult to reproduce in manufactured foods because processes such as extrusion cooking tend to disrupt cell walls and increase the availability of digestible carbohydrate.

There has been considerable interest in the commercial use of isolated fibre supplements in order to delay the absorption of glucose derived from sucrose and starch. Wheat bran is ineffective when administered in combination with a liquid test meal containing glucose but oral doses of around 10–20 g of highly viscous soluble polysaccharides, such as guar gum, pectin and oat β-glucan, do slow the absorption of glucose (Jenkins *et al.*, 1978). The primary mechanism appears to be increased viscosity of the contents of the small intestine, which inhibits stirring in the boundary layer close to the mucosal surface and increases the distance across which nutrients must diffuse before absorption (Johnson and Gee, 1981; Blackburn *et al.*, 1984). This rate-limiting effect delays rather than prevents absorption of glucose, but it can limit the glycaemic response to starchy foods in both healthy volunteers and diabetics, and products based on this principle have been developed successfully (Apling and Ellis, 1982).

There is also good evidence that certain soluble polysaccharides can reduce plasma cholesterol levels in hypercholesterolaemic individuals to a degree that can significantly reduce the risk of developing atheromatous plaque. The most effective polysaccharides appear to be pectin and oat β-glucan, but other types of fibre such as isphagula husk and modified cellulose gums have also been shown to be hypocholesterolaemic in experimental animals and humans. Truswell and Beynen (1992) have estimated that about 10 g of pectin must be consumed each day to lower the plasma total cholesterol by 5–10%. This would require the consumption of about 1 kg of fruit and vegetables if this level of pectin were to be derived from natural sources alone. The mechanism of action is not clearly established, but it may be due to an inhibition of cholesterol and bile salt absorption causing a shift in hepatic cholesterol metabolism in favour of reduced low density lipoprotein (LDL). Provision of soluble fibre from oat gum to reduce plasma cholesterol has recently been recognized by the US Food and Drug Administration as a permissible claim for a functional food product.

The large intestine. The colon is primarily an organ of salvage of energy from food residues and endogenous materials that have escaped digestion and absorption in the small bowel, and of formation and storage of faeces. The proximal colon provides a watery, nutrient-rich environment, constantly supplied with fresh substrates from the small bowel, and it is the main site of permanent bacterial colonization in the human alimentary tract (Johnson, 1996). There are about 200 g of such material in the right colon, some of which is transferred at intervals into the transverse and distal segments for partial dehydration and storage as nascent faeces.

The faecal micro-organisms degrade many, but not all, components of dietary fibre, as well as undigested starch, to yield the volatile fatty acids butyrate, propionate and acetate, which are transported into and across the colonic mucosa. Around three-quarters of the caloric value of the non-starch polysaccharides becomes available to the body by these routes. The poorly fermentable components of fibre – principally insoluble cereal brans – and the bacterial cells produced as a result of the metabolism of fermentable fibre, both contribute to faecal bulk. The mildly laxative properties of wheat bran have been recognized since classical times and the importance of this aspect of fibre for the well-being of the colon was emphasized by the founders of the dietary fibre hypothesis. However, they went further by proposing that chronic constipation was virtually universal, but largely unrecognized, in Western industrialized societies and that a low consumption of dietary fibre could cause a variety of diseases of the large bowel ranging from haemorrhoids to cancer. This direct causal link has been difficult to prove conclusively but there is good epidemiological evidence linking the risk of colorectal cancer to slow transit and low faecal bulk (Cummings *et al.*, 1992).

In general a high intake of dietary fibre does lead to a faster transit time through the colon, probably because a high intraluminal mass stimulates smooth muscle activity, but the efficacy of any particular source of fibre depends to a great extent on its chemical composition (Stephen and Cummings, 1980). Wheat bran, which is insoluble and highly lignified, resists fermentation and tends to retain water during transit. The increment in stool mass caused by wheat bran depends to some extent on particle size, but to a rough approximation the output of stool is increased by between 3 and 5 g for every 1 g of wheat bran consumed. Other sources of dietary fibre that also favour water retention, such as isphagula husk, which is a mucilaginous material derived from Psyllium, can also work effectively as mild laxatives. However, polysaccharides such as pectin, guar and oat β-glucan, which are readily fermented by anaerobic bacteria, are much less effective as laxatives, although the bacterial cells formed do make some contribution to the total faecal output. It is vitally important that when sources of fibre are being considered for the development of new functional food products these important differences in the behaviour of different components of fibre are taken into account. It is extremely difficult to draw general conclusions about the physiological effect of any food simply on the basis of a single analytical measure of total fibre content.

Colonic butyrate

Apart from increasing the availability of energy from dietary fibre, saccharolytic fermentation has the important effect of regulating the physical and chemical environment of the colonic lumen. The mucosal surfaces of the intestinal tract are among the main sites of cell replication in the human body. In the healthy colon the dividing cells are confined to the basal regions of the crypts, and their progeny differentiate as they ascend the crypt column. Fully mature cells emerge onto the luminal surface and are eventually shed into the colonic lumen after a few days of life. Under normal circumstances cell production is exactly matched by exfoliation, so that the morphology of the mucosa remains stable. According to the widely accepted adenoma–carcinoma model of colonic carcinogenesis, cancer develops because of a progressive deregulation of this sequence of events associated with acquisition of mutations by stem cells (Vogelstein et al., 1988). The first recognizable abnormality is an increase in the rate of mitosis and a loss of the normal spatial distribution of dividing cells within the crypt. The abnormally dividing cells eventually give rise to an adenomatous polyp, an initially benign lesion that occurs in over 50% of the elderly population in the UK and the USA. A small proportion of these polyps eventually develop into malignant tumours. During carbohydrate fermentation the luminal pH becomes more acidic and the quantity of butyrate available to the mucosal cells increases, which may help to inhibit the adenoma–carcinoma sequence.

Interest in the possible role of butyrate as an antineoplastic component of the faeces has developed because of its known ability to inhibit the growth of mammalian tumour cell lines in vitro (Van Wijk et al., 1981; Czerniac et al., 1987; Barnard and Warwick, 1993). The reduced proliferative activity of cultured tumour cells exposed to butyrate is usually accompanied by other changes that suggest a shift toward the normal, non-transformed cell phenotype. Butyrate is a preferred metabolic substrate for colonic mucosal cells (Roediger, 1980). Although it stimulates colorectal mucosal cell proliferation in animals, this effect is usually regarded as a physiological response rather than as a pre-neoplastic phenomenon. The importance of butyrate as a metabolic substrate for the colonocytes, coupled with its ability to inhibit the growth of tumour cells *in vitro*, and the fact that abnormally low levels of butyrate production have been observed in colorectal cancer patients, have encouraged speculation that an increased supply of butyrate might delay or reverse the neoplastic process in the human colon (Hill, 1996). There is considerable interest in the development of foods designed to deliver fermentable substrates capable of yielding a high level of butyrate to the distal colon. Resistant starch-containing retrograded amylose and amylopectin are particularly attractive candidates because they can be read-ily created in processed foods and give a relatively high level of butyrate during fermentation (Englyst *et al.*, 1987).

The difficulty of manipulating colonic butyrate production *in vivo* has hampered attempts to explore its effects in humans. The largest and most detailed study published to date is that of Kashtan *et al.* (1992), who set out to explore the effect of soluble fibre derived from oat bran on faecal short-chain fatty acids (SCFAs) and mucosal markers of crypt cell proliferation in a large group of patients, with or without a history of adenomatous polyps. Half of the patients were given oat bran, which is rich in fermentable β-glucan (Lund and Johnson, 1991), for two weeks and the control group received wheat bran. The oat bran was associated with a significant decrease in faecal pH, but faecal SCFA and butyrate levels actually fell, to an extent that approached statistical significance. There was no significant effect of either supplement on biomarkers of proliferation in the rectal mucosa. Although it is reasonable to assume that consumption of oat bran led to an increased supply of butyrate in the proximal large bowel, this was not measured and without the appropriate data the study must be regarded as inconclusive. Before leaving this topic it is important to note that Wasan and Goodlad (1996) regard the hyperproliferative effect of fermentable carbohydrate in animal models as potentially cancer-promoting and have called for caution in the development and consumption of highly fermentable dietary fibre supplements. This view is based on some extent on animal studies (Jacobs and Lupton, 1986) but the argument is largely theoretical and the issue remains highly controversial.

Conclusion

The dietary fibre hypothesis has provided the food industry with many opportu-nities to develop food products with physiological effects beyond the simple provision of nutrients. Cereal products rich in wheat bran, to provide roughage, were developed early in the twentieth century and in general the research that followed several decades later has confirmed their value. Most sources of dietary fibre are based on foods that are already widely accepted and there are few if any safety issues associated with them. A few rare cases of intestinal obstruction due to over-consumption of fibre have been reported, but these have usually been caused by very unusual dietary practices (Kang and Dow, 1979) or underlying disease (Cooper and Tracey, 1989) or both. There appears to be continuing scope for the development of new products based on the physiological effects outlined above (Thebaudin *et al.*, 1997). It must be emphasized, however, that the biophysical and chemical properties of any fibre component used in such foods must be thoroughly understood in relation to the health-related function that the food is intended to improve (Johnson, 1993). Whatever the analytical method used, fibre sources must not be chosen purely on the basis of a single analytical value for dietary fibre or non-starch polysaccharides (Johnson, 1990).

Antioxidant nutrients and β-carotene

Living tissues that undertake aerobic metabolism as a source of energy are under constant threat of damage by reactive oxygen derivatives. Such free radicals are usually short-lived species but they possess a single unpaired electron, rendering them highly reactive against biologically important macromolecules including DNA, proteins and membrane lipids. To counteract this threat to their integrity, cells have evolved a variety of defence systems based on both water- and lipid-soluble antioxidant species, and on antioxidant enzymes. These various systems are deployed throughout the intra- and extracellular environments at sites most vulnerable to pro-oxidant damage. A high proportion of the antioxidant systems of the human body are dependent on dietary constitutents, several of which are recognized as vitamins. The most important water-soluble antioxidant in human metabolism is ascorbate (vitamin C), which, unlike most vertebrates, human beings cannot synthesize. Vitamin E (RRR-α-tocopherol) is the most important lipid-phase antioxidant, but the antioxidant effects of β-carotene and other carotenoids are now thought to be of considerable importance in human metabolism. Plant foods are the main source of these compounds in the human diet. If human beings have become adapted to a relatively high intake of antioxidant nutrients from fruits and vegetables during the course of evolution, then ideally a modern diet should also provide an optimal supply of these substances by one means or another.

Vitamin C

The only wholly undisputed function of vitamin C is that of preventing scurvy and it is principally on this that official dietary recommendations for its intake are based. However, vitamin C has a variety of other probable or proposed effects on human health, including the promotion of iron absorption (Hunt *et al.*, 1990), the regulation of cholesterol metabolism (Ginter *et al.*, 1977) and the modulation of various immune parameters (Anderson *et al.*, 1980). The vitamin function of ascorbate is complex. It acts principally as an electron donor and in this role it is known to be an essential cofactor in at least eight different enzyme systems that have been characterized *in vitro*. These include prolyl and lysyl hydroxylases involved in collagen metabolism, but the precise role of ascorbate in the pathophysiology of scurvy has not been fully determined (England and Seifter, 1986). In a paper on the need to develop a mechanistic understanding of the optimal vitamin C requirements for human beings, Levine *et al.* (1995) drew attention to the paucity of information on the reaction kinetics of ascorbate at the concentrations present in the tissues *in vivo*.

The optimal level of vitamin C intake for the preservation of health is still uncertain (Levine *et al.*, 1995). Mild scurvy develops in adults whose intake of vitamin C is restricted to around 1 mg/day, but 10 mg/day is sufficient to prevent or alleviate symptoms under experimental conditions (Bartley *et al.*, 1953). The current reference nutrient intake for vitamin C in the UK is 40 mg/day in adults (Department of Health, 1991), while in the USA the recommended dietary allowance (RDA) is 60 mg/day. These figures are based on the need to provide a reasonable margin of safety over and above the level of intake needed to prevent scurvy in most individuals. However, plasma levels of ascorbate do not achieve saturation in adults until daily intakes reach 70 to 100 mg (Bates *et al.*, 1979). The toxicity of vitamin C is very low, but there is some risk of kidney stone formation in susceptible individuals when intakes exceed 500 mg/day (Urivetsky *et al.*, 1992). Based on these and other considerations Levine *et al.* (1995) suggest an optimum vitamin C intake of about 200 mg/day.

What evidence is there for a protective effect of such high vitamin C intakes against degenerative diseases? Ascorbate is probably the most effective water-soluble antioxidant in the plasma and, judging from studies carried out *in vitro*, it is a prime candidate for a protective role against oxidative damage to cell membranes and LDL cholesterol (Frei *et al.*, 1989; Jialal *et al.*, 1980). However, as with many other aspects of the 'antioxidant hypothesis', although the epidemiological evidence is consistent with a protective effect of vitamin C against cancer (Block, 1991) and heart disease (Gey *et al.*, 1993a), it remains inconclusive because of the sheer complexity of the composition of fruits and vegetables, which are the main source of the vitamin in the unsupplemented diet. Byers and Guerrero (1995) addressed this issue directly in a meta-analysis of epidemiological studies on cancer and antioxidant vitamins. They analysed a series of case-control and cohort studies in which intakes of fruits and vegetables, and of vitamins C and E from food or from supplements, were determined. As in previous reviews of this type (Steinmetz and Potter 1991; Block *et al.*, 1992) there was a strong and consistent protective effect of fruits and vegetables against cancers of the alimentary tract and lung. There was also a consistent correlation with estimated vitamin C intake based on fruit and vegetable composition, but the authors found the evidence for a protective effect of vitamin C from supplements much less convincing. One obvious interpretation of these observations is that in fact fruits and vegetables exert their protective effects because of constituents other than vitamin C.

A substantial proportion of the population in the USA and in Europe now take daily vitamin C supplements, but most of the vitamin C in human diets is derived from natural sources. Consumers who follow the '5-a-day' guidelines that are being widely adopted in the USA and Europe could obtain as much as 200 mg of ascorbate per day. This is well in excess of the currently recommended levels, but much less than the level at which any toxic effects are likely. However, vitamin C is generally regarded as the most labile of the vitamins (Bender, 1978) and there is certainly a need to minimize losses in the food chain. Vitamin C is readily lost from foods during storage, by enzymic destruction or during processing, through leaching or by oxidation. Enzymic destruction begins in leafy vegetables as soon as the plants are harvested. However, vitamin C is relatively stable under anaerobic conditions and at low temperatures. Packaged fruit juices are an important source of vitamin C in the diet, but careful formulation, processing and storage are necessary if the consumer is to derive the full benefit from the product.

Various ascorbates are produced commercially for nutritional supplementation of foods and as antioxidants to improve the keeping qualities of products such as fruit juices, as flour improvers and as a preservative used in curing meats including bacon. The use of ascorbates as processing aids is not generally considered to be nutritionally important. However, as Bender (1978) has pointed out, ascorbate levels reach as high as 150–500 mg/kg in bacon and around 50% of this can survive average storage and cooking conditions. Thus vitamin C derived from commercial meat products could be of considerable nutritional significance to individuals who consume little or no fresh fruit and vegetables.

Vitamin E

The tocopherols are a group of compounds originally identified as essential for the maintenance of fertility, and for growth and development of the foetus in rats. Vitamin E is a collective term for eight compounds: α-, β-, γ- and δ-tocopherol, α-, β-, γ- and δ-tocotrienol. The naturally occurring isomer is RRR-α-tocopherol and this accounts for 90% of endogenous vitamin E activity in humans. Any mixture of tocopherols and tocotrienols is referred to as vitamin E but since the biological potency of the compounds varies, their activities are expressed conventionally in terms of milligram equivalents of RRR-α-tocopherol. Vitamin E is lipid soluble and was first isolated from wheatgerm oil. The main sources in the human diet are nuts and seeds, and oils derived from them, particularly soya and groundnut oils.

All the tocopherols and tocotrienols contain a hydroxyl-bearing aromatic ring structure, which accounts for their ability to donate hydrogen to free radicals and thus act as biological antioxidants (Tappel, 1972). The unpaired electron that results from hydrogen donation is delocalized into the ring structure of the toco-pherol, which renders it relatively stable and unreactive. Being lipid soluble, vitamin E is readily incorporated into cell membranes and lipoprotein particles. These structures are rich in polyunsaturated fatty acids, which are highly suscep-tible to damage by free radicals derived from the metabolic activity of cells and from other sources. Damage initiated by a single hydroxyl radical can give rise to a self-propagating chain reaction, but the chain can be broken by donation of hydrogen and formation of a stable radical as a result of interaction with vitamin E. It is probable that vitamin E is then regenerated by vitamin C (Doba et al., 1985), or by other mechanisms, so that cellular antioxidant surveillance is main-tained. In animal models of vitamin E deficiency the various symptoms that develop are consistent with membrane damage. In humans, frank symptoms of vitamin E deficiency are only seen in premature infants and in malabsorption states. However, it seems entirely plausible that intakes of vitamin E higher than those required to protect against symptoms of deficiency may provide increased protection against free-radical mediated damage to DNA. Thus vitamin E may be anticarcinogenic, particularly in smokers, whose lungs are exposed to high levels of free-radicals that have been reported to be reduced by supplementation with vitamin E (Duthie et al., 1991).

Apart from cell membranes, vitamin E is now thought to play a major role in the protection of LDL from oxidative damage (Steinberg, 1991). High levels of LDL have long been regarded as a risk factor for coronary heart disease and oxidatively damaged LDL is thought to be recognized and preferentially taken up by macrophages associated with arterial wall, thus creating foam cells that initiate the formation of atheromatous plaque. Vitamin E is the major lipid-solu-ble antioxidant in human plasma (Burton et al., 1982) and it is incorporated into LDL particles in vivo. Using in vitro techniques, it has been shown that vitamin E protects LDL against oxidative damage induced by free radicals. Furthermore α-tocopherol may also inhibit other stages in the atherogenic process by reduc-ing the proliferation of arterial smooth muscle cells (Azzi et al., 1995). Thus vitamin E, whether by itself or in combination with other plasma coantioxidants (Thomas et al., 1995), has come to be regarded as a major protective factor against coronary heart disease.

Although the mechanisms by which vitamin E can protect cells against disease processes leading to cancer and coronary heart disease seem very plausi-ble, the hypothesis remains unproven because of the inconclusive results of epidemiological studies and intervention trials. Ecological studies show a strong inverse correlation between risk of coronary heart disease and plasma vitamin E concentrations at the population level (Gey et al., 1987, 1993b), but the associa-tion is not necessarily borne out when individuals within a population are stud-ied (Hense et al., 1993). Intervention trials, which enable the hypothesis to be tested directly, have so far proven inconclusive (Stampfer and Rimm, 1995). Similarly, evidence for a protective effect of vitamin E supplements against cancer remains weak. For example, in the α-tocopherol, β-carotene (ATBC) study groups of smokers received supplementation with vitamin E and other antioxidant vitamins under placebo-controlled, double-blind conditions (Alpha-Tocopherol, Beta-Carotene Cancer Prevention Study Group, 1994). There was no significant protective effect of vitamin E against lung cancer but lower than expected rates of prostate and bowel cancer were observed. Interestingly, as in previous ecological studies, lower rates of lung cancer were obtained in those subjects who had the highest plasma levels of vitamin E and β-carotene at entry (Albanes *et al.*, 1995). Perhaps these vitamins exert protective effects only when the individual has been exposed to them for a large proportion of his or her lifespan. Alternatively, they may be acting as markers for other unidentified protective factors present in plant foods. At any rate the putative protective effects of antioxidant nutrients are not yet recognized as a basis for increasing the recommended levels of intake in the UK and the most recent Department of Health guidelines on vitamin E recommend only that the issue should be kept under review (Department of Health, 1991).

Carotenoids

The carotenoids are a diverse group of lipid-soluble pigments derived from vegetables and fruits. Of the 500 or so carotenoids known to exist in the human food chain, β-carotene is by far the most well known and intensively studied because of its important role as a precursor for vitamin A. However, in the present context the most important characteristic of the carotenoids is the fact that their molecular structure includes an extended chain of double bonds, which enables them to function as antioxidants. This is presumably their primary role in green plants, which generate singlet oxygen as a damaging by-product of photosynthesis. The carotenoids of green plants are located in the chloroplasts; under experimental conditions the absence of these carotenoids during photosynthesis leads rapidly to the free-radical mediated destruction of both chlorophyll and chloroplast membranes (Halliwell and Gutteridge, 1993). A variety of dietary carotenoids is released from plant foods in the small intestine and absorbed in conjunction with dietary fat. Conversion of β-carotene to vitamin A in the intestinal mucosa is not complete and β-carotene is detectable in human plasma at levels that are related positively to the dietary intake of fruits and vegetables. At least 10 other carotenoids have been recorded in blood including lutein and lycopene, which is present at higher concentrations than β-carotene.

As with other dietary antioxidants, interest in carotenoids as protective factors against degenerative disease has been stimulated by a combination of experimental and observational studies. The realization that carotenoids might express antioxidant activity in human tissues, thereby protecting cell membranes, proteins and DNA against damage by free radicals, provides a satisfying rationale for the frequently observed inverse relationship between carotenoid consumption and risk of cancer and heart disease. Certainly there is consistent evidence from both case-control and cohort studies that a low dietary intake of β-carotene or a relatively low concentration of β-carotene in plasma is a significant risk factor for lung cancer and stomach cancer, and there is weaker evidence for cancer at other sites (Ziegler, 1991; van Poppel and Goldbohm, 1995). With regard to cardiovascular disease, a similar pattern of inverse relationships between risk of disease and various markers of β-carotene exposure, including dietary intake, plasma and adipose tissue levels, has been observed (Kohlmeier and Hastings, 1995).

Despite the consistency and plausibility of the evidence for a direct protective effect of carotenoids against cancer and heart disease, intervention trials with β-carotene have proved disappointing. In particular, the ATBC study, which involved over 29 000 male smokers and included a cohort given 20 mg of β-carotene daily for up to 8 years, produced no evidence for a protective effect against cancer at any site. On the contrary, there was a higher incidence of lung, prostate and stomach cancer in the β-carotene group (Albanes *et al.*, 1995; Alpha-Tocopherol, Beta-Carotene Cancer Prevention Study Group, 1994). Although the trial was primarily designed to investigate the effect of intervention with antioxidants on lung cancer, 1473 men also died of cardiovascular disease during the trial. Again there was a higher rate of both coronary heart disease and stroke in the group receiving ß-carotene compared to the control group (Albanes *et al.*, 1995; Alpha-Tocopherol, Beta-Carotene Cancer Prevention Study Group, 1994).

In the current state of uncertainty there are various explanations for the failure of intervention trials to confirm the protective effects of carotenoids against degenerative diseases. One possibility is that β-carotene is indeed a protective antioxidant but its beneficial effects are somehow obscured by an inappropriate experimental design. The induction of most tumours, including lung cancer, is a lengthy multistage process involving both initiation and promotion of precancerous cells in the target tissue. The lungs of the smokers used in the ATBC study had been exposed to cigarette smoke for many years and the tumours that developed during the trial must have been initiated before the intervention began. Possibly exposure to increased levels of β-carotene at this late stage is ineffective, or perhaps even serves to promote carcinogenesis in some way. There is no suggestion, however, that β-carotene is toxic in any other circumstances, even when given at pharmacological doses for long periods to treat photosensitivity disorders (Diplock, 1997). An alternative explanation is that β-carotene has no protective effect in itself but merely serves as a marker for some other aspect of the environment or behaviour of individuals at lower risk of cancer. Thus β-carotene is associated in the diet with other carotenoids, including lycopene, which has a significantly higher free radical quenching capacity. Of course the protective effects of fruits and vegetables against cancer might be due to other classes of biologically active phytochemicals acting through entirely different anticarcinogenic mechanisms, a possibility that will be discussed more fully later in this chapter. Until these issues are resolved it would not be appropriate to encourage the development and consumption of functional foods designed to provide consumers with high doses of carotenoids, but the general advice to increase fruit and vegetable consumption remains prudent.

Whereas performed vitamin A is derived from animal sources such as liver, fish and dairy products, carotenoids are obtained principally from dark leafy vegetables, coloured fruits and some oils such as palm oil. Carrots are a rich source of β-carotene and tomatoes contain mostly lycopene. β-carotene is also an important food additive, used for colouring and as a dietary supplement. It has been given 'generally recognized as safe' (GRAS) status by the US Food and Drug Administration. Being lipid soluble, carotenoids are resistant to leaching losses during processing and cooking but they can undergo oxidation and isomerization during heat treatment, which reduces the vitamin A potency of β-carotene and probably modifies the antioxidant activity as well. On the other hand the availability of carotenoids for intestinal absorption is increased by the physical disruption of the food matrix. It should be noted that consumption of sucrose polyesters leads to the formation of a non-absorbable lipid phase in the intestinal lumen into which fat-soluble substances are partitioned. This reduces the bioavailability of fat-soluble vitamins and carotenoids. The nutritional significance of this effect remains to be established.

Conclusions

There is strong circumstantial evidence that high intakes of the antioxidant nutrients are associated with a reduced risk of coronary heart disease and cancer, and there are sound mechanistic hypotheses to explain this relationship. On the other hand, the results of intervention studies have not been conclusive and other constituents of fruit and vegetables may be responsible for the protective effects associated with these complex foods. A recent international conference on antioxidant vitamins, β-carotene and disease prevention included a panel discussion on the current status of the antioxidant hypothesis and the conclusion was that the available evidence was still not sufficient to enable public health recommendations regarding the efficacy and safety of the compounds for preventing disease (Sies and Krinsky, 1995). Under these circumstances the development of functional foods supplemented with antioxidant vitamins is probably not justifiable at this stage but there is a considerable amount of research in progress that may change the outlook radically in the next few years. In the mean time, for the individual, maintenance of antioxidant vitamin status at a level equivalent to that of the upper quintile of the general population seems prudent, preferably by consumption of ample quantities of fruit and vegetables.

Non-nutrient phytochemicals

Apart from the recognized nutrients and dietary fibre, plant foods also provide a rich variety of biologically active phytochemicals that may play a role in the prevention of degenerative diseases. Secondary plant metabolites often function as natural pesticides and it has been emphasized that even in modern Western diets such compounds exceed synthetic pesticide contaminants by around 1000-fold (Ames *et al.*, 1990). Many of these compounds have commonly been regarded as toxicants but in recent years there has been something of a revolution in thinking as interest in their possible role as protective factors has developed. A host of compounds has been shown to exhibit potentially beneficial biological effects, including chlorophyll derivatives, protease inhibitors, organosulphur compounds from alliums and *d*-limonene, a constituent of citrus oils (Johnson *et al.*, 1994). Although there is ever-growing interest in the non-nutrient phyto-chemicals, for the scientists and for the food manufacturer wishing to exploit their potential they remain the most challenging of all the dietary constituents derived from plant foods. In this section the biological properties and the possible implications for human health of two of the major classes of phytochemicals, the phenolic compounds and the glucosinolates, are briefly reviewed.

Phenolic compounds

Phenolic compounds contain one or more aromatic rings bearing hydroxyl groups, together with other functional groups. Their complex derivatives are responsible for much of the flavour, colour and, indirectly, the texture of plant foods, and they are also the major soluble constituents of tea, coffee and wine. The simpler phenolic substances include monophenols with a single benzene ring, found abundantly in fruits and seeds. The hydroxycinnamic acid group are derived from *p*-coumaric acid, caffeic and ferulic acid. A still more complex group containing two or more benzene rings includes catechins, proantho-cyanins, anthocyanidins and flavonols. The tannins are a large and rather ill-defined class of water-soluble phenolics with molecular weights ranging from 500 to several thousand. One of the principle characteristics of almost any diet rich in plant foods is the considerable quantity and variety of phenolic substances that it provides. The dietary burden in the UK is difficult to calculate but intakes may lie in the range 1 to 10 g per day in vegetarians and heavy tea drinkers. Only a brief discussion of the phenolic compounds and their signifi-cance for health is possible in this chapter. Emphasis is given to the flavonoids and phytoestrogens because of the current interest in their potential as protective factors against cancer and heart disease.

Flavonoids

Flavonoids consist of a three-ring structure with two aromatic centres (C_6–C_3–C_6). They were first identified by Szent-Gyorgi in the 1930s and have since received considerable attention as putative vitamins (vitamin P), potential toxicants and more recently as antioxidants and anticarcinogens (Havsteen,

1983; Formica and Regelson, 1995). There are about 2000 identified flavonoids. They occur throughout the plant kingdom, providing colour, flavour, antifungal and anti-bacterial activity, as well as contributing to other aspects of plant physiology through interactions with auxin metabolism. Most plant tissues can synthesize flavonoids; they commonly occur in leaves and fruits used as human food in the form of water-soluble glycosides. Among the most common and thoroughly studied are the flavan-3,4 diols quercetin, myrecetin and kaempferol, which in western Europe are probably obtained mainly from apples, onions and black tea (Hertog *et al.*, 1993).

Flavonoid glycosides are fairly resistant to processing, cooking and digestion, and occur intact in the small intestinal lumen, where they have usually been regarded as unavailable for intestinal absorption. However, flavonoid aglycones are known to be released from their sugar moieties by bacterial hydrolases in the large bowel and some absorption of quercetin is thought to occur there. This view has been challenged by Hollman *et al.* (1995, 1996), who have obtained evidence for small intestinal absorption of intact quercetin glycosides in humans. To explain these findings Hollman has proposed that the sugar moieties of some quercetin glycosides interact with the intestinal monosaccharide transport pathway so as to facilitate absorption of the intact molecule (Hollman, 1997). Further studies on the interaction between quercetin glycosides and the sodium-dependent glucose/galactose transporter of rat small intestine provide some additional support for this hypothesis (Gee *et al.*, 1998).

The most common flavonoids in the human diet, quercetin and kaempherol, have been shown to be mutagenic in the Ames test, with or without metabolic activation with S9, and quercetin is also genotoxic in a number of *in vitro* mutagenicity assays based on mammalian cell lines (Bjeldans and Chong, 1977). However, these effects appear to be dependent on the ability of flavonoids to behave as pro-oxidants in the presence of heavy metals and under conditions of relatively high oxygen tension, which occur in these tests (Hatcher and Bryan, 1985). These conditions probably have little relevance to the behaviour of flavonoids *in vivo*. At any rate there is very little evidence that quercetin and other flavonoids are carcinogenic in rodent assays (Formica and Regelson, 1995).

Blocking activity. The presence of hydrogen-donating hydroxyl groups associated with an aromatic ring structure into which the unpaired electron can become delocalized enables flavonoids to function as antioxidants in a similar way to α-tocopherol, under the redox conditions of living tissues. It is this property that has attracted most attention recently. Both quercetin itself and many of its glycosides have been shown to scavenge superoxide radicals, singlet oxygen and lipid peroxy radicals (Takahama, 1985; Robak and Gryglewski, 1988) and this property enables quercetin to inhibit free-radical dependent mechanisms of carcinogenesis.

Anticarcinogens can be classified broadly as substances that suppress the onset of neoplasia in animals or human beings. Carcinogenesis is a prolonged multistage process and for most tumours it is extremely difficult to study directly in human beings. The majority of the research on putative natural anti-carcinogens from food has been done using tissue culture systems or experimental animals exposed to chemical carcinogens. Using these techniques anticarcinogenic compounds have been classified either as *blocking agents*, which prevent the formation of carcinogens, enhance their detoxification or otherwise inhibit their activity, or as *suppressing agents*, which interfere with the promotion of tumour development after the initial genotoxic event (Wattenberg, 1990). Inhibition of free-radical mediated DNA damage is one mechanism by which flavonols are thought to block initiation of tumour cells (Newmark, 1992). The ability of the liver and intestinal mucosa to intercept and metabolize toxic chemicals provides another important defence against environmental carcinogens, which may be upregulated by dietary phenolics. Phase I enzymes metabolize hydrophobic species to oxygenated products, which provide substrates for conjugation by phase II enzymes. The conjugated products of the latter are water-soluble species that can be readily transported out of the cell. Several phenolic compounds, including quercetin, have been shown to induce one such enzyme, quinone reductase, *in vitro* (De Long *et al.*, 1986).

Suppressing activity. The concept of a suppressing agent was introduced by Wattenberg (1990) to describe the behaviour of isolated compounds such as sodium cyanate, tert-butylisocyanate and benzyl isothiocyanate, as well as foods of plant origin including Brassicas, green coffee beans, green Brazilian cocoa beans and orange oil (Wattenberg, 1981; Wattenberg, 1990). The essential characteristic of an oral suppressing agent is its ability to inhibit the appearance of tumours, even when fed to animals some considerable time after exposure to the carcinogen that initiated the neoplasia. The definition of suppressing agents is therefore largely a functional one and in most cases the mechanism of action is unknown and probably multifactorial. However, one probable mechanism is inhibition of the cyclo-oxygenase pathway of arachidonic acid metabolism, which regulates prostaglandin metabolism. Quercetin has been shown to inhibit cycloxygenase *in vitro* and this may account for its ability to inhibit promotion of mouse skin tumours by phorbol esters (Kato *et al.*, 1983).

Cardiovascular effects. The ability of flavonoids to scavenge free radicals, block lipid peroxidation and inhibit cyclo-oxygenase metabolism raises the possibility that they may act as protective factors against coronary heart disease. As mentioned earlier, the formation of atheromatous plaque begins as macrophages in the arterial wall accumulate oxidatively damaged LDL to become foam cells. In the presence of α-tocopherol, flavonols have been shown to protect LDL from oxidation *in vitro* (de Whalley *et al.*, 1990; Frankel *et al.*, 1993a) and this effect extends to phenolic substances derived from red wine (Frankel *et al.*, 1993b). If flavonoids are absorbed from food, and if the circulating forms retain their antioxidant activity *in vivo*, then they may provide an important degree of protection against the formation of atherogenic LDL. Several epidemiological studies support this hypothesis. In one recent investigation, Hertog *et al.* (1993) measured flavonoid intake in a group of 805 elderly Dutch men. The average intake of flavonoids at entry into the study was 25.9 mg/day, most of which was derived from tea, apples and onions. There was a significant inverse relationship between flavonoid intake and subsequent coronary heart disease such that the relative risk in men in the highest tertile of intake was 42% of the risk for those in the lowest tertile. Similar findings have recently been reported for a group of over 5000 younger Finnish men and women (Knekt *et al.*, 1996).

Flavonols exhibit other biological effects that may enable them to inhibit later events in the pathophysiology of coronary heart disease (Formica and Regelson, 1995). Acute blockage of coronary arteries occurs when clots form on the surface of atheromatous plaque and occlude the vessel lumen. Quercetin blocks aggregation of platelets by inhibiting eicosanoid metabolism and apparently by blocking thromboxane receptors at the platelet surface (Tzeng *et al.*, 1991). Flavonoids have also been shown to enhance vasodilation by a mechanism involving interactions with nitric oxide metabolism (Fitzpatrick *et al.*, 1993).

Phytoestrogens

Another class of food-borne phenolic compounds, the phytoestrogens, deserve particular mention because of the strong epidemiological evidence for their having a protective effect against hormone-dependent cancers. Interest in the oestrogenic activity of plant constituents began with the observation that hormone-dependent reproductive disorders in Australian sheep were caused by substances derived from the clover that formed a major part of their diet (Bennetts *et al.*, 1946). The oestrogen-like compounds were later shown to be diphenolic isoflavones, genistein and daidzein, present in the plant as the glycosides genistin and daidzin or as the methylated derivatives biochanin A or formononentin (Schutt *et al.*, 1970). Like many other secondary plant metabolites, isoflavanoid derivatives are thought to be metabolized to biologically active forms by the intestinal microflora. The glycosides are broken down to release the free aglycones genistein and daidzein, which may be absorbed or further metabolized to various other biologically available derivatives including equol (4', 7-dihydroxyisoflavan) and dihydro- and tetrahydrodaidzein. Many of these compounds, including genistein, daidzein and equol, occur in human urine, mostly as glucuronide conjugates (Axelson *et al.*, 1982; Bannwart *et al.*, 1984; Adlercreutz *et al.*, 1986, 1991a, b). Isoflavonoids are derived chiefly from legumes and particularly from processed soy products (Setchell *et al.*, 1984). The lignans enterolactone and enterodiol are a second group of diphenolic phytoestrogens, which appear in the circulation and in the urine after consumption of various plant foods containing their precursors.

The principle on which phytoestrogens are thought to act is comparable to that of tamoxifem, a weak oestrogen-like drug that is used in the chemotherapy and chemoprevention of breast cancer. By binding to the oestrogen receptor in breast tissue, and in hormone-dependent tumour cells derived from breast tissue, the drug inhibits the growth-promoting activity of endogenous oestrogen (Powles, 1992). Lignans and isoflavanoids are excreted in high concentration in the urine of vegetarians eating large quantities of cereals and pulses (Adlercreutz *et al.*, 1991a) and high levels of isoflavanoids occur in Asian populations eating large quantities of soy products (Adlercreutz *et al.*, 1991b).

The consumption of oestrogen-like compounds from the diet might conceivably have adverse as well as beneficial physiological effects. It is probably fair to say that the balance of risk and benefit has not been explored to an extent that would justify the development of functional foods based on the exploitation of phytoestrogens. However, at the present time the balance of evidence appears to be in favour of a protective effect of these compounds against oestrogen-dependent diseases including breast cancer, benign prostatic enlargement and prostate cancer (Griffiths *et al.*, 1996). All of these conditions are major causes of morbidity and death in Western countries but they have a much lower prevalence in many Asian countries. Indeed the incidence of both breast and prostate cancer in Western countries is 5–8-fold greater than in many oriental countries, but Asian immigrants to the West eventually experience the same disease risk as the local population. One explanation for these differences is suppression of the disease process by phytoestrogens derived from certain Oriental diets.

Conclusion

As we have seen, the antioxidant and antitumour activities of many food-borne phenolics are the subject of much current research activity and in principle they are ideal candidates as constituents of functional foods. However, very little is known of their absorption and metabolism in man. The identity and concentrations of compounds reaching the target tissues from food is poorly understood in many cases and it is therefore extremely difficult to interpret the significance of mechanisms identified *in vitro*. Detailed studies on the bioavailability of phenolics are urgently required in order to design properly focused epidemiological investigations and to assess the potential for the development of functional foods and nutraceuticals. The case for the physiological activity of phytoestrogens in human beings seems particularly compelling in view of the combined evidence from observational and experimental work with animals, epidemiological studies and mechanistic studies *in vitro* (Griffiths *et al.*, 1996). However, direct experimental evidence of health benefits based on intervention trials is missing. Caution is also necessary because of the complexity of human reproductive endocrinology and the unknown effects of chronic exposure to oestrogens at various stages of the lifecycle. Nevertheless, experimental trials using well-established dietary components such as soy products to elevate circulating levels of phytoestrogens to those which are normal in Oriental populations are probably ethically justifiable. The rational exploitation of phytoestrogens may well provide important opportunities for the food industry in the medium and long term.

Glucosinolates

The glucosinolates are a large class of sulphur-containing secondary metabolites found in the Brassica vegetables. Brassica tissue has been shown to inhibit tumour formation in animals and to modulate phase II enzyme activity in human subjects, and there is good evidence that the glucosinolates are at least partially responsible. More than 100 different glucosinolates have been characterized but on the basis of their side chains they are classified into three main categories comprising an aliphatic/alkenyl group, an aromatic group and an indolyl group. All glucosinolates are conjugated with glucose and remain stable within storage vacuoles in the plant tissue. However, on disruption by processing or mastication they are rapidly hydrolysed by an endogenous cytosolic thioglucosidase called myrosinase. The aglycones are unstable and undergo a spontaneous rearrangement, releasing sulphate and a variety of different unstable products, which vary according to the conditions of the reaction and the identity of the side chain in the parent compound. The main groups of breakdown products are isothiocyanates (ITC), thiocyanates, nitriles, epithionitriles and indoles. The chemistry and biology of glucosinolates has been reviewed elsewhere (Fenwick et al., 1983, 1989).

The breakdown products of glucosinolates contribute significantly to the flavour and odour of Brassicas and they have been shown to exhibit a range of important physiological and biochemical activities in humans and experimental animals. Rapeseed is rich in glucosinolates and the commercial importance of this crop has previously focused much attention on the antinutritional effects of isothiocyanates, nitriles, oxazolidine-2-thiones and epi-thionitriles (Fenwick et al., 1989), but it is now generally accepted that there is no convincing evidence for adverse effects in humans consuming normal levels of Brassica vegetables (McMillan et al., 1986). More recently there has been an upsurge of interest in glucosinolates as a source of dietary anticarcinogens (Jongen, 1996). In their extensive review of fruits and vegetables in general, Steinmetz and Potter (1991) conclude that a high consumption of Brassica vegetables is associated with a reduction in risk of cancer at many sites. There was a particularly strong association with a lower risk of colon cancer and this was independent of fibre content. The evidence for the anticarcinogenic effects of Brassica vegetables in human populations is strongly supported by evidence obtained with experimental animals.

The anticarcinogenic effects of glucosinolates appear to involve both blocking and suppression of tumourigenesis. Cell culture is being used extensively to assay compounds or foods for their ability to induce phase II enzymes (Zhang et al., 1992; Prochaska et al., 1992; Tawfiq et al., 1995). Such assays often give positive results for extracts from Brassicas and for isolated glucosinolate break-down products, but not for the parent compounds. There is also strong evidence to show that Brassica vegetables and components from them induce phase II enzymes in a number of different organs, and in general this is associated with a reduction in the formation of DNA adducts (Whitty and Bjeldanes, 1987). For example, broccoli added to the diet of rats reduced the binding of aflatoxin B1 or its metabolites to hepatic DNA (Ramsdell and Eaton, 1988). Brussels sprouts or, crucially, a glucosinolate-containing fraction from Brussels sprouts have been shown to inhibit aflatoxin altered foci in rats (Godlewski *et al.*, 1985). There is some evidence that consumption of Brussels sprouts can induce phase II activity, with potentially beneficial effects, in human subjects as well (Bogaards *et al.*, 1994; Verhagen *et al.*, 1995).

Wattenberg (1981) showed that both cruciferous vegetables and compounds such as benzyl isothiocyanate, which is a breakdown product of glucosinolates found in a number of cruciferous vegetables, could inhibit the appearance of mammary tumours in experimental animals, even when given days or weeks after exposure to a chemical carcinogen. The number of tumours in the treatment group was 40–50% lower than in the control groups, and the average number of tumours per rat was approximately halved. Similarly, the introduction of allyl isothiocyanate (AITC) into the diet of rats treated with the specific colon carcinogen dimethyl hydrazine (DMH) leads to a significant reduction in the numbers of precancerous colonic lesions present 42 days later (Smith *et al.*, 1996, 1998). Colorectal carcinoma is the second most common cause of death from cancer in many European populations and in the USA. The protective effect of Brassica vegetables in epidemiological studies, coupled with the emerging evidence for a specific suppressing effect of AITC against neoplastic lesions of the colorectal mucosa, suggests a special need to understand the effects of glucosinolate breakdown products on proliferation and apoptotic cell death in the colonic crypt.

The bioavailability of the glucosinolates poses a particular problem in that they are rapidly depleted during the processing and cooking of vegetables, and their breakdown products are unstable. It is therefore not clear what biologically active forms are present in ingested vegetables and in the different regions of the alimentary tract. Nor is it yet clear whether isothiocyanates act only after absorption into the circulation from the small intestine or whether, for example, AITC might act locally on the colonic mucosa. Intact glucosinolates are known to be hydrolysed by the colonic microflora and this could expose the colonic mucosa to particularly high levels of breakdown products (Rabot *et al.*, 1993; Michaelsen *et al.*, 1994). Thus the pattern of intake of glucosinolates and their breakdown products varies according to the production, cooking and consumption patterns of Brassica vegetables. These variables evidently determine the biological activities of the glucosinolate breakdown products in food but it is not yet clear whether they can be optimized to enhance the protective effects of glucosinolates in the diet.

Conclusion

It seems prudent to assume that human beings are adapted to a high intake of plant foods and that at least some the body's biochemical defence mechanisms can be enhanced by secondary plant metabolites. The constant provision of these substances should perhaps be regarded as a normal aspect of nutrition (Johnson *et al.*, 1994). There is virtually no epidemiological evidence to suggest adverse effects of fruits and vegetables when consumed in substantial quantities as part of a mixed diet. Public health education should therefore emphasize the need to increase consumption of fruits and vegetables but in view of the current level of uncertainty as to the mechanism of action of anticarcinogens it would seem premature to frame such advice so that any particular group of fruits or vegetables is strongly favoured.

The full exploitation of the beneficial effects of plant foods may in the future justify the development of new products that can, in effect, be used as tools for chemoprevention, but this will require a much more thorough understanding of the relevant biochemical mechanisms than we possess at present. It may well be that the mechanisms reviewed in this chapter act synergistically in the context of complex human eating patterns, so that no single product could ever fully match the protective effects of diets rich in fruits and vegetables. Another problem is that many of the biologically active components of fruits and vegetables might also be regarded as potential antinutritional factors or natural toxins. Some of the glucosinolate derivatives have been shown to be genotoxic using *in vitro* assays (Musk *et al.*, 1995; Kassie *et al.*, 1996) and this paradox needs to be resolved by further research.

Although fruits and vegetables are undoubtedly protective when consumed as part of a conventional diet, there may be a U-shaped relationship between intake and risk that could lead to hazards if isolated compounds are consumed in large quantities. Even when the protective mechanisms of particular phytochemicals are fully established, plant breeders and food technologists will always need to proceed cautiously with the enrichment of plant foods by genetic manipulation or with the development of concentrated dietary supplements.

References

Adlercreutz, H., Fotsis, T., Bannwart, C., Wahala, K., Makela, T., Brunow, G. and Hase, T. (1986) Determination of urinary lignans and phytoestrogen metabolites, potential antiestrogens and anticarcinogens in urine of women on various habitual diets. *Journal of Steroid Biochemistry*, **25**, 791–797.

Adlercreutz, H., Honjo, H., Higashi, A., Fotsis, T., Hamalainen, E., Hasegawa, T. and Okada, H. (1991a) Urinary excretion of lignan and isoflavanoid phytoestrogens in Japanese men and women consuming traditional Japanese diet. *American Journal of Clinical Nutrition*, **54**, 1093–1100.

Adlercreutz, H., Fotsis, T., Bannwart, C., Wahala, K., Brunow, G. and Hase, T. (1991b) Isotope dilution gas chromatographic–mass spectrometric method for the determination of lignans and isoflavanoids in human urine, including identification of genestein. *Clinical Chimica Acta*, **199**, 263–278.

Albanes, D., Heinonen, O.P., Huttunen, J.K., Taylor, P.R., Virtamo, J., Edwards, B.K., Haapakoski, J., Rautalahti, M., Hartman, A.M., Palmgren, J. and Greenwald, P. (1995) Effects of alpha-tocopherol and beta-carotene supplements on cancer incidence in the alpha-tocopherol beta-carotene cancer prevention study. *American Journal of Clinical Nutrition*, **62** (suppl.), 1427–1430.

Alpha-Tocopherol, Beta-Carotene Cancer Prevention Study Group (1994) The effect of vitamin E and beta-carotene on the incidence of lung cancer and other cancers in male smokers. *New England Journal of Medicine*, **330**, 1029–1035.

Ames, B.N., Profet, M. and Gold, L.S. (1990) Dietary pesticides (99.9% all natural). *Proceedings of the National Academy of Sciences*, **87**, 7777–7781.

Anderson, R., Oosthuizen, R., Maritz, R., Theron, A. and Van Rensberg, A.J. (1980) The effects of increasing weekly doses of ascorbate on certain cellular and humoral immune functions in normal volunteers. *American Journal of Clinical Nutrition*, **33**, 71–76.

Apling, E.C. and Ellis, P.R. (1983) Guar bread, concept to application. *Chemistry and Industry*, 950–954.

Axelson, M., Kirk, D.N., Farrant, R.D., Cooley, G., Lawson, A.M. and Setchell, K.D.R. (1982) The identification of the weak oestrogen equol (7-hydroxy-3-(4'hydroxyphenyl) chroman) in human urine. *Biochemical Journal*, **201**, 353–357.

Azzi, A., Boscoboinik, D., Marilley, D., Özer, N.K., Säuble, B. and Tasinato, A. (1995) Vitamin E: a sensor and an information transducer of the cell oxidation state. *American Journal of Clinical Nutrition*, **62** (suppl.), 1337S–1346S.

Bannwart, C., Fotsis, T., Heikkinen, R. and Adlercreutz, H. (1984) Identification of the isoflavonic phytoestrogen daidzein in human urine. *Clinical Chimica Acta*, **136**, 165–172.

Barnard, J.A. and Warwick, G. (1993) Butyrate rapidly induces growth inhibition and differentiation in HT-29 cells. *Cell Growth and Differentiation*, **4**, 495–501.

Barnard, N.D., Nicholson, A. and Howard, J.L. (1995) The medical costs attributable to meat consumption. *Preventive Medicine*, **24**, 646–655.

Bartley, W., Krebs, H.A. and O'Brien, J.P. (1953) *Vitamin C Requirements of Human Adults*, MRC Special Report Series 280, HMSO, London.

Bates, C.J., Rutishauser, I.H.E. and Black A.E. (1979) Long-term vitamin status and dietary intake of healthy elderly subjects. *British Journal of Nutrition*, **42**, 43–56.

Bender, A.E. (1978) Vitamins, in *Food Processing and Nutrition*, Academic Press, London, pp. 27–57.

Bennetts, H.W., Underwood, E.J. and Sheir, F.L. (1946) A specific breeding problem of sheep on subterranean clover pastures in Western Australia. *Australian Veterinary Journal*, **22**, 2–12.

Bjeldans, L.F. and Chong, G.W. (1977) Mutagenic activity of quercetin and related compounds. *Science*, **197**, 577–578.

Blackburn, N.A., Redfern, J.S., Holgate, A.M., Hanning, I., Scarpello, J.H.B., Johnson, I.T. and Read, N.W. (1984) The mechanism of action of guar gum in improving glucose tolerance in man. *Clinical Science*, **52**, 371–380.

Block, G. (1991) Vitamin C and cancer prevention: the epidemiologic evidence. *American Journal of Clinical Nutrition*, **53** (suppl.), 270S–283S.

Block, G., Patterson, B. and Subar, A. (1992) Fruit, vegetables and cancer prevention: a review of the epidemiological evidence. *Nutrition and Cancer*, **18**, 1–29.

Bogaards, J.J.P., Verhagen, H. and Willems, M.I. (1994) Consumption of Brussels sprouts results in elevated alpha-class glutathione s-transferase levels in human blood plasma. *Carcinogenesis*, **15**, 1073–1075.

Burton, G.W., Joyce, A. and Ingold, K.U. (1982) First proof that vitamin E is the major lipid-soluble chain-breaking antioxidant in human blood plasma. *Lancet*, **2**, 327–328.

Byers, T. and Guerrero, N. (1995) Epidemiologic evidence for vitamin C and vitamin E in cancer prevention. *American Journal of Clinical Nutrition*, **62** (suppl.), 1385S–1392S.

Cannon, G. (1992) *Food and Health: The Experts Agree*, Consumers Association, London.

Cleave, T.L., Campbell, G.D. and Painter, N.S. (1969) *Diabetes, Coronary Thrombosis and the Saccharine Disease*, 2nd edn, Wright, Bristol.

Cooper, S.G. and Tracey, E.J. (1989) Small bowel obstruction caused by oat bran bezoar. *New England Journal of Medicine*, **320**, 1148–1149.

Cummings, J.H., Bingham, S.A., Heaton, K.W. and Eastwood, M.A. (1992) Fecal weight, colon cancer risk, and dietary intake of nonstarch polysaccharides (dietary fibre). *Gastroenterology*, **103**, 1783–1789.

Czerniac, B., Herz, F. and Wersto, R.P. (1987) Modification of H-ras oncogene p-21 expression and cell cycle progression in the human colon cancer cell line HT-29. *Cancer Research*, **47**, 2826–2830.

De Long, M.J., Prochaska, H.J. and Talalay, P. (1986) Induction of NAD(P)H: quinone reductase in murine hepatoma cells by phenolic antioxidants, azo dyes and other chemoprotectors: a model system for the study of anticarcinogens. *Proceedings of the National Academy of Sciences USA*, **83**, 787–791.

Department of Health (1991) *Dietary Reference Values for Food Energy and Nutrients for the United Kingdom*, Report on Health and Social Subjects 41, HMSO, London.

de Whalley, C.V., Rankin, S.M., Hoult, J.R.S., Jessup, W. and Leake, D.E. (1990) Flavonoids inhibit the oxidative modification of low density lipoproteins by macrophages. *Biochemical Pharmacology*, **39**, 1743–1750.

Diplock, A. (1997) The safety of ß-carotene and the antioxidant vitamins C and E, in *Antioxidants and Disease Prevention* (ed. H.S. Garewal), CRC Press, Boca Raton, Florida, pp. 3–17.

Doba, T., Burton, G.W. and Ingold, K.U. (1985) Antioxidant and cooxidant activity of vitamin C. The effect of vitamin C either alone or in the presence of vitamin E or a water soluble vitamin E analogue upon the peroxidation of aqueous multilamellar phospholipid liposomes. *Biochemica Biophysica Acta*, **835**, 298–302.

Doll, R. and Peto, R. (1981) The causes of cancer: quantitative estimates of avoidable risks of cancer in the United States today. *Journal of the National Cancer Institute*, **66**, 1191–1308.

Duthie, G.G., Arthur, J.R. and James, W.P.T. (1991) Effects of smoking and vitamin E on blood antioxidant status. *American Journal of Clinical Nutrition*, **53**, 1061S–1063S.

England, S. and Seifter, S. (1986) The biochemical functions of ascorbic acid. *Annual Review of Nutrition*, **6**, 365–406.

Englyst, H.N., Hay, S. and MacFarlane, G.T. (1987) Polysaccharide breakdown by mixed populations of human faecal bacteria. *Microbial Ecology*, **95**, 163–171.

Englyst, H.N., Kingman, S.M. and Cummings, J.H. (1992) Classification and measurement of nutritionally important starch fractions. *European Journal of Clinical Nutrition*, **46** (suppl. 2), S33–S50.

Fenwick, G.R., Heaney, R.K. and Mullin, W.J. (1983) Glucosinolates and their breakdown products in foods and food plants. *CRC Critical Reviews in Food Science and Nutrition*, **18**, 123–201.

Fenwick, G.R., Heaney, R.K. and Mawson, R. (1989) *Glucosinolates, in Toxicants of Plant Origin Vol II, Glycosides* (ed. P.R. Cheeke), CRC Press, Boca Raton, pp. 1–41.

Fitzpatrick, D.F., Hirschfield, S.L. and Coffey, R.G. (1993) Endothelium dependent vasorelaxing activity of wine and other grape products. *American Journal of Physiology*, **265**, H774–H778.

Formica, J.V. and Regelson, W. (1995) Review of the biology of quercetin and related bioflavonoids. *Food and Chemical Toxicology*, **33**, 1061–1080.

Frankel, E.N., Waterhouse, A.L. and Kinsella, J.E. (1993a) Inhibition of human LDL oxidation by resveratrol. *Lancet*, **341**, 1103–1104.

Frankel, E.N., Kanner, J., German, J.B., Parks, E. and Kinsella, J.E. (1993b) Inhibition of oxidation of human low density lipoprotein by phenolic substances in red wine. *Lancet*, **341**, 454–457.

Frei, B., England, L. and Ames, B.N. (1989) Ascorbate is an outstanding antioxidant in human plasma. *Proceedings of the National Academy of Sciences USA*, **86**, 6377–6381.

Gee, J.M., Dupont, S., Rhodes, M.J.C. and Johnson, I.T. (1998) Quercetin glycosides interact with the intestinal glucose transport pathway. *Free Radical Biology and Medicine* (in press).

Gey, K.F., Brubacher, G.F. and Stähelin, H.B. (1987) Plasma levels of antioxidant vitamins in relation to ischemic heart disease and cancer. *American Journal of Clinical Nutrition*, **45** (suppl.), 1368–1377.

Gey, K.F., Stähelin, H.B., Eichholzer, M. and Lüdin, E. (1993a) Poor plasma status of carotene and vitamin C is associated with higher mortality from ischaemic heart disease and stroke: prospective basel study. *Clinical Investigation*, **7**, 3–6.

Gey, K.F., Moser, U.K., Jordan, P. (1993b) Increased risk of cardiovascular disease at suboptimal plasma concentrations of essential antioxidants: an epidemiological update with special attention to carotene and vitamin C. *American Journal of Clinical Nutrition*, **57** (suppl.), 787S–797S.

Ginter, E., Cerna, O., Budlovsky, J., Balaz, V., Hruba, F., Roch, V. and Sasko, E. (1977) Effect of ascorbic acid on plasma cholesterol in a long term experiment. *International Journal of Vitamin Research*, **47**, 123–144.

Godlewski, C.E., Boyd, J.N., Sherman, W.K., Anderson, J.L. and Stoewsand, G.S. (1985) Hepatic glutathione S-transferase activity and aflatoxin B1-induced enzyme altered foci in rats fed fractions of Brussels sprouts. *Cancer Letters*, **28**, 151–157.

Griffiths, K., Adlercreutz, H., Boyle, P., Denis, L., Nicholson, R.I. and Morton, M.S. (1996) in *Nutrition and Cancer*, Isis Medical Media, Oxford, pp. 55–98.

Halliwell, B.H. and Gutteridge, J.M.C. (1993) *Free Radicals in Biology and Medicine*, 2nd edn, Oxford University Press, Oxford, pp. 277–298.

Hatcher, J.F. and Bryan, G.T. (1985) Factors affecting the mutagenic activity of quercetin for Salmonella typhimurium TA98: metals, antioxidants and pH. *Mutation Research*, **148**, 13–23.

Havsteen, B. (1983) Flavonoids, a class of natural products of high pharmacological potency. *Biochemical Pharmacology*, **32**, 1141–1148.

Hense, H.W., Stender, M., Bors, W. and Keil, U. (1993) Lack of an association between serum vitamin E and myocardial infarction in a population with high vitamin E levels. *Atherosclerosis*, **103**, 21–28.

Hertog, M.G., Feskens, E.J., Hollman, P.C.H., Katan, M.B. and Kromhout, D. (1993) Dietary antioxidant flavonoids and risk of coronary heart disease: the zutphen elderly study. *Lancet*, **342**, 1007–1011.

Hill, M.J. (1996) Introduction: dietary fibre, butyrate and colorectal cancer. *European Journal of Cancer Prevention*, **4**, 341–343.

Hipsley, E.H. (1953) Dietary 'fibre' and pregnancy toxaemia. *British Medical Journal*, ii, 420–422.

Hollman, P.C.H. (1997) Determinants of the absorption of the dietary flavonoid quercetin in man, Ph.D. Thesis, Agricultural University of Wageningen.

Hollman, P.C.H., de Vries, J.H.M., van Leeuwen, S.D., Mengelers, M.J.B. and Katan, M.B. (1995) Absorption of dietary quercetin glycosides and quercetin in healthy ileostomy volunteers. *American Journal of Clinical Nutrition*, **62**, 1276–1282.

Hollman, P.C.H., Gaag, M.V.D., Mengelers, M.J.B., van Trup, J.M.P., de Vries, J.H.M. and Katan, M.B. (1996) Absorption and disposition kinetics of the dietary antioxidant quercetin in man. *Free Radical Biology and Medicine*, **21**, 703–707.

Hunt, J.R., Mullen, L.M., Lykken, G.I., Gallagher, S.K. and Nielsen, F.H. (1990) Ascorbic acid: effect on ongoing iron absorption and status in iron-depleted young women. *American Journal of Clinical Nutrition*, **51**, 649–655.

Jacobs, L.R. and Lupton, J.R. (1986) Relationship between colonic luminal pH, cell proliferation, and colon carcinogenesis in 1,2-dimethylhydrazine treated rats fed high fiber diets. *Cancer Research*, **46**, 1727–1734.

Jenkins, D.J.A., Wolever, T.M.S. and Leeds, A.R. (1978) Dietary fibres, fibre analogues and glucose tolerance: importance of viscosity. *British Medical Journal*, **1**, 1392–1394.

Jenkins, D.J.A., Wolever, T.M.S. and Taylor, R.H. (1981) Glycaemic index of foods: a physiological basis for carbohydrate exchange. *American Journal of Clinical Nutrition*, **34**, 362–366.

Jialal, I., Vega, J.L. and Grundy, S.M. (1990) Physiologic levels of ascorbate inhibit the oxidative modification of low density lipoprotein. *Atherosclerosis*, **82**, 151–191.

Johnson, I.T. (1990) Fibre sources for the food industry. *Proceedings of the Nutrition Society*, **49**, 31–38.

Johnson, I.T. (1993) Soluble fibre – a useful concept? in *Plant Polymeric Carbohydrates* (eds F. Meuser, D.J. Manner and W. Seibel), Royal Society of Chemistry, Cambridge, pp. 147–153.

Johnson, I.T. (1996) Substrates for fermentation in the large bowel. *Biochemical Society Transactions*, **24**, 824–828.

Johnson, I.T. and Gee, J.M. (1981) The effect of gel-forming gums on the intestinal unstirred layer and sugar transport *in vitro*. *Gut*, **22**, 398–403.

Johnson, I.T., Williamson, G.M. and Musk, S.R.R. (1994) Anticarcinogenic factors in plant foods: a new class of nutrients? *Nutrition Research Reviews*, **7**, 175–204.

Jongen, W.M.F. (1996) Glucosinolates in Brassica: occurrence and significance as cancer-modulating agents. *Proceedings of the Nutrition Society*, **55**, 433–446.

Kang, J.Y. and Dow, W.F. (1979) Unprocessed bran causing intestinal obstruction. *British Medical Journal*, **1**, 1249–1250.

Kashtan, H., Stern, H.S. and Jenkins, D.J.A. (1992) Colonic fermentation and markers of colorectal-cancer risk. *American Journal of Clinical Nutrition*, **55**, 723–728.

Kassie, F., Parzefall, W., Musk, S., Johnson, I.T., Lamprecht, G., Sontag, G. and Knäsmuller S. (1996) Detection of genotoxic effects of crude extracts from Brassica vegetables and phytopharmaceutical preparations and spices from cruciferous plants in bacterial and mammalian cells. *Chemical Biological Interactions*, **102**, 1–16.

Kato, R., Makadate, S., Yamamoto, S. and Sugimura, T. (1983) Inhibition of 12-O-tetradecanoylphorbol-13-acetate-induced tumor promotion and ornithine decarboxylase activity by quercetin: possible involvement of lipoxygenase inhibition. *Carcinogensis*, **5**, 1301–1305.

Keys, A. (1980) *Seven Countries: a Multivariate Analysis of Death and Coronary Heart Disease*, Harvard University Press, Harvard.

Knekt, P., Jarvinen, R. and Reunanen, A. (1996) Flavonoid intake and coronary mortality in Finland: a cohort study. *British Medical Journal*, **312**, 478–481.

Kohlmeier, L. and Hastings, S.B. (1995) Epidemiologic evidence of a role of carotenoids in cardiovascular disease prevention. *American Journal of Clinical Nutrition*, **62**, 1370S–1376S.

Levine, M., Dhariwal, K.R. and Welch, R.W. (1995) Determination of optimal vitamin C requirements in humans. *American Journal of Clinical Nutrition*, **62** (suppl.), 1347S–1356S.

Lund, E.K. and Johnson, I.T. (1991) Fermentable carbohydrate reaching the colon after ingestion of oats in humans. *Journal of Nutrition*, **121**, 311–317.

McMillan, M., Spinks, E.A. and Fenwick, G.R. (1986) Preliminary observations on the effects of dietary Brussels sprouts on thyroid function. *Human Toxicology*, **5**, 15–19.

Michaelsen, S., Otte, J., Simonsen, L.-O. and Sörensen, H. (1994) Absorption and degradation of individual intact glucosinolates in the digestive tract of rodents. *Acta Agriculturae Scandinavica*, **44**, 25–37.

Musk, S.R.R., Smith, T.K. and Johnson, I.T. (1995) On the cytotoxicity and genotoxicity of allyl and phenethyl isothiocyanates and their parent glucosinolates sinigrin and gluconasturtin. *Mutation Research Letters*, **348**, 19–23.

Newmark, H.L. (1992) Plant phenolic compounds as inhibitors of mutagenesis and carcinogenesis, in *Phenolic Compounds in Food and Their Effects on Health II* (eds Mou-Tuan Huang, Chi-Tang Ho and Chang Y Lee), ACS Symposium Series 507, ACS, Washington, pp. 48–52.

Peters, C.R. and O'Brien, E.M. (1981) The early hominid plant-food niche: insights from an analysis of plant exploitation by Homo, Pan and Papio in Eastern and Southern Africa. *Current Anthropology*, **22**, 127–140.

Powles, T.J. (1992) The case for clinical trials of tamoxifen for prevention of breast cancer. *Lancet*, **340**, 1145–1147.

Prochaska, H.J., Santamaria, A.B. and Talalay, P. (1992) Rapid detection of inducers of enzymes that protect against carcinogens. *Proceedings of the National Academy of Sciences USA*, **89**, 2394–2398.

Rabot, S., Nugon-Baudon, L., Railbaud, P. and Szylit, O. (1993) Rape-seed meal toxicity in gnotobiotic rats influence of a whole human faecal flora or single human strains of Escherichia coli and Bacteroides vulgatus. *British Journal of Nutrition*, **70**, 323–331.

Ramsdell, H.S. and Eaton, D.L. (1988) Modification of aflatoxin B1 biotransformations in vitro and DNA binding in vivo by dietary broccoli in rats. *Journal of Toxicology and Environmental Health*, **25**, 269–275.

Robak, J. and Gryglewski, R.J. (1988) Flavonoids are scavengers of superoxide anion. *Biochemical Pharmacology*, **37**, 83–88.

Roediger, W.E.W. (1980) Role of anaerobic bacteria in the metabolic welfare of the colonic mucosa in man. *Gut*, **21**, 793–798.

Schutt, D.A., Weston, R.A. and Hogan, J.P. (1970) Quantitative aspects of phyto-oestrogen metabolism in sheep fed on subterranean clover (*Trifolium subterranean* cultivar clare) or red clover (*Trifolium pratense*). *Australian Journal of Agricultural Research*, **21**, 713–722.

Selvendran, R.R., Stevens, B.J.H. and Dupont, M.S. (1987) Dietary fibre: chemistry, analysis and properties. *Advances in Food Research*, **31**, 117–209.

Setchell, K.D.R., Borriello, S.P., Hulme, P., Kirk, D.N. and Axelson, M. (1984) Nonsteroidal oestrogens of dietary origin: possible roles in hormone-dependent disease. *American Journal of Clinical Nutrition*, **40**, 569–578.

Sies, H. and Krinsky, N.I. (1995) The present status of antioxidant vitamins and β-carotene. *American Journal of Clinical Nutrition*, **62**, 1299S–1300S.

Smith, T.K., Musk, S.R.R. and Johnson, I.T. (1996) Allyl isothiocyanate selectively kills undifferentiated HT29 cells in vitro and suppresses aberrant crypt foci in the colonic mucosa of rats. *Biochemical Society Transactions*, **24**, 606S.

Smith, T.K., Lund, E.K. and Johnson, I.T. (1998) Inhibition of DMH-induced aberrant crypt foci and induction of apoptosis in rat colon following oral administration of the glucosinolate sinigrin. *Carcinogenesis*, **19**, 267-273.

Stampfer, M.J. and Rimm, E.B. (1995) Epidemiologic evidence for vitamin E in prevention of cardiovascular disease. *American Journal of Clinical Nutrition*, **62** (suppl.), 1365S–1369S.

Steinberg, D. (1991) Antioxidants and atherosclerosis. A current assessment. *Circulation*, **84**, 1420–1425.

Steinmetz, K.A. and Potter, J.D. (1991) Vegetables, fruit and cancer. I. Epidemiology. *Cancer Causes and Control*, **2**, 325–357.

Stephen, A.M. and Cummings, J.H. (1980) Mechanism of action of dietary fibre in the colon. *Nature*, **284**, 283–284.

Takahama, U. (1985) Inhibition of lipoxygenase-dependent lipid peroxidation by quercetin: mechanism of antioxidant function. *Phytochemistry*, **24**, 1443–1446.

Tappel, A.L. (1972) Vitamin E and free radical peroxidation of lipids. *Annals of the New York Academy of Sciences*, **203**, 12–28.

Tawfiq, N., Heaney, R.K. and Plumb, J.A. (1995) Dietary glucosinolates as blocking agents against carcinogenesis: correlation between glucosinolate structure and induction of quinone reductase in murine hepalclc7 cells. *Carcinogenesis*, **16**, 1191–1194.

Thebaudin, J.Y., Lefebvre, A.C., Harrington, M. and Bourgeois, C.M. (1997) Dietary fibres: nutritional and technological interest. *Trends in Food Science and Technology*, **8**, 41–48.

Thomas, S.R., Neuzil, J., Mohr, D. et al. (1995) Coantioxidants make alpha-tocopherol an efficient antioxidant for low-density lipoprotein. *American Journal of Clinical Nutrition*, **62** (suppl.), 1357S–1364S.

Thorogood, M., Mann, J., Appleby, P. and MaPherson, K. (1994) Risk of death from cancer and aschaemic heart disease in meat and non-meat eaters. *British Medical Journal*, **308**, 1667–1671.

Trowell, H.C. (1972) Ischemic heart disease and dietary fiber. *American Journal of Clinical Nutrition*, **25**, 926–932.

Trowell, H.C., Southgate, D.A.T., Wolever, T.M.S., Leeds, A.R., Gassull, M.A. and Jenkins, D.J.A. (1976) Dietary fibre redefined. *Lancet*, **i**, 967.

Trowell, H.C., Burkitt, D.P. and Heaton, K. (1985) Dietary Fibre, Fibre-Depleted Foods and Disease, Academic Press, London and New York.

Truswell, A.S. and Beynen, A.C. (1992) Dietary fibre and plasma lipids: potential for prevention and treatment of hyperlipidaemia, in Dietary Fibre – A Component of Food (eds T.F. Schweizer and C.A. Edwards), Springer Verlag, London, pp. 295–332.

Tzeng, S.H., Ko, W.C., Ko, F.N. and Teng, C.M. (1991) Inhibition of platelet aggregation by some flavonoids. *Thrombosis Research*, **64**, 91–100.

Urivetsky, M., Kessaris, D. and Smith, A.D. (1992) Ascorbic acid overdosing: a risk factor for calcium oxalate nephrolithiasis. *Journal of Urology*, **147**, 1215–1218.

van Poppel, G. and Goldbohm, R.A. (1995) Epidemiological evidence for beta-carotene and cancer prevention. *American Journal of Clinical Nutrition*, **62**, 1393S–1402S.

van Wijk, R., Tichonicky, L. and Kruth, J. (1981) Effect of sodium butyrate on the hepatoma cell cycle: possible use for cell synchronization. *In Vitro*, **17**, 859–864.

Verhagen, H., Poulsen, H.E., Loft, S., van Poppel, Willems, M.I. and van Bladeren, P.J. (1995) Reduction of oxidative damage in humans by Brussels sprouts. *Carinogenesis*, **16**, 969–970.

Vogelstein, B., Fearon, E.R. and Hamilton, S.R. (1988) Genetic alterations during colorectal tumour development. *New England Journal of Medicine*, **319**, 525–533.

Wasan, H.S. and Goodlad, R.A. (1996) Fibre-supplemented foods may damage your health. *Lancet*, **348**, 319–320.

Wattenberg, L.W. (1981) Inhibition of carcinogen-induced neoplasia by sodium cyanante, tertbutylisocyanate and benzyl isothiocyanate administered subsequent to carcinogen exposure. *Cancer Research*, **41**, 2991–2994.

Wattenberg, L.W. (1990) Inhibition of carcinogenesis by minor anutrient constituents of the diet. *Proceedings of the Nutrition Society*, **49**, 173–183.

Whitty, J.P. and Bjeldanes, L.F. (1987) The effects of dietary cabbage on xenobiotic-metabolising enzymes and the binding of aflatoxin B1 to hepatic DNA in rats. *Food and Chemical Toxicology*, **25**, 581–587.

Zhang, Y., Talalay, P., Cho, C.-G. and Posner, G.H. (1992) A major inducer of anticarcinogenic protective enzymes from broccoli: isolation and elucidation of structure. *Proceedings of the National Academy of Sciences*, **89**, 2399–2403.

Ziegler, R.G. (1991) Vegetables, fruits, and carotenoids and the risk of cancer. *American Journal of Clinical Nutrition*, **53**, 251S–259S.

8   Nutritional labelling and claims
URSULA ARENS

The provision of nutrition information on food labelling is a major aspect of food policy considered by nutritionists, by government and regulatory bodies, and by the food industry. With the adoption of legislation and guidelines to support and consistent provision of information, consumers have come to expect nutrient content declaration on the labelling of all or most foods. However, attempts to provide information will be of limited benefit in influencing food choice if, at the same time, no effort is made to increase consumer understanding of the application of such data. Furthermore, there are many issues relating to the appropriate presentation of nutrition information still to be resolved and legislation must evolve with scientific and with consumer understanding of food choice in relation to health.

Definitions

Nutrient declarations provide nutrition information about a food per unit weight and/or per serving. Nutrient declarations usually include energy and the macronutrients (fat, protein and carbohydrate), and may also include a further breakdown of the macronutrients (e.g. saturates, sugars) as well as vitamin and mineral declarations. This information is usually given in a standard format within a nutrient panel on the label.

Nutrient (or content) claims state that a food contains, or has particular amounts of one or several nutrients. Claims usually use a descriptor, e.g. 'high', 'reduced' or 'low', in relation to the nutrient referred to on the label. Nutrient declarations are not considered to be nutrient claims under food labelling legislation.

Health claims state that a food is in some way beneficial to health and well-being. There are three main types of health claim:

- reference to a disease risk factor (e.g. 'can help lower blood cholesterol')
- reference to a nutrient's effect on a physiological function (e.g. 'calcium is needed to build strong bones and teeth')
- general non-specific claims (e.g. 'suitable for an active lifestyle').

Medicinal claims state that a food can prevent, treat or cure a disease or a symptom of a disease. Medicinal claims are not permitted unless a food is licensed as a medicine.

Claims for particular nutritional uses are statements that a food is suitable for people with particular nutritional requirements, for example:

- those whose digestive process or metabolism is disturbed (e.g. diabetics)
- those who, because of special physiological conditions, benefit from the consumption of certain substances (e.g. infants).

The historical development of legislation and guidelines

Nutrition labelling is increasingly subject to statutory control, with the USA being particularly comprehensive in its legislation. With the advent of global marketing, and the removal of legislative barriers within the European Union (EU) to further enhance trade, decision-making on labelling legislation has progressed beyond national control.

USA

The USA first introduced nutrition labelling legislation in 1973. This was voluntary unless a nutrient claim was made or if the product had been fortified. When information was provided it had to be in a standard format based on a serving of the food. Although over 70% of all packaged foods in the USA displayed nutrition information in the defined format, dissatisfaction with the labelling provisions among consumers, scientists and industry experts resulted in a complete review of the legislation under the Nutrition Labelling and Education Act (NLEA). This was passed by the US Congress in 1990, and required the Food and Drug Administration (FDA) to issue new proposals for mandatory nutrition labelling legislation. The intentions of the Act were to recognize the role of nutrition labelling of foods beyond the mere provision of information to a supportive role for nutrition education. The FDA issued proposals that were widely debated and final regulations were issued in January 1993 (Food and Drug Administration, 1993).

The regulations established mandatory labelling of all packaged food products sold in the USA. Products exempted included foods of no nutritional significance, e.g. herbs, food with less than 12 square inches of labelling surface and ready-to-eat foods if prepared on the premises from which they were sold.

EU

Considerable discussion within the EU resulted in decisions to harmonize food law and to provide consumers with more information on labelling. Although initial proposals were developed for vertical harmonization of legislation (i.e. defining detailed specifications for particular foods), the considerable variation of foods consumed within different European countries resulted in progress that was too slow to meet requirements for flexible and innovative food marketing. As a result, most activity is now via horizontal harmonization (i.e. defining general criteria and labelling across a range of foods). Thus while the emphasis on compositional standards has been reduced, increased focus has been put on the comprehensive labelling of foods.

Specific impetus for nutrition labelling came from a growing public interest in the relationship between diet and health. It was considered that a basic knowledge of nutrition and appropriate nutrition labelling of foods would jointly contribute towards enabling the consumer to select 'healthier' diets, and thus help to reduce the risk of some diseases.

The Directive on nutrition labelling for foodstuffs was formally adopted by the Council of the EU in September 1990 (European Commission, 1990). All Member States were instructed to prohibit trade of products not in compliance with the Directive from October 1993. Nutrition labelling would not be mandatory unless triggered by a nutrient claim on labelling, but where information was provided it would have to be in the format defined within the Directive. Bottled water and 'diet integrators' were exempted from the Directive because it was assumed that other Directives would specify the labelling requirements of these products.

Although comprehensive nutrition labelling was agreed to be ideal, there was concern that because knowledge on the subject of nutrition was often poor, the information provided should be simple and easily understood by the average consumer. It was also believed that the gradual introduction of detailed requirements would encourage smaller food companies to provide nutrition labelling.

The Directive defined energy conversion figures and component declarations for macronutrients, and labelling of recommended daily allowance (RDA) values and criteria for declarations for the micronutrients. The Directive also stated that the additional provision of nutrition information in a graphical format could be defined in future 'in a format to be determined'. There was provision for a formal review of the Directive in 1998.

UK

The catalyst for widespread nutrition labelling in the UK was the 1984 COMA Report on Diet and Cardiovascular Disease (Department of Health and Social Security, 1984). However, a considerable number of Regulations and Codes of Practice had already provided specific details for the labelling of nutrients. The Labelling of Food Regulations 1970 (Statutory Instrument 400, 1970) provided criteria for vitamin and mineral claims, and introduced requirements for claims on energy content or the suitability of products for diabetics or slimmers.

The Food Labelling Regulations 1970 were extended, and previous Codes of Practice were formally recognized, with the issue of the Food Labelling Regulations 1984 (SI 1305, 1984). Although the Food Labelling Regulations 1984 did not specifically address the format and scope of nutrition labelling, they defined criteria for the declaration of macro- and micronutrients, and set out conditions for some nutrient claims.

As not all criteria relating to the presentation of information and format were defined within the Food Labelling Regulations 1984, a plethora of nutrition information formats appeared on food labelling from the mid 1980s. The increase in information provision followed pressure for nutrition labelling from consumers and health professionals, as well as some sectors of the food industry seeing a marketing advantage from the provision of such data. Various food retailers made decisions to provide information on *all* products and this was matched by similar actions by some food trade groups and manufacturing companies. Although these food industry moves were considered positive and helpful, there was concern that the different formats that appeared could contribute to consumer confusion.

In 1987 the UK Ministry of Agriculture, Fisheries and Food (MAFF) issued proposals to require the mandatory labelling of most foods with total fat and saturated fat content values (Ministry of Agriculture, Fisheries and Food, 1987). The proposals required the inclusion of *trans* fatty acid values within the calculation of the saturates. Because such unilateral labelling legislation would have been considered a technical barrier to European trade, and the EU Commission had stated that nutrition labelling was an area of food law that would be covered by a directive, MAFF revoked the proposals for regulation and developed guidelines for the format of nutrition labelling. The guidelines were widely adopted, but some manufacturers and retailers had developed their own schemes to an extent that they did not amend their labelling formats until the EU Directive on nutrition labelling was issued.

In 1988 MAFF's Food Advisory Committee reviewed labelling legislation and practices. Although the final report principally considered criteria for nutrient claims, it recommended that full nutrition information should be required if a claim was made on labelling (Ministry of Agriculture, Fisheries and Food, 1991).

FAO/WHO

The Codex Alimentarius Commission was established in 1962 to implement the Food and Agriculture Organisation/World Health Organization (FAO/WHO) food standards programme. It is a intergovernmental organization and currently represents 138 countries. The Codex Committee on Food Labelling has issued guidelines on nutrition labelling to support the provision of information on the nutrient content of foods where claims are made, to ensure that such information is not false or misleading and to strive towards increasingly consistent formats around the world.

The Codex guidelines on nutrition labelling, although advisory rather than binding on governments, had an important influence on the development of the EU Directive on nutrition labelling (European Commission, 1990). Regular meetings of both the Codex Food Labelling Committee and other related committees continue to review and update guidelines for nutrient declarations in line with current consensus views, and these provide a principal reference point in international discussions on nutrition labelling.

Requirements for nutrient declarations

Consumer perceptions of the nutrient content of food can vary widely depending on the format of the labelling on food products. Information provided on labels is the outcome of a balance between complete data about the nutrient character-istics of a product and the need for such information to be simple and fit into the space on labelling. Legislation defining requirements for nutrient declarations ensures consistency on labelling, which is an essential basis for public nutrition education in relation to food choice. Nutrient declarations are usually presented within a defined area on labelling (the nutrition panel or box) and, as the criteria controlling nutrient declarations have become more defined within legislation, the presentation of information has become progressively standardized.

USA

The NLEA defines the most comprehensive nutrient declaration regulations in the world. The regulations require information to be boxed and headed with the title 'Nutrition Facts' (see Figure 8.1) and further details provided must include:

- serving size (in household units and metric weight)
- number of servings
- energy: calories per serving and from fat
- macronutrients: amounts per serving and percentage daily value per serving (based on a 2000 calorie intake)
- macronutrients: percentage reference daily intake (RDI)
- standard information on macronutrient energy conversion factors
- standard information on macronutrient levels representing daily value (for a 2000 and 2500 calorie intake).

Nutrition panels must include all the nutrients listed below; simplified formats are permitted only if a product contains insignificant quantities of seven or more of the mandatory nutrients.

Calories. The number of calories per serving expressed in 5 calorie increments below 50 calories, and in 10 calorie increments above 50 calories.

Calories from fat. The number of calories from fat.

Total fat. The grams of fat per serving in 0.5 g increments below 3 g and then to

Nutrition Facts

Serving Size 1/2 cup (114g)
Servings Per Container 4

Amount Per Serving

Calories 260	Calories from fat 120

	% Daily Value*
Total Fat 13 g	**20%**
Saturated Fat 5g	**25%**
Cholesterol 30mg	**10%**
Sodium 660mg	**28%**
Total Carbohydrate 31g	**11%**
Dietary Fiber 0g	**0%**
Sugars 13g	
Protein 5g	

Vitamin A 4%	•	Vitamin C 2%
Calcium 15%	•	Iron 4%

*Percent Daily Values are based on a 2000 calorie diet. Your Daily Values may vary higher or lower depending on your calorie needs:

Nutrient	Calories	2000	2500
Total Fat	Less than	65g	80g
Sat. Fat	Less than	20g	25g
Cholesterol	Less than	300mg	300mg
Sodium	Less than	2,400mg	2,400mg
Total Carbohydrate		300g	375g
Dietary Fiber		25g	30g

Calories per gram:
Fat 9 - Carbohydrates 4 - Protein 4

Figure 8.1 Example of nutrition labelling.

the nearest gram; fat must also be expressed as a percentage of the daily value of 65 g, i.e. 30% of calories from fat on a 2000 calorie intake.

Saturated fat. The grams of saturated fat per serving expressed in 0.5 g increments; saturated fat must also be expressed as a percentage of the daily value of 20 g.

Cholesterol. The milligrams of cholesterol per serving in 5 mg increments; cholesterol must also be expressed as a percentage of the daily value of 300 mg.

Sodium. The milligrams of sodium per serving in 5 mg increments up to 140 mg, and 10 mg increments at higher levels; sodium must also be expressed as a percentage of the daily value of 2400 mg.

Total carbohydrate. The grams of carbohydrate per serving in 1 g increments; in addition information must be expressed as a percentage of the daily value of 300 g.

Dietary fibre. The grams of fibre per serving in 1 g increments and also expressed as a percentage of the daily value of 25 g.

Sugars. The grams of sugars per serving in 1 g increments; additional information relating sugar levels to a daily value is not required.

Protein. The grams of protein per serving in 1 g increments; additional information is only required if claims are made about protein, in which case a percentage of the daily value for protein of 50 g must be declared.

Vitamin A. The percentage of the RDI of 5000 iu (= 1500 μg) per serving; the contribution of β-carotene to vitamin A activity may be indicated as a percentage, e.g. 'vitamin A 20% (50% as β-carotene)'. This indicates that half of the vitamin A activity, in a product providing a fifth of the RDI of vitamin A per serving, comes from β-carotene.

Vitamin C. The percentage of the RDI of 60 mg per serving.

Calcium. The percentage of the RDI of 1000 mg per serving.

Iron. The percentage of the RDI of 18 mg per serving.

EU

The EU Directive on nutrition labelling defines the scope and format of labelling. Where it is provided, all information on energy values and the macronutrients must be expressed per 100 g or 100 ml; information for vitamins and minerals must also be presented as a percentage of the RDA. Nutrients can also be declared as a per serving or a per portion figure providing that these are described on the label, e.g. 'per 30 g serving'.

Further criteria defined in the Directive are:

- the energy value of the food must be described in kilojoules (kJ) and in kilocalories (kcal)
- the amounts of protein, carbohydrate and fat must be described in grams (g)
- the amounts of sugars, saturates, fibre and sodium can be presented. If a nutrient claim is made on labelling, then the declaration of all of these nutrients is mandatory.
- information on starches, polyols, monosaturates, polysaturates or cholesterol can also be provided, and is required if specific mention to any of these items is made on the labelling.

In calculating the energy content of the macronutrients the prescribed conversion factors are:

1 g carbohydrate	=	17 kJ (4 kcal)
1 g polyols	=	10 kJ (2.4 kcal)
1 g protein	=	17 kJ (4 kcal)
1 g fat	=	37 kJ (9 kcal)
1 g alcohol (ethanol)	=	29 kJ (7 kcal)
1 g organic acid	=	13 kJ (3 kcal)

Reference to a vitamin or mineral on labelling can only be made if a food contains a 'significant amount' (15% of the RDA in 100 g or 100 ml of a product or per single portion package) (Table 8.1).

Nutrition information should be provided as an average value (defined as 'the figure which best represents the amount of a nutrient considering allowances for seasonal variability, patterns of consumption, and other factors which may cause an actual value to vary'). Acceptable sources of information for nutrient declarations are the manufacturer's analysis of the food, a calculation from values of the ingredients used in the food or from generally established and accepted data.

UK

Nutrient declaration formats are defined with the Food Labelling Regulations 1996 (SI 1499, 1996). These incorporate all the requirements defined within the EU Directive on nutrition labelling (European Commission, 1990).

Requirements for nutrient claims

Nutrition claims describe and usually emphasize a particular nutrient on the labelling; nutrient declarations within nutrient panels are specifically not consid-

Table 8.1 Criteria for micronutrient claims

	RDA[a]	Source claim: minimum amount per daily serving	Rich source claim: minimum amount per daily serving	Label declaration: minimum amount per 100g or 100 ml[b]
Vitamin A (μg)	800	133	400	120
Vitamin D (μg)	5	0.83	2.5	0.75
Vitamin E (mg)	10	1.7	5	1.5
Vitamin C (mg)	60	10	30	9
Thiamin (Vitamin B_1) (mg)	1.4	0.23	0.7	0.21
Riboflavin (Vitamin B_2) (mg)	16	0.27	0.8	0.24
Niacin (mg)	18	3	9	2.7
Vitamin B_3 (mg)	2	0.3	1	0.3
Folic acid (μg)	200	33.3	100	30
Vitamin B_{12} (μg)	1	0.16	0.5	0.15
Biotin (mg)	0.15	0.025	0.075	0.023
Pantothenic acid (mg)	6		3	0.9
Calcium (mg)	800	133	400	120
Phosphorus (mg)	800	133	400	120
Iron (mg)	14	3	7	2.1
Magnesium (mg)	300	33.3	150	45
Zinc (mg)	15	2.5	7.5	2.25
Iodine (μg)	150	25	75	22.5

Source: Statutory Instrument 1499, 1996.

[a] The RDA figures defined within labelling legislation are not the same figures as the reference nutrient intake (RNI) figures for micronutrients defined by the UK Department of Health.

[b] These minimum levels apply as a rule although exceptions have not been defined.

ered to be claims. While nutrient declarations provide comprehensive data on a product, consumers find claims useful to support food purchase decisions, e.g. 'low fat' claims may be of particular interest to some consumers, and support appropriate food selection without more detailed (time-consuming) examination of nutrient data. Nutrient claims can be absolute, e.g. less than 5 g fat per 100 g, or relative, e.g. 25% less fat.

Because of the greater ease of use of nutrient claims compared to nutrient declarations, criteria for claims should be defined in legislation so that they are not misleading. Absolute claims may incorrectly emphasize nutrients if the consumer cannot relate the information to typical intakes of the nutrient. Relative claims may be misleading in relation to nutrient level modification in a food depending on baseline amounts in a standard product; thus a '10% reduced fat' version of a high-fat food, e.g. cheese, could provide a useful reduction in fat consumed per serving; in contrast a '10% reduced fat' version of a low-fat food, e.g. yoghurt, may not provide significantly less fat per serving.

USA

The NLEA established defined nutrition labelling and nutrient claims. The NLEA regulations considered claims to include direct statements about the levels of nutrients and implied claims, e.g. 'high in rice bran', would be considered as a claim relating to the fibre content of a food. Nutrient claims (described in the regulations as 'nutrient descriptors') relate absolute or relative criteria per serving and/or as a percentage of a daily value figure. The NLEA regulators also prescribe critera for general claims, e.g. the term 'healthy' requires a product to be low in fat and in saturated fat, and to contain at least 10% of the RDI of vitamins A or C, or calcium or iron. A claim that a food contains an ingredient known to contain a particular nutrient can be made but must comply with the 'good source' definition of the nutrient, e.g. a 'contains bran' claim needs to comply with the 'source of fibre' criteria (at least 2.5 g fibre per serving). Avoidance claims, e.g. 'gluten-free' or 'contains no dairy ingredients', are not considered to be implied nutrient claims.

The extensive NLEA regulations have generally been welcomed by the US food industry, although initial implementation costs (food analysis, repackaging, etc.) have been considerable. Consumer understanding requires evaluation to indicate whether nutrient declarations on labels influence food choice and to guide subsequent consumer education programmes.

EU

The Directive on nutrition labelling defined a nutrient claim as any representation that states, suggests or implies that a food has particular nutritional properties owing to the energy or nutrients it contains, or does not contain (European Commission, 1990). Claims are permitted for protein, carbohydrate, fat, fibre, sodium or their components, or any of the scheduled vitamins or minerals (Table 8.1). When nutrient claims are made, nutrition labelling becomes compulsory.

The European Commission has issued several draft directives for the regulation of nutrient claims. Previous drafts proposed specific criteria for claims, e.g. with defined cut-off values per 100 g food, and also more general proposals that all claims should be permitted provided that they are 'well-founded and justifiable and formulated with "due precision"' (European Commission, 1994a). Until an EU Directive on claims is adopted, the provisions of national legislation, where they exist, apply in individual EU member countries.

A framework Directive (one setting out general principles for subsequent more detailed Directives) defined nine categories of foods intended for particular nutritional uses (PARNUTS) (European Commision, 1989). It was later suggested that specific legislation should only be drafted for four categories of foods, namely infant formula and follow-on formula, baby foods, low-energy (slimming) foods and foods for specific medical purposes (European Commission, 1994b). PARNUTS foods need to comply with the general legislation applying to all foods, but there are further specific requirements for composition, labelling and marketing, e.g. the Directive on infant and follow-on formula defines specific nutrient claims that apply only to this category of foods (Table 8.3).

Table 8.2 MAFF guidelines for nutrient claims

Claims	Fat	Saturates	Sugars	Fibre	Sodium
Free	<0.15 g/100 g	<0.1 g/100 g	<0.2 g/100 g	—	<5 mg/100 g
Low	<5 g/100 g *and* per serving	<3 g/100 g *and* per serving	<5 g/100 g *and* per serving	—	<40 g/100 g *and* per serving
Reduced	25% less	25% less	25% less	—	25% less
Less	x% less	x% less	x% less		x% less
No added	—	—	No sugars or foods composed mainly of sugars added to the food or any of its ingredients		No salts of sodium have been added to the food or any of its ingredients
Increased	—	—	—	25% more *and* >3 g/100 g *and* per serving	—
More	—	—	—	x% more	—
Source	—	—	—	>3 g/100 g *or* per serving	—
High/rich source	—	—	—	>6 g/100 g *or* per serving	—

Source: Ministry of Agriculture, Fisheries and Food, 1993.

Table 8.3 Claims criteria for infant formulae

Claim	Conditions
Adapted protein	The protein content is lower than 0.6 g/100 kJ (2.5 g/100 kcal) and the whey protein/casein ratio is not less than 1.0
Low sodium	The sodium content is lower than 9 mg/100 kJ (39 mg/100 kcal)
Sucrose free	No sucrose is present
Lactose only	Lactose is the only carbohydrate present
Lactose free	No lactose is present
Iron enriched	Iron is added

Source: Statutory Instrument 77, 1995.

UK

Claims made on food labelling in the UK are subject to the Food Safety Act 1990, which makes it an offence to 'falsely describe food, or to mislead as to its nature, substance or quality'. A low-fat claim for a high-fat food would be a false description and/or misleading as to the nature of that food, and thus be in breach of the Act. There are also specific provisions in the Food Labelling Regulations 1996 (SI 1499, 1996) which define criteria for claims for energy, protein, cholesterol and for vitamins and/or minerals as follows:

Energy
Reduced = <75% of a similar or standard food
Low = <167 kJ (40 kcal) per 100 g (or 100 ml) and per normal serving. (Note: there is separate provision for the term 'low calorie' for soft drinks: products may not contain more than 10 kcals per 100 ml (SI 1499, 1996).)

Protein
Source = >12% energy from protein and >12 g protein
Rich source = >20% energy from protein and >12 g protein in the quantity of food that can reasonably be expected to be consumed in one day.

Cholesterol
Absence = <0.005% cholesterol.

Micronutrients (vitamins/minerals)
Source = >17% of the RDA
Rich source = >50% of the RDA of the micronutrient (Table 8.1) in the quantity of food that can be reasonably be expected to be consumed in one day.

In 1991 the UK Food Advisory Committee published a review of food labelling and presented proposals for controlling both absolute and relative nutrient claims and their components. These proposals were formally issued for consultation and, subsequent to discussion and slight modification, MAFF issued guidelines (Table 8.2) (Ministry of Agriculture, Fisheries and Food, 1993). These guidelines were advisory and had no legal effect (other than, perhaps, as a point of reference in case of legal dispute), but it was hoped that food manufacturers would adhere to the criteria issued. Subsequent UK legislative developments are unlikely ahead of EU actions and because of MAFF general policy to support deregulation.

Requirements for health claims

These are many food labels that currently make general statements about health aspects of products. However, it has been particularly difficult to define criteria and formalize legislation for such claims. It is not always evident where health claims begin and medicinal claims (which are expressly prohibited) end. While there are concerns that some information on labelling could be potentially misleading, the over-stringent regulation of health claims could impair communication to the interested consumer of clear and valid food–health relationships.

The legislative options are:

- to prohibit health claims
- to allow defined statements on labelling about some food–health relationships
- to require experts to approve health claims on labelling prior to marketing on case-by-case or a category basis
- to issue general guidelines.

USA

The NLEA required the FDA to develop regulations for labelling claims 'based on the totality of publicly available scientific evidence, and where there was substantial agreement amongst qualified experts that the claims were supported by the evidence'.

Health claims on labelling:

- have to use the terms 'may' or 'might' to describe a food–health link
- have to describe what role non-dietary factors have on a health parameter
- must not describe the degree of risk reduction linked to the altered intake of a nutrient
- have to describe a balanced and healthy diet
- can only be made if a food naturally contains at least 10% of the RDI of vitamins A or C, or calcium or iron.

The NLEA established a mechanism allowing claims to be made on food labels. The detailed health claims granted 'official' legal status may have a considerable impact on the promotion of certain foods and monitoring will indicate whether explicit statements about health on labelling support dietary changes in the population.

Health claims are not permitted on foods for infants and young children, or for foods exceeding maximum defined amounts of fat, saturated fat, cholesterol or sodium. Model health claims are described in the Regulations (Table 8.4)

Table 8.4 Health claims allowed on US food labels

Food characteristics	Health claim – reduced risk of	Model claim statements
High in (bioavailable) calcium	Osteoporosis	Regular exercise and a healthy diet with enough calcium helps teens and young adult white and Asian women maintain good bone health and may reduce their high risk of osteoporosis later in life
Low sodium	Hypertension	Diets low in sodium may reduce the risk of high blood pressure, a disease associated with many factors
Low fat	Cancer	Development of cancer depends on many factors. A diet low in total fat may reduce the risk of some cancers
Low saturated fat, low cholesterol and low fat	Coronary heart disease	While many factors affect heart disease, diets low in saturated fat and cholesterol may reduce the risk of this disease
Grain products, fruits or vegetables that contain dietary fibre; low fat	Cancer	Low-fat diets rich in fibre-containing grain products, fruits and vegetables may reduce the risk of some types of cancer, a disease associated with many factors
Fruit, vegetable or grain products that contain fibre; low saturated fat; low cholesterol; low fat	Coronary heart disease	Diets low in saturated fat and cholesterol and rich in fruits, vegetables and grain products that contain some types of dietary fibre, particularly soluble fibre, may reduce the risk of heart disease, a disease associated with many factors
A fruit or vegetble; low fat; good source (without fortification) of vitamin A, vitamin C or dietary fibre	Cancer	Low-fat diets rich in fruits and vegetables (foods that are low in fat and may contain dietary fibre, vitamin A and vitamin C) may reduce the risk of some types of cancers, a disease associated with many factors
Good source of folate	Neural tube defects	Women who consume adequate amounts of folate, a B vitamin, daily throughout their childbearing years may reduce their risk of having a child with a neural tube birth defect. Such birth defects, while not widespread, are very serious. They can have many causes. Adequate amounts of folate can be obtained from diets rich in fruits, dark-green leafy vegetables and legumes, enriched grain products, fortified cereals or a supplement. Folate consumption should be limited to 1000 µg per day from all sources

Source: Food and Drug Administration, 1993

although manufacturers may develop their own text to describe approved relationship claims, providing all the specific requirements for such claims are fulfilled.

The Dietary Supplement Health and Education Act adopted in 1994 subsequently made separate provision for the regulation of health claims on the labelling of dietary supplements.

EU

The European Commission has drafted several Directives on claims in the labelling and advertising of foods. Drafts issued describe general provisions for 'well-founded and justifiable' claims (European Commission, 1994a), however, detailed specific criteria for health claims do not appear likely. Specific directives for foods intended for particular nutritional uses (PARNUTS) do not make references to general health claims but they do detail labelling requirements and/or restrictions in relation to information about health and dietary use for people with specific health requirements or conditions.

UK

The Food Labelling Regulations 1996 (SI 1499, 1996) expressly prohibit medicinal claims but they do allow claims relating to particular nutritional use. Products making such claims need to be supported by relevant information on the labelling about nutrient characteristics to justify the statements made. Information provided only to health professionals is exempted from restrictions on claims. The other point of reference in the UK relating to health claims is the very broad provision within the Food Safety Act 1990 (Ministry of Agriculture, Fisheries and Food, 1990). This states that food should not be injurious to health and should be of the nature, substance of quality (including nutrient and health quality) demanded by the purchaser (Ministry of Agriculture, Fisheries and Food, 1990).

In a review of food labelling by the Food Advisory Committee in 1990, caution was expressed about the value of health claims, whether or not they could be substantiated, in relation to balanced consumer health education (Ministry of Agriculture, Fisheries and Food, 1991). In the limited space on labelling it is difficult to put a claim into context and further qualifications might be easily lost within all the other information provided on labelling. The Committee specifically recommended that claims relating to deficiency diseases be prohibited because such claims could be misleading, as the impression conveyed could be that an ordinary diet was not sufficient to prevent such disease. They also recommended that health endorsements by organizations, or by individuals (testimonials), be banned as these gave considerable scope for misleading consumers.

The Food Advisory Committee considered that certain health claims relating to chronic diseases could provide useful information, provided the scientific basis of such claims was controlled. The recommendations were to permit such health claims provided that:

- the claim was supported by recommendations made by the UK Chief Medical Officer
- the claim related to the food as eaten, rather than to the properties of any individual ingredients
- the product was able to fulfil the claim when consumed in normal amounts
- the product displayed full nutrition labelling to demonstrate that the claim was justified
- the role of the specific food was explained in relation to an overall diet (e.g. 'as part of a low fat diet').

These proposals were not used to draft labelling legislation because health claims were to be addressed by an EU Directive on claims, which would subsequently override any national legislation.

In 1996 the Food Advisory Committee again considered the principles underlying health claims, particularly in relation to foods marketed specifically for health-promoting properties ('functional foods') (Ministry of Agriculture, Fisheries and Food, 1996). A consultation document described the Food Advisory Committee conclusions as follows:

- references to a specific disease or disease risk factor should not be made on labelling
- positive messages linking food and health, e.g. nutrient function claims or statements based on officially endorsed good dietary practice, are helpful
- health claims not based on official recommendations must be substantiated by valid data demonstrating physiological effects in humans
- claims should not infer health benefits from additional or reduced intakes of particular nutrients where this is not justified
- claims must be valid for foods (not just ingredients or components) eaten in normal quantities
- claims should be accompanied by full nutrition labelling.

Views on the merits of guidelines versus statutory rules on health claims were to be considered prior to a formal recommendation by the Food Advisory Committee. In the interim, advice on health claims to companies and to enforcement officers should be provided by trade associations and the Local Authorities Co-ordinating Body on Food and Trading Standards (LACOTS).

Medicinal claims are expressly prohibited by the Food Labelling Regulations 1996. Any food product making such a claim would be classed as a medicine and would require authorization from the Medicines Control Authority (MCA). The MCA has issued guidelines for use by manufacturers and by those responsible for the enforcement of legislation on the types of claims considered to be medicinal (Medicines Control Agency, 1995).

References

British Nutrition Foundation (1996) *Nutrition Claims* (briefing paper), British Nutrition Foundation, London.

Department of Health and Social Security (1984) Diet and Cardiovascular Disease, *Report on Health and Social Subjects 28*, HMSO, London.

European Commission (1989) Council Directive 89/398/EEC on the approximation of laws of the Member States relating to foodstuffs intended for particular nutritional use. *Official Journal of the European Communities*, **L186**, 27–32.

European Commission (1990) Council Directive 90/496/EEC on nutrition labelling of foodstuffs, *Official Journal of the European Communities*, **L276**, 40–44.

European Commission (1994a) Consumer Policy Service (CPS) proposal on claims in the labelling and advertising of foodstuffs, European Commission, Brussels.

European Commission (1994b) Proposal amending Council Directive 89/398/ECC on the approximation of the laws of the Member States relating to foodstuffs intended for particular nutritional uses, European Commission, Brussels.

Food and Drug Administration (1993) Department of Health and Human Services. Final rules – food labelling (etc.). *Federal Register*, **58**, 3.

Medicines Control Agency (1995) A guide to what is a medicinal product, *Medicines Act Leaflet 8*, Medicines Control Agency, London.

Ministry of Agriculture, Fisheries and Food (1987) Proposals for Fat Content in Food (Labelling) Regulations, MAFF, London.

Ministry of Agriculture, Fisheries and Food (1990) The Food Safety Act 1990, MAFF, London.

Ministry of Agriculture, Fisheries and Food (1991) Food Advisory Committee Report of its Review of Food Labelling and Advertising 1990, HMSO, London.

Ministry of Agriculture, Fisheries and Food (1993) Guidelines for the use of certain nutrient claims of food labelling and advertising, Consumer Protection Division, MAFF, London.

Ministry of Agriculture, Fisheries and Foods (1996) Food Advisory Committee Review of Functional Foods and Health Claims, MAFF, London.

Statutory Instrument 400 (1970) The Labelling of Food Regulations 1970, HMSO, London.

Statutory Instrument 1305 (1984) The Food Labelling Regulations 1984, HMSO, London.

Statutory Instrument 77 (1995) The Infant Formula and Follow-on Formula Regulations 1995, HMSO, London.

Statutory Instrument 1499 (1996) The Food Labelling Regulations 1996, HMSO, London.

Index

Page numbers appearing in *italic* refer to tables.